INTIMATE WARFARE

Other titles in the
Systemic Thinking and Practice Series:
edited by David Campbell and Ros Draper
published and distributed by Karnac

Asen, E., Neil Dawson, N., & McHugh, B. *Multiple Family Therapy: The Marlborough Model and Its Wider Applications*

Baum, S., & Lynggaard, H. (Eds.) *Intellectual Disabilities: A Systemic Approach*

Bentovim, A. *Trauma-Organized Systems. Systemic Understanding of Family Violence: Physical and Sexual Abuse*

Boscolo, L., & Bertrando, P. *Systemic Therapy with Individuals*

Burck, C., & Daniel, G. *Gender and Family Therapy*

Campbell, D., Draper, R., & Huffington, C. *Second Thoughts on the Theory and Practice of the Milan Approach to Family Therapy*

Campbell, D., Draper, R., & Huffington, C. *Teaching Systemic Thinking*

Campbell, D., & Mason, B. (Eds.) *Perspectives on Supervision*

Cecchin, G., Lane, G., & Ray, W. A. *The Cybernetics of Prejudices in the Practice of Psychotherapy*

Cecchin, G., Lane, G., & Ray, W. A. *Irreverence: A Strategy for Therapists' Survival*

Dallos, R. Interacting Stories: *Narratives, Family Beliefs, and Therapy*

Draper, R., Gower, M., & Huffington, C. *Teaching Family Therapy*

Farmer, C. *Psychodrama and Systemic Therapy*

Flaskas, C., & Perlesz, A. (Eds.) *The Therapeutic Relationship in Systemic Therapy*

Flaskas, C., & Pocock, D. *Systems and Psychoanalysis: Contemporary Integrations in Family Therapy*

Flaskas, C., Mason, B., & Perlesz, A. *The Space Between: Experience, Context, and Process in the Therapeutic Relationship*

Fredman, G. *Death Talk: Conversations with Children and Families*

Hildebrand, J. *Bridging the Gap: A Training Module in Personal and Professional Development*

Hoffman, L. *Exchanging Voices: A Collaborative Approach to Family Therapy*

Jones, E. *Working with Adult Survivors of Child Sexual Abuse*

Jones, E., & Asen, E. *Systemic Couple Therapy and Depression*

Krause, I.-B. *Culture and System in Family Therapy*

Mason, B., & Sawyerr, A. (Eds.) *Exploring the Unsaid: Creativity, Risks, and Dilemmas in Working Cross-Culturally*

Robinson, M. *Divorce as Family Transition: When Private Sorrow Becomes a Public Matter*

Seikkula, J., & Arnkil, T. E. *Dialogical Meetings in Social Networks*

Smith, G. *Systemic Approaches to Training in Child Protection*

Wilson, J. *Child-Focused Practice: A Collaborative Systemic Approach*

Credit card orders, Tel: +44(0) 20-7431-1075; Fax: +44(0) 20-7435-9076
Email: shop@karnacbooks.com

INTIMATE WARFARE
Regarding the Fragility of Family Relations

Martine Groen and
Justine van Lawick

Systemic Thinking and Practice Series:

Series Editor
Ros Draper

KARNAC

First published in 2009 by
Karnac Books Ltd
118 Finchley Road, London NW3 5HT

British Library Cataloguing in Publication Data

A C.I.P. for this book is available from the British Library

ISBN: 978 1 85575 521 5

Translated by Martha M. Otten & Marcel Otten

Edited, designed and produced by The Studio Publishing Services Ltd
www.publishingservicesuk.co.uk
e-mail: studio@publishingservicesuk.co.uk

www.karnacbooks.com

CONTENTS

ABOUT THE AUTHORS   vii

SERIES EDITOR'S FOREWORD   ix

FOREWORD   xi

INTRODUCTION   xv

CHAPTER ONE
Domestic violence: characteristics and size   1
 Justine van Lawick

CHAPTER TWO
Together you will progress   19
 Justine van Lawick

CHAPTER THREE
The downward spiral of violence between partners   25
 Justine van Lawick

CHAPTER FOUR
From ill-behaviour to relational behaviour   71
 Justine van Lawick

CHAPTER FIVE
Escalation and de-escalation   93
Justine van Lawick

CHAPTER SIX
Violence in families of various cultural backgrounds   99
Martine Groen

CHAPTER SEVEN
The coherence between shame and violence   151
Martine Groen

CHAPTER EIGHT
Rituals of revenge   169
Martine Groen

CHAPTER NINE
The reproduction of violence   183
Martine Groen

CHAPTER TEN
Of young rulers and the terror at home   201
Justine van Lawick

CHAPTER ELEVEN
The therapist as a person   229
Martine Groen

CHAPTER TWELVE
Apprehensive heroes   253
Martine Groen

CONCLUSION   273

REFERENCES   279

INDEX   293

ABOUT THE AUTHORS

Martine Groen is a clinical psychologist and psychotherapist, who has specialized in the effects of violence and trauma in families. She is also a trainer, consultant, coach, and mediator in non-profit organizations. She has been consulting and training traumatized women, families, and organizations from 1995 to 2005 in former Yugoslavia. She took part in a conflict resolutions scheme between various organizations in Bosnia. She has published several books on prostitution, intimate war, domestic violence, shame and violence.

Justine van Lawick is clinical psychologist, family therapist, and director of training in the Lorentzhuis, a centre for systemic therapy, training and consultation in Haarlem, the Netherlands. Her areas of interest focus on addressing violent behaviour in families with compassion for all involved family members and without blaming. Another area of interest is working with marginalized families. Justine has published many articles and a book.

It is an honour to include the second edition of this book in our series. Cultural and societal taboos about talking about domestic violence as well as the consequences of such violence, frequently leaving perpetrators and victims either in hiding or in the public domain of the justice system, mean that professionals constrained by agency requirements easily omit addressing the systemic complexities in cases of domestic violence. In highlighting the systemic complexities of domestic violence, this book seeks also to inspire excellence among professionals who recognize that where multiple agencies are involved with the different needs of different clients in any domestic violence situation, collaborative working and co-creation is in the best interests of all their clients. This book is for professionals working as sole practitioners as well as those involved in multi-agency working.

Written by two well-recognized experts in their field, this book brings to the reader a vast storehouse of wisdom and experience for understanding and intervening with clarity and compassion in the lives of wounded and damaged people.

The authors, Martine Groen and Justine van Lawick, are well known nationally in Holland, a country with a long history of forward thinking in the provision of services for the marginalized members of society, perpetrators and victims of domestic violence being no exception. The international experience and reputations of the authors in war-torn countries, where abuse and violence have become synonymous with names of villages and towns, also means that readers of this book can benefit from the distillation of their accumulated wisdom and experience, over the years, as clinicians, researchers, and pioneers in the field of therapeutic work with clients involved in domestic violence.

Being well aware themselves of the potential for contamination when working with such toxic subject matter, the authors not only include a chapter specifically addressing needs of therapists working self-reflexively with domestic violence situations, but also ensure that each chapter in the book stands alone for readers to consult and access, if they wish, on a need-to-know, case-by-case basis. Even with the possibility available for readers to avoid facing over-exposure at any one time to such painful material, the many perspectives addressed in the various chapters of the book, far from adding to complexity, will, one hopes, enable readers, with a sigh of relief at the recognition found in these pages, to connect specific aspects of any current piece of their work to a topic from the field of domestic violence so ably and carefully explored by Groen and Lawick. There is a richness in each chapter in the detail and care with which the authors address taboo issues, managing to name without either blaming or shaming.

The scope of this book and its wealth of knowledge and information means it will be of use to any professionals, not just family therapists required to work with domestic violence issues in their daily work, and, as such, is in keeping with the vision and ethos of this series to disseminate systemic thinking and practice among the helping professions and show its usefulness to as wide a professional audience as possible. As series editor, I hope this book will inspire more professionals to champion joined-up working, so promoting better services, awareness raising, and preventative work for those driven to communicate through acts of domestic violence and those they injure, thus reducing the need for "intimate warfare".

Ros Draper
Series Editor
Hampshire 2009

FOREWORD

The family is commonly viewed as the primary setting for nurturing and an alleged "safe haven". In reality, it is also a very dangerous place to live in. We are much more likely to be physically or sexually assaulted by a member of our family than by a stranger. Like tobacco and other toxic substances, the family should carry a Government Health Warning, as it can seriously damage your well-being. Violence within the family (intra-family violence) is a major public health issue and takes many forms, from child abuse to sibling abuse, from spouse abuse to elder abuse. The more narrow term "domestic violence" refers specifically to the exercise of control and the misuse of power, physical, emotional, mental, financial, and/or sexual by one person, usually a man, over another, usually a woman, within the context of an intimate relationship.

Intimate Warfare puts intra-family violence into context, that is, the close relationships and the wider social system(s) of which families are part. It is written by two passionate and highly experienced psychotherapists from the Netherlands, whose knowledge of the subject is far reaching and transcends the Dutch borders. In Europe, domestic violence is the major cause of death and disability for women aged 19–44 and accounts for more death and ill health than cancer or traffic accidents (Amnesty International, 2004, Government National Plan for Domestic Violence, 2005). In England and Wales almost half of all women killed every year die at the hands of an intimate male partner or ex-partner (Women's Aid, 2001). In the UK (British Crime Survey, 2000) it is estimated that one third of violent reported crime is domestic assault, now renamed as "intimate violence". Such violence is not at all uncommon: 48% of women and 33% of men reported that they had suffered more than one form of intimate violence since the age of sixteen (Dewar Research Government Statistics on Domestic Violence, 2007). There are also increasing reports of domestic violence by men, but since many young males tend not to regard domestic violence as a crime, or do not wish to admit it, the true incidence is likely to be much higher.

It is a sad fact, but most violence is "home grown". It is estimated that 65–90% of domestic violence incidents are witnessed by children, and many of these children develop emotional and behavioural difficulties that mirror those of children who have been the actual victims of abuse. *Intimate Warfare* shows how violence emerges in the family context and is reproduced in the offspring. While there are plenty of publications in the field of domestic violence, from learned papers to comprehensive text books, *Intimate Warfare* is a unique contribution in that it covers the subject from a whole range of different perspectives. It describes systemic ways of working individually with perpetrators, using a systemic frame. It addresses violent partner relationships, as well as teenage violence against parents. It presents many pragmatic ideas and techniques that systemic practitioners can use in their daily practice. There are fascinating accounts of how the seeming "fit" between experiences of shame and violence can feed and perpetuate the "downward spiral" of violent escalation. Unusual for a book of this kind, particularly in the systemic field, there is a chapter with the sole focus on the therapist and on transference and countertransference issues and how these manifest themselves in different work contexts. The authors build useful bridges between systemic and psychodynamic frameworks: for example, when they show how circular interviewing techniques stimulate reflective ability and mentalizing functions. Clients are helped to learn to regulate their emotions and impulses better, resulting in their enhanced awareness of emotions, cognitions and desires in others, leading to the development of new and different social and moral awareness.

Intimate Warfare describes brilliantly how tensions build up in families, how these can spiral into violence, how such violence can be curbed, and how people can be taught different ways of managing conflictual situations. The book refers to the changing roles of men and women in recent decades and the confusion and tensions that go with this. The authors convincingly relate their approach to the ever-changing historical and political settings and contextualize violent behaviours by embedding these in the social and family environment.

Intimate Warfare deserves a wide readership, and not only among systemically orientated clinicians. It is essential reading for all those who are passionate about working with violence in families. This book not only complements other recent publications on this important subject, but is a significant new contribution to make the family—and the world—a safer place.

Eia Asen, MD, FRCPsych
Systemic Practitioner
Consultant Child, Adolescent and Family Psychiatrist
Marlborough Family Service, London NW8
London, August 2009

Introduction

The community in which children are nursed, the family, should by all accounts be a safe haven. However, it is not. People within family relationships are likely to be threatened, humiliated, smacked, raped, or murdered.

Such violence in the domestic circle conjures up a lot of questions. For years we have been working with this problematical issue, and we are trying to make the dynamics of violence within the family more understandable. This book is a reflection of our dialogue.

The first edition of this book was published in 1998. Much has changed over the intervening years. The results of the1997 Intomart survey, which showed that 45% of the Dutch population has experienced violence within the domestic circle, made the government become aware of the scale and gravity of the problem. Funds were made available for projects which dealt with the recognition, prevention, care, and treatment of domestic violence. The projects on domestic violence have led to establishing several networks in which the police, support centres for domestic violence, general practitioners, shelters, centres for victim aid, social services, municipal health care agencies, centres for child welfare, psychiatry, care and treatment of drug-addicts, probation services, social workers, psychotherapists, and systemic-therapists co-operate. As to the effectiveness of this approach, future research will tell.

The Dutch police have created a special registration of domestic violence and calculated that, in a year, they receive more than 57,000 reports of domestic violence. It is a known fact that only 12% of all the cases are being reported. This means that every year about 500,000 acts of violence occur on a scale of 16,000,000 inhabitants. Many of these incidents are witnessed by children. Because of this, these children have an increased risk of developing psychosocial or behavioural problems.

In April 2007, the University of Leiden published the results of a major research about child abuse. The results are shocking. Yearly, 107,200 children are being abused in the Netherlands. About 45% is being neglected; 24,000 children are victims of physical abuse. This means that, in the Netherlands, about thirty out of 1000 children are being abused. A quarter of the cases concern sexual abuse, three quarters physical abuse. Only the cases which led to visual traces are included.

Quite new research with the Conflict Tactics Scale shows that women also can be violent in couple relationships.

All together, we have to admit that domestic violence is one of the largest and most influential social problems in society.

The Dutch government made prevention and diminishing of domestic violence one of the core issues of the current cabinet (2007–2011).

From March 2009 onwards, a new law makes it possible to place the perpetrator of violence out of the family home for ten days or longer. During this time intensive help is offered for all the involved family members. The pilots that were being started before this in four big cities showed that this barring of perpetrators worked well in getting the family into an effective helping programme. Most perpetrators also suffer, and want the violence to stop. Most couples want to end the violence, not the relationship.

The new Dutch law of 25 April 2007 forbids all physical punishment of children. Although this will not prevent all parental smacks, it will make it impossible for parents to hide behind a pedagogical argument when confronted with maltreatment of their children.

In March 2007, a Dutch Commission started to create a scientifically based official professional guideline on how to recognize, acknowledge, diagnose, and treat domestic violence. Systemic thinking is the basis of this guideline.

A systemic perspective also forms the foundation of this book. That means that we try to understand the systemic dynamics that are connected to family violence and that we want to work with all involved to stop and prevent violence. We try to work with all on non-violent ways of conflict resolution.

In this book, we concentrate on couple violence and the consequences for children (Chapter Nine). One chapter addresses the violence of adolescents directed against parents (Chapter Ten).

The reader will notice that a lot of questions will remain unanswered. You will also find that the authors' points of view and modes of thought may differ at times. Each chapter identifies the author. However, the ideas of both authors have been incorporated in all chapters.

You can read each of the twelve chapters in which the different aspect of domestic violence are discussed independently.

In this edition, two chapters are added: one about escalating and de-escalating acts (Chapter Five) and one about violence in migrant families.

In the first chapter, "Characteristics and size of domestic violence", we address questions about the definition, size, and characteristics of domestic violence. The second chapter, "Together you will progress", is of a practical nature and discusses the possibilities of involving partners (usually men) in couple therapy. The third chapter, "The downward spiral of violence between partners" discusses the possibility of ending violence in a relationship. A model is presented of a therapy in which a great deal of attention is given to the gender division of roles between men and women. The fourth chapter, "From ill-behaviour to relational behaviour", elaborates on the previous chapter and examines on a more in-depth level the possibilities of couple therapy with regard to the issue of violence. The fifth chapter is a new one about escalating and de-escalating acts, followed by a new chapter on violence in migrant families. Chapter Seven, "The coherence between shame and violence", discusses shame, the emotion that nurtures and fortifies the downward spiral of violence between men and women. Chapter

Eight deals with the importance of "Rituals of vengeance" to make someone pay for the suffering and to create the ability to reconcile. Chapter Nine, "The reproduction of violence", deals with children who almost always lose out where domestic violence is concerned. Practical examples are given to demonstrate the importance of rituals in therapy. The following chapter (Chapter Ten) "Of young rulers and the terror at home", discusses adolescent violence that is directed towards the parents. In Chapter Eleven, "The therapist as a person", the therapist is the focal point. Secondary trauma, negative transference, the context of work, and possible preventions are discussed.

The final chapter, "Apprehensive heroes", is a theoretical chapter in which new points of view on the issue of violence are given and possible consequences discussed. In the conclusion, we give suggestions for future reference.

Some important themes, such as sexual violence, violence in gay and lesbian relationships, violence against children, and violence between siblings, are absent. The fact that we do not discuss these themes does not mean that we underestimate their importance. However, we have limited ourselves to those issues with which we have gained more experience and which we have given considerable thought. Our reference is a private practice in a network of colleagues. It would be a mistake to assume that a private practice only encounters the less severe cases. Both our practices deal with a broad spectrum of cases which vary from the less severe to the very serious. We have both clients who are first time help-seekers, as well as clients who have already travelled the well-trodden path of social help and mental health care. Because we have agreements with healthcare insurers, we are able to provide therapy to a broad spectrum of the social classes.

Working together with other professional helpers is part of our systemic therapies.

We hope to inspire you with our ideas and experiences.

CHAPTER ONE

Domestic violence: characteristics and size

Justine van Lawick

Introduction

I n this chapter we deal with some of the prime issues regarding domestic violence. How come the "safe haven" that the family unit is supposed to be is, in fact, often a hotbed of violence? What part does gender identity play in both the perpetrators' and the victims' case? Are the perpetrators mostly male and females mostly the victims? What is the influence of education and culture? In what way are psychopathology and violence connected?

From the second half of the past century, worldwide research has been carried out into violence within families, especially violence of men against women. Only in the last three or four decades has one come to realize that domestic violence is not an exception to the rule, but a serious social, medical, and psychological problem. People are more likely to be hit, kicked, humiliated, threatened, raped, seriously physically abused, hurt, or killed by family members in their own home, then anywhere else. This seems to be the case all over the world (Jasinski & Williams, 1998). It is hard to accept the image of the family unit as the most violent institution of society. One rather clings to the image of the warm,

1

intimate, safe, and relaxing nest, the "haven in a heartless world" (Lasch, 1977).

Size

In the Netherlands, a broad public debate has been set in motion after the national survey that bureau Intomart, assigned by the Department of Justice, conducted in 1997, which showed that 45% of the Dutch population had at some point experienced violence in the domestic circle (van Dijk, 1997). The research focused on physical, sexual, and psychological violence. Twenty-one per cent of the interviewees had experienced violence that continued for more than five years. According to the researchers, boys and men are victims in equal measure with girls and women. In 80% of the cases, the perpetrators are male. Apparently, there is a strong taboo: only 12% of the victims report to the police and only half of them actually press charges. Innovative to the Intomart research is that boys and men were interviewed as well as women; earlier research and publications have mostly dealt with the victimhood of women (Bograd & Yllo, 1988; Gelles, 1997; Jasinski & Williams, 1998; Römkens, 1992; Stark & Flitcraft, 1996; Walker, 1984). Towards the end of the past century and from the beginning of the present century, interest has arisen in the dynamics within couples (Cooper & Vetere, 2005; Goldner, Penn, Sheinberg, & Walker, 1990; Kik & Baars, 2000; van Lawick & Groen, 1998; Vetere & Cooper, 2007), and the psychology and dynamics of violent men (Bancroft & Silverman, 2002; Dutton, Golant, & Pijnaker, 2000; Jacobson & Gottman, 1998a,b; Scalia, 2002).

The international discourse on domestic violence has been complicated through thorough research on conflict management in couples. The central instrument in this research is the Conflict Tactics Scale, developed by Straus in 1979. The original has been tested, adapted, validated, and revised several times. The most recent and often used version is the Revised Conflict Tactics Scale (CTS 2, Straus, 1999). The CTS consists of seventy-eight questions: the respondent has to mention the frequency of violent acts on a scale from 0 (never happened) to 6 (happened more than twenty times in the past year). The behaviours that are mentioned vary from insults to broken bones. Every odd number question is put from the perspective of the respondent: "I did . . . against my partner", while every even number question takes the perspective of the partner: "my partner did . . . against me". The scale measures three dimensions: psychological aggression, physical aggression, and injuries. The last part, about injuries, is added to counter the criticism that this scale only measures light forms of violence.

The conclusion of this research is that women are as violent as men in partner relationships. There seems to be no significant difference in the scale of violence in heterosexual or homosexual couples.

Many studies address the individual characteristics and psychodynamics of perpetrators (men) or victims (women). We prefer to study the dynamic of the couple.

Johnson carried out research on relational profiles with violent couples (Johnson, 1995, 2000). He suggested four categories:

- Intimate Terrorism (IT): controlling aggression directed against the partner. This dynamic is charactarized by escalations of violence that serve to control the partner. This contains physical violence and psychological violence, such as forced isolation, threatening, humiliation, and economical dependency. This group consists mainly of men.
- Violent Resistence (VR). This group refers to the dynamic of defending against the attacks of a violent partner: mainly women.
- Mutual Violent Control (MVC): two terrorizing partners who want to control the other; they both use violence. This group consists of men and women.
- Common Couple Violence (CCV). Violence as a consequence of fights that get out of hand. In this group, men and women turn out to be equally violent.

Graham-Kevan and Archer (2002) researched a mixed group of women in shelters and their partners (N=86); male and female students (N=208); and males in a batterer programme and their wives (N=192) to classify the categories of Johnson. Respondents had to fill in questionnaires about physical aggression, injuries, escalations, and controlling behaviour. Respondents coming from shelters and batterer programmes could be connected more to the IT, VR, and MVC categories, and the students and part of the former group to CCV.

These figures trigger strong reactions. People who are convinced that domestic violence is mainly directed against women by men who want to dominate them question the outcomes of research that shows that women are as violent as men. They criticize the methodology of the research and suggest that the CTS only addresses mild forms of family violence. It strikes me that opponents never question research when the outcomes support their own ideas. I suppose the confusion is connected to the fact that we talk about different groups of violent persons. One group consists mainly of men terrorizing women, and this is the group we tend to think about when we consider domestic violence.

In relationships where one terrorizes the other, or both partners try to terrorize each other, *controlling* behaviour seems to be central. In couples where violence occurs when conflicts escalate and get out of hand, *loss of control* is central. We do not know exactly the size of these two different groups. But, when studying the huge figures on domestic violence, we have to realize that part of this is a group of men and women who fight each other and are equally violent. They experience light or severe forms of violence when conflicts escalate and explode. This group fits best into systemic couple therapy.

Men, women, and violence

In clinical practice, we also recognize that a lot of women use physical violence in conflict with their male partners. An often expressed example is that they try to prevent their spouse from leaving if he wants to go. We often hear that women are the provokers: they attack their spouse out of pure frustration, and the men in these cases state that violence is their only source of defence. Of course, even in these cases there are men who do not hesitate to hit and hurt their spouse.

Men and women use psychological violence. Men can humiliate and threaten women, but women can also belittle and undermine men. Dutton (2005) revised his perspective on couple violence. He started his research and treatment of male batterers from a feminist point of view. He supposed that violence in intimate relationships was used by men who had internalized values from patriarchy and wanted to dominate women. After twenty-five years of research, analysing, meta-analysing, and experiences with treatment of male batterers, he changed his mind. Metastudies showed that batterer programs built on the idea that batterers want to dominate women were not effective, recidives were extremely high (Babcock, Green, & Robie, 2004). Dutton started to think that feminist theory confused the issue by making men perpetrators and women victims. Violent behaviour by women was concealed. He still recognizes patriarchal terrorism in a small group, but he also recognizes matriarchal terrorism, and he found that 45% of couple violence is mutual. Much research addressed only women as victims, and this blurred the whole issue. Dutton now thinks that it is psychopathology that is the problem, not patriarchy. He concentrates on attachment injuries in violent persons.

I am afraid that he is focusing the subject too much on an individual perspective. Contextualizing violence is crucial. Social circumstances are of utmost importance: housing, financial resources (debts!), illness, work, neighbourhood, culture, discrimination, and other context-bound factors.

Dutton states that about 4% of severely violent men and women merit a gaol sentence, with treatment, but for the other 96% he suggests a combination of treatment directed to personality problems, self control, and couple therapy. We agree with these suggestions.

Violence and systemic therapy

If we let the results of all the different researches percolate, it is hard to believe that we, in our role as systemic therapists, have not become aware of the gravity and scale of the violence issue within the domestic circle much sooner. It is only due to the critical notes from the feminist perspective (Goldner, 1985, 1998; Hare-Mustin, 1978; Luepnitz, 1988) that emerged into our field of expertise some twenty or so years ago that we started to acknowledge this blind spot. We kept focusing on the reciprocation of interactions in which the perpetrator can be seen as a victim, too, and *vice versa*. Systemic therapists wanted to disengage from the reduced linear thinking which focuses on the cause of problems and instead concentrate on the circularity in order to search for a chain of interconnected symptoms. Neutrality was high on the agenda; systemic therapists had to keep an open mind towards both parties, immerse themselves with all involved, and refrain from any moral judgement. Thus, the possibility was created to keep the influence of gender, class, and culture out of the frame in the theoretical consideration and the analysis of the issue. This made it possible to overlook balances of power between family members, and in turn, for example, incest and abuse were either not recognized or ignored.

Defining violence

When we talk about violence in this book, we mean physical, psychological, and sexual violence. How do we define violence? Concerning content, it does seem impossible to answer this question properly. A slap could mean physical violence, but it can also be part of a cheerful frolic. Even injuries cannot be directly linked to physical violence. We have come to a definition that puts the relationship at centre-stage. We talk about violence when a family member damages the integrity of another family member and hurts the other psychologically and/or physically.

We have to distinguish between violence that is intentional and violence that is not-intentional. When one person terrorizes the other, violent behaviour has the *intention* to control the other. With common couple violence, people lose control during escalations and do not have the intention to harm the other person.

When we talk about terrorizing behaviour, we define violence as follows: a person abuses his or her physical and psychological dominance to threaten or hurt the other in order to create fear and, thus, maintain a superior position and keep the other in a subordinate position. Thus, a relational context is created in which the dominant person can impose his/her will on the subordinate one against their will.

We have already stated that sometimes this terrorizing and controlling behaviour is mutual. Both try to occupy the dominant position. This dynamic can lead to severe injuries, or even death.

With common violence, we refer to conflicts that get out of hand. In this context, it is much more difficult to talk about intention.

Violence has many faces: psychological, physical, and sexual, which can be from light to severe forms. It can be directed against children, adults, parents, the elderly. Brothers and sisters can be violent; other family members, grandparents, aunts and uncles, or close friends can be involved. Sometimes a power difference is crucial, as with parents and children; sometimes a power balance seems to exist.

We started to concentrate on physical violence, but our clients taught us to change our position on this. In the first place, physical and psychological violence go together; humiliation, threatening, and scolding often precede slapping. Second, many people say, after the violence has stopped, "I can forget about the beating, but I cannot forget about the words". A parent who learnt not to use physical punishment but who is shouting, "I wish you hadn't entered my life, you are spoiling my whole life, I wish you were dead" is probably causing even more harm. We want to distinguish these issues from incest: serious violence with a different dynamic. Perpetrators of incest have different motives and the relational dynamic is quite different from the dynamic of violent escalations. We do not address this issue in this book. Many other publications inform readers about incest and families (Bentovim, 1988; Lamers-Winkelman, 2000; Sheinberg, 2001).

The influence of gender

Gender development influences behaviour, also violent behaviour of men and women. We would like to use the definition of gender by Meulenbelt (1997). She defines gender at different levels:

> The biological difference, thus creating a gender-identity, interconnected with the early stages of personality development. This is influenced by a set of codes for masculinity and femininity that may differ with culture, timeframe and social background. Subsequently this is linked to the social context: the distribution of labour, money and power. [pp. 10–11]

This elaborate description (Meulenbelt goes further) does justice to the complexity of the concept. We will dwell on the different elements of the definition.

The biological difference

Whether "masculine" and "feminine" behaviour are explained by biological principles and cerebral differences is a recurring discussion. A lot of research is available which shows that male and female brains work differently. These differences are more connected to power differences and different positions in society than with essential, innate differences. These differences are connected with the influence of hormones as well (Kimura, 1992).Women are said to use both halves of their brain more and they divide their attention better than men. They can interpret non-verbal signals well, are good at languages, and focused on co-operation. The left half of the brain seems to be dominant with men. They can hold and focus their attention, have a well developed spatial awareness, are problem-solving, and prepared to go into action themselves. This, of course, is a generalization; each individual will have a unique combination of qualities. These differences have been formed during the course of evolution and are intertwined with the different roles that men and women fulfil in society. If these divisions of tasks change significantly, and if this lasts for generations, these differences may change. It is striking, for instance, when observing men who serve women in power to find how good they are in interpreting the non-verbal signals of their female boss and, for example, bring water when needed.

It is striking how many people give a sigh of relief when once again it is "discovered" that the difference between men and women stems from different neurological connections in the brain. "No point in worrying, everything is written in stone already", seems to be the general idea. One easily abandons the broadly accepted conviction that body and soul, or "soma" and "psyche", form an indivisible unit and one opts for biological determinism. Circularity is easily swapped for linear causality: the brains differ, *ergo* women and men differ, herein lies the cause. I like to come full circle: it is not possible to conclude where "nature" stops and "nurture" takes over, genes and environmental factors form an indivisible unit and can only be comprehended within this context.

Gender identity

Gender identity is formed in the first years of one's life and is anchored in the primal layers of the personality. Freud thought that gender identity developed only from the fourth year onwards. It has transpired, through the work of Stoller (1968) and Delfos (2001), that children "know" that they are a boy or a girl from a very early age and subsequently behave as such. Parents and others react differently towards a boy or a girl, as does society. With a male baby, taking initiative, for example, is stimulated. This starts while in the womb: if there is a lot of activity and movement in the belly then it will probably be a "real" boy. The code for masculine behaviour expects and approves initiative in almost all cultures. The same goes for wooing a female. The expectation that the young women will have to keep relationships going stems from gender identity, too. Girls are stimulated to co-operate properly from an early age onwards. This transpires beautifully from Tannen's (1990) language research. As toddlers, girls are already busying themselves to find solutions when opinions differ so that they can play together, while boys defend their territory and will be likely to start a fight. Girls say, "Shall we . . .", and boys say, "I want . . ." There is something to be said for both attitudes. Precisely because this gender identity is so deeply anchored within us, it has a wide-ranging influence on our behaviour even though we are often unaware of this.

The codes that are imposed on girls and boys, women and men, differ with culture, class, and time frame. There are numerous examples. We will name a few.

A man behind a stroller or with a baby in a pouch on the belly meets the criteria of the new male code of North-Western Europe. It is much less so in Southern Europe and unthinkable in, for example, a traditional Creole family. Despite this, an unemployed Dutch father refused point-blank the suggestion that he should take his little boy to school, "because", he stated, "I am not one of those softies who carry their child on their bikes in a child's saddle." Obviously this image did not fit in his code of masculinity. At the beginning of the twentieth century, going to university was regarded in our culture as unfeminine. It was even believed that too much study would result in a woman losing her fertility. Nowadays, girls as well as boys are stimulated to learn, and, on average, girls achieve higher grades than boys at secondary level. In many university courses the majority of students consists of women, including in medicine and law. Boys seem to be the vulnerable sex nowadays; they are uncertain of what is expected from them and of their role when women study, work, and deliver children and care.

In traditional religious education, a distinction between girls' and boys' subjects is still made. The code for femininity and masculinity is more stringent in a traditional context. Turkish girls are not allowed to glance at, or kiss, a man. Only when they are married can they "give" themselves to their husbands. It is, therefore, important to examine time and again how masculinity and femininity are outlined in a specific culture, within a specific time frame, with *these* people from *this* family.

The social context

This is a dimension which is often ignored in psychological literature. Studies in the fields of sociology and anthropology show convincingly that the influence of division of labour, money, and care is a strong defining factor. Interesting in this regard is the study of Gilmore (1990), who researched the code for masculinity all over the world. He arrived at the conclusion that the differences between the sexes are more distinct if the means of living are dwindling and the environment (e.g., climate) is harsher. He found only two cultures where the difference between men and women is not emphasized. These turned out to be groups (the Semi and Tahitians) where there has always been an abundance of means of sustenance and, as a result, a warring tradition was non-existent. Given that we live in an affluent society, this creates the possibility of putting less emphasis on gender difference. Economically harsher times, however, will immediately put more pressure on the division of work and money. The "given right" of men to work often gets priority over the employment of women.

Yet another example: the fact that so many women cut down their working hours with the arrival of children has far-reaching consequences for the economy. Men often work longer hours given the same situation, and in doing so make career leaps. Women put their careers on the back burner and fall behind in the job market. It seems almost impossible to catch up and it has significant economic consequences. This inequality causes financial dependency of women and the results are painful if the marriage ends in a divorce. The humiliating position in which many mothers on welfare or on a minimal income find themselves is common know-ledge. Worldwide poverty seems to be a women's issue. Around the turn of the century, 80% of the world population who live below the poverty line were women.

When we talk about gender formation in this book, we mean the complexity of male and female behaviour that is based on all the aforementioned levels. This concept will be used extensively in Chapter Three, regarding the downward spiral of violence between men and women.

The influence of personal history

Next to social and cultural context and gender, personal history plays a meaningful role. People can be raised in a family where regulating emotions is problematic. Families can be unsafe. In an unsafe context, children have to survive by finding solutions; fight-ing others can be one way.

When children grow up in a family where they can find safe attachments to care-givers, they can learn to regulate their emotions in these safe relationships. They also learn to care for other people without fear of losing their autonomy. In unsafe relationships with care-givers, development of the ability to regulate emotions is hindered in children, and these people are more easily triggered to use violence in relationships.

In the context of this book, we cannot elaborate on this issue, but other publications do explain more deeply this developmental process (Fonagy, 2001; Johnson, 2004).

We think all human beings can be violent under certain circum-stances, but people who develop well in a safe and loving environ-ment learn to regulate aggression and can avoid violent escalations.

So, assessing personality problems is very important. Other psy-chopathology, such as depression, mania, psychosis, and other psy-chiatric syndromes, also can be connected to interpersonal violence, but it is beyond the remit of this book to go into this issue deeply.

Substance abuse

Addiction to alcohol, medicine, drugs, or gambling enhances the chance of violent explosions. These substances do not directly lead to violence, but the brake on violent behaviour does not work well. Treatment of addiction is crucial when aiming at stopping violence.

Changes in the balance of power within the family unit

In the past forty years, a change has come about in the development between male–female relationships in our Western culture. Far into the 1950s, an imbalance of power between men and women was an accepted fact. The matrimonial ideal was of compliance; husband and wife were supposed to complement each other. Inequality was not experienced or seen as an imbalance of power, and did not carry the notion of suppression of the wife by the husband's dominance. In the 1960s, things changed in this regard. The matrimonial ideal shifted towards more equality between men and women. Nowadays, the imbalance of power is not readily accepted and in a lot of marriages there is an ongoing battle (silent or more vocal) about the division of care. The authoritarian father or partner is no longer popular in our Western culture. Husbands who hit their wives used to be met with understanding, support even, because women were seen as subordinate: they had to obey their husbands. Today, a man who hits his spouse will be met with disapproval.

Men who hit ought to be ashamed of themselves. Research has shown that attitudes towards men who hit their spouses are changing. In the USA, 13% of interviewees in 1990 were of the opinion that, under certain circumstances, a husband is allowed to hit his wife; in 1992 this was down to 12% and it decreased even more, to 10%, in 1994 (Gelles, 1997).

Among the young there is an awareness of the norm that men are not allowed to hit women. This became evident to me when my daughter, aged seventeen at the time, managed to stop a fight between some young men. I asked her and my then fifteen-year-old son why they thought that girls are more successful in stopping a fight and why boys, if they try to intervene, probably get knocked about themselves. My son knew the answer immediately. "If you hit a girl, you're a pansy; you just don't hit a girl." My daughter added that there is no reason for fearing a girl might join the fight, because girls do not fight. I asked what their thoughts were on girls who do fight. "Those are bitches," was their response. It did not sound very uplifting.

The guidelines along which we educate our children have undergone changes as well. When we read contemporary pedagogical literature which gives advice to parents and professionals alike, we detect a strong shift towards less physical violence. In the 1950s, physical punishment was regarded as a necessary part of child-rearing. Parents and teachers were expected to teach the children how to behave in a civilized manner and in accordance with the prevailing norm. Despite the fact that the norms on civilized and proper behaviour have changed with the times, the guidelines along which we educate our children have not changed that much in general. "The hand that rocks the cradle is the hand that rules the world" and "Spare the rod, spoil the child" were perennially popular sayings. Parents and teachers raised children with authority. In cases where a child did not accept their authority, physical punishment was regarded as quite normal and even advisable. "A household of commands", as De Swaan (1982) calls it.

That these practices have not entirely vanished transpired when an eighteen-year-old Belgian girl applied for the job of baby-sitter for my children. In our interview, she admitted that she regarded hitting as an integral part of raising children. She herself had been hit many times by her own father, but she saw no grounds to reject him. "He loved me and I had it coming." I decided to look for another baby-sitter. During a television broadcast about counselling Moroccan youths who are running riot (6 January, 1998), a Moroccan father who clearly loved his children and who would do almost anything for them elaborated extensively about the fact that raising children is impossible without hitting them. He was of the opinion that if the Dutch police would hit more often and harder, those boys would stop their criminal behaviour.

In the past century, ideas about child-raising have changed slowly but surely in Western European and North American culture. Psychological theories emerged in the modes of thought about child development. Sigmund Freud, and, later on, his daughter Anna Freud, have had a significant influence. Children were no longer regarded as somewhat flawed adults who had to be reared with a tight grip into civil human beings, but as emotional young people who could get damaged and hurt. The authoritarian style of educating gave way to a more democratic style. The ideal became: proper contact with the child in order for it to develop within a safe attachment (especially with the mother). As an extreme counter-movement, anti-authoritarian education and anti-authoritarian daycare centres were created, with the idea that children should grow up properly, wholly and totally free, if they were not hindered in any way. It is common knowledge that this extreme form could not survive in our culture. Democratic education became the dominant norm. The "household of commands" shifted towards the "household of negotiations" (De Swaan, 1982). Children were allowed to voice their own opinions and they were heard. The accepted ideal was *not* to hit children. In the public domain, physical punishment was prohibited by law. If a teacher hits a child, the parents can sue him or her. In the private domain, parents can still spank their children without causing any judicial action, even though physical punishment is banned in the European Treaty of Human Rights, Clause 3.

Disappearing acts

Just because the balance of power within the family unit has undergone changes and the use of violence is frowned upon in our culture, this does not imply a factual decrease.

Gelles (1997) finds that 84% to 97% of all parents around the world apply physical punishment to their children. Physical punishment does not cease when the children are mature enough to partake in discussions. Gelles quotes research conducted in the USA which concluded that 50% of the young were still being hit when they were high-school seniors. Baartman (1993), too, convincingly shows in his study about violence in child-raising matters how the rearing culture is drenched with heavy-handed treatment of children. Meanwhile, women's magazines, family magazines, and books about child-rearing from the 1950s onwards tell us time and again: "A good parent does not hit his/her child". Consequently, parents who do hit their children, more or less out of despair, feel guilty: they do not fit the image of a good parent that they themselves, in all probability, have internalized; the parent who has a good relationship with the child, who can listen and discuss in order to arrive at solutions together, does not hit. Educational spanking of a child is still allowed, although acceptance is declining. Again in the USA, in 1983, some 83% still found it necessary to spank a child at times; in 1991, this was down to 73%. In the Scandinavian countries, the spanking of children is now prohibited by law; there was an ongoing discussion in the Netherlands about this in 2002, but a bill which prohibits parents from ever hitting their children was not passed.

The statistics of what people find acceptable differ significantly from the statistics about what actually happens between men and women, parents and children. Even though the "PC" offensive has turned against violence within human relations, we cannot therefore conclude the actual decline of violence. The notion of progress, the philosophical idea that through more discussion civilization will yield a more peaceful existence between men (Elias, 1982), does not hold true. There was (is?) this notion that people in the Middle Ages were still primitive in glorifying violence: public tortures and burnings were, after all, a magnet for a day out. We are supposed to be more civilized. However, when we consider what has happened in the past century with regard to wars, street violence, and domestic violence, and how the beginning of this century is already drenched in menace and violence, we will have to acknowledge that we, as a species, are very limited creatures, that we are easily influenced, and that violence between human beings is not "civilized away" that easily. Even though physical violence is forbidden by law, it does not seem to be declining. Violence on the streets and in the domestic circle seems to be on the increase. Violent interactions have proved to be not that easily banned.

We have developed ideas about the discrepancy between the fact that physical violence between people in our culture is ever more repudiated and the fact that physical violence between people seems to be increasing, rather than decreasing.

Precisely because of public repudiation of physical violence in human relations, this phenomenon finds itself in the domain of taboo. Because violence is "not done", and is attached to shame, it goes "underground" in both interpersonal (hitting within the walls of one's home has to remain a secret) and intra-personal (the violence must not become part of oneself; it is repressed or split off) relationships. Responsibility for violent behaviour is laid at the doorstep of the other. Responsibility for one's actions are laid outside the person; self-control therefore becomes problematic.

Precisely this can lead to boundless violent behaviour. Shame is a contributing factor as well. In Chapter Seven, Martine Groen will elaborate on the theme of shame.

A comparison can be made with eating disorders. A lot of women with eating disorders tell me that they have no control over it. Although they resist, "something takes over". Once the feeding-frenzy has started, there is no stopping it, ". . . because I lost out already, I don't care one way or the other". A man recalls his violence in this manner: "If she has cornered me into hitting her, I think, you're going to get it now, 'cause this is what you wanted, didn't you?" We think it is paramount to reclaim the theme "aggression in relationships" from the shadowland of taboo and acknowledge that the capacity for aggression is as much a part of oneself as the capacity to love.

Consequences for therapeutic practice

As we stated before, shame leads to disassociation. This, in turn, leads to major problems for psychotherapy as well. Dissociation results in not experiencing one's behaviour as an integral part of oneself. "This isn't me, I'm not violent; something alien to me is letting me do this." Responsibility is not taken because it is placed outside oneself.

These two consequences of the taboo-and-shame complex make it very hard to find points of departure for psychotherapy. Two questions are at the centre: how can we entice our clients to reclaim their violent behaviour in order to make them say, "Yes, this is me, I can be a violent person", and how can we tempt our clients to take responsibility for the way in which they express their violent tendencies? Are there any forms of expressing aggression linked to frustration which do not damage another?

Here, we enter difficult territory. When we entice people to reclaim their aggressive tendencies, we legitimize its existence. Therefore, we must be prepared to acknowledge that our own aggressive feelings are just as much part of ourselves as our capacity to love and form attachments. As psychotherapists, we must be prepared to explore our own aggression and violent tendencies, and acknowledge its existence within ourselves.

We regard aggression as an existential part of human behaviour. When aggression is rejected or denied, there is a potential danger that aggressive feelings can fester and thus create boundlessness.

So, we arrive at the following conclusions. Psychotherapists, social workers, and others would be advised to examine their own aggression, to get to know it and deal with it. In this way, they can recognize and examine aggression and aggressive expressions of others (among whom will be some of their clients) without being overcome by fear. If the therapist has not dealt with his/her own aggression and aggressive experiences in his/her own life properly, then it is most likely that this therapist will ignore the clients' aggression, entirely repudiate it, or not recognize it. Adequate care for one's own safety in working with aggression still remains a necessary condition.

It is paramount to find new forms in which aggression can be expressed in a structured manner without inflicting damage on other persons.

CHAPTER TWO

Together you will progress

Justine van Lawick

Most issues on violence within partner relationships only come to light when a woman seeks help within the framework of individual care, from either the GP, A & E departments, social services, the police force, lawyers, Victim Aid, Child Care, primary health care psychologists, addiction care, psychotherapy, or psychiatry. In this chapter, we will discuss the possibility of engaging partners in therapy in order to enhance its effectiveness and speed. In most cases, the woman, categorized as victim, is the one who starts talking, either willingly or because a therapist asks the right questions. Sharing the secret of abuse with a therapist offers relief, but it often comes with the client's injunction not to mention the abuse to others, including the abusive partner. The help given will focus mainly on survival strategies for the woman and ways to leave the abusive partner. Shelters for abused women and their children can be a temporary refuge.

This individual approach can create a stand-off, and sometimes even take a turn for the worse. If the spouse grows more confident and shows more resistance, either on her own or through a group for abused women, this could prove threatening for the husband and, in turn, increase the violence. This could lead to even more control over the spouse and to increased isolation, thus leading to the cancellation of appointments. When the spouse threatens divorce, the situation can escalate even more, because the husband's violence will increase when his fear of abandonment grows. In some cases, an abused spouse will receive help from social services over a long period of time without any noticeable change in her situation. Whenever the social worker insists on a joint interview with the husband, the request will be repudiated for whatever reason, while, during the course of every interview, the spouse will mention the unbearable situation at home. Thus, the social worker gets sucked into the victim's helplessness and contributes to the status quo. The one most likely to need to change, the partner, remains scot-free of having to take any responsibility, and therefore does not receive any support in any process of change. The spouse is in a position where she takes responsibility by asking for help, but, more often than not, she is incapable of changing the situation at home.

The partner can come into the picture when the woman is stimulated to report to the police, and this can lead to obligatory therapy programmes for batterers. The problem here is that research shows that batterer treatment programmes have very little effect and high recidivist outcomes (Babcock & LaTaillade, 2000).

The conclusion must be that individual treatment is less effective because the couple dynamic and the behaviour of the woman stays concealed. In women's groups for victims of violence, it is not permissible to talk about the violent behaviour of women: "He is responsible, women tend to take too much responsibility all the time, HE has to control himself and keep you safe". In programmes for batterers, men cannot talk about the violent behaviour of their female partners. If they say, "But often she attacks me first", therapists ask them not to externalize and blame others for their behaviour; they are responsible for controlling themselves, whatever the woman does. So, in both groups, the violent behaviour of woman is out of court and cannot be investigated, and the couple dynamic stays out of sight.

We prefer a mutual approach for the couple in order to invite both partners to take responsibility for promoting safety in the home and stopping violent behaviour. It is crucial to focus on the couple dynamic and on the personality problems of the individuals.

A clear differentiation can be made between complementary and symmetrical dynamics. In the complementary violent dynamic, one takes the power and the other has to submit. The one in power controls and dominates the partner. If the partner is opposing the one in power, the dominant one increases the acts of control and domination. Psychological and physical violence, or threatening with violence, are instrumental. The subordinate partner gets frightened and tries to avoid escalations; this triggers subordinate behaviour and, as a result of this spiral, the power difference grows. This is the group in which one partner terrorizes the other, as described in Chapter One.

In the symmetrical dynamic, a continuing struggle for power is central. Each tries to get hold of the other or the situation through psychological, physical, or sexual interventions. The aggression of one invites the aggression of the other. Such situations can escalate until they become a harsh fight, sometimes resulting in actual wounds.

When one partner is terrorizing, controlling, intimidating, and isolating the other, couple therapy is not the first choice of action. Safety for the threatened partner must be provided first. This group is a small group; most couples become violent because conflicts get out of hand.

Stith, Rosen, McCollum, and Thomsen (2004) carried out research on couple therapy as a treatment module for couple violence, comparing individual couple therapy and couple groups. The outcome was that couple therapy in couple groups was effective in reducing recidivism even more than individual couple therapy.

A treatment model that involves both partners is more effective, safer, and offers more prospects for a future without violence. Partners who hurt each other can also have a strong bond. Many do not want a divorce; they want the violence to stop. A joint treatment programme opens up the possibility of inviting both partners to take responsibility for changing their behaviour in order to stop the violence. Others, too, such as children and family members, can be involved. This contextualizing of violence seems to be much more effective than an individual focus.

Exceptions can be caused by addiction, lack of motivation to stay together, destructive antisocial behaviour, or serious psychopathology.

So, when couple therapy seems to be indicated as an effective solution, how do we motive clients to bring in their partners?

In both batterer treatment programmes and treatment programmes for victims, it turns out to be very difficult to involve partners. When a man is in a treatment programme for perpetrators, the wife is often so relieved that he now has to change his behaviour that she is not willing to go into treatment herself. She wants him back when he is more friendly and co-operative, and when he learns to stop violent behaviour. The danger is that her behaviour is hidden. For instance, if she enjoys the power of her new role as legitimated victim and uses this to control him, this dynamic can be the catalyst for new violence.

When victims ask for help, they often do not want their partners to be involved because they are afraid of what would happen. They want to do it themselves. We think that this is always a pitfall, and that seeing both partners together is nearly always the best way to go, at least for assessment. In treatment programmes for perpetrators, couple sessions ought to be part of the treatment routine. When a man returns home after treatment, couple sessions are necessary.

It seems to be more complicated to involve a partner when the wife asks for professional help. In this chapter, we concentrate on this situation and we offer some ideas on how to proceed to involve a partner in treatment.

One of the key abilities of every therapist is the ability to motivate the client to bring the partner or important others to the interview. With the issue on violence come additional barriers to motivating the partner to partake in therapy; we would like to elaborate on these.

The abused partner, almost always a woman, objects to inviting her abusive husband because she is scared. "If he knows that I come here to talk about it, he will beat me up." Often, there is also the presumption that he will not come anyway. "That's not like him, he's not the talking kind, he thinks this is all nonsense, he doesn't believe in it, he will never come." The sex of the counsellor may be used as a reason: "He never takes a woman seriously; he will never listen to you". Culture can play a part, too: "My husband does not wish to talk to a woman".

It is paramount, in our experience, to involve the husband in the therapy at the earliest possible stage of the therapeutic process. If the wife has already established a long-standing contact with the therapist, she will become ever more entangled with the wife and her story and suffering, which interferes with a dual position. It will become more difficult and threatening for the husband to show up. "They only want to tell me off, they believe everything she says anyway, I can do without that, thank you very much."

Groen (2001) cites a few possible questions to put to the wife that can help her in motivating the husband to come along: the possible damage that might be inflicted on the children, which he surely would want to prevent, a possible divorce if the situation at home does not improve, or to prevent pressing charges with the police, which might jeopardize his job as well. It might be helpful for her to consider whether her husband would want a wife who is scared of him, and to examine the possibilities of lessening his sense of shame.

If all this does not help and the wife is unwilling to invite her husband herself, or if she says she asked him but he refuses, it might be a good strategy for the counsellor to try to contact the husband. One can discuss with the wife an appropriate time to call him. In our experience, almost all men are willing to come if you emphasize that you want to hear their side of the story. Even the husbands whose wives were adamant that they would never oblige are remarkably easy to persuade to make an appointment. It might be a good idea to talk to him one-on-one, in order for the husband to experience your willingness to listen to him. It is, however, paramount to make it crystal clear during the course of the one-on-one interview that you do not condone physical violence within family relationships and that counselling is meant to find other ways to solve conflicts. If you, alongside all this, are really intent on listening to his version of the situation, it is often not difficult to make an appointment for a mutual interview afterwards. Dutton, Golant, and Pijnaker (2000) emphasize the fear of abandonment with violent men. We will return to this later on in this book, but for now I mention it because it helps me to realize that almost all men want to prevent a divorce, and this can be a significant motivation to accept therapy and to change.

There are cases where one cannot persuade the partner to come for an appointment, and this leaves you with three options.

First, one can examine through which important others the partner might be motivated. This could be a family member, such as a respected uncle or a brother, or a respected member of the community: the GP, the vicar, imam, or another respectable figure. It is vital, after discussing it with the spouse, to contact this middleman to examine whether this would be a correct interpretation of things.

The second option is coaching the spouse into going to the police or to press charges. Taking the judicial road can sometimes be a good way into couple therapy, because it has been made clear from the start that the violent behaviour of the partner is against the law. In the projects for domestic violence that have been up and running for a couple of years in several municipalities in the Netherlands, it is common practice to start enforced therapy after a report to, or pressing of charges with, the police; the opportunity for therapy is offered, but if a batterer is unwilling to co-operate, criminal proceedings will be started and then it is all up to the Department of Public Prosecutions. From January 2009 onwards, a new law in the Netherlands makes it possible to exclude the perpetrator from the family home for ten days, with the possibility of prolongation. During this time, intensive help for the whole family is initiated.

A third possibility is for the wife to leave the home with her children and find refuge in a shelter for abused women and children. Nowadays, it is mainly migrant women who choose this option; it is often the only way for them to escape a life-threatening situation. In cases where one can presume the partner to be a psychopathic abuser (see Chapters Four and Nine for further details) it can be the best possible route to take.

To conclude, it is important to mention that not all couple therapy will lead to maintaining the relationship. In some cases, it is clear that a divorce could be the best option. It is mostly the wife who sets the wheels in motion for a divorce, especially when she feels safer. In such cases, relationship therapy offers better prospects for future security for all concerned and it increases the chance of preventing future violence after the divorce, in the form of stalking, for example.

If, aided by the possibilities offered in this chapter, one succeeds in motivating both partners to take on couple sessions, the first session will follow suit. The next chapter will handle this subject.

CHAPTER THREE

The downward spiral of violence between partners

Justine van Lawick

Introduction

I clearly recall Peter and Ella, two good-looking, young, and successful people who came to me in the outpatients clinic of a psychiatric centre two days after Ella had attempted suicide by using drugs. Peter had found her just in time, and the hospital where Ella was admitted first referred them to me. Pressing for the reason as to why she had tried to commit suicide, I realized that Ella saw herself as worthless. Despite her shiny career as a manager of a medium-sized company, a beautiful house, a good income, social life, and travels abroad, she still felt unhappy and worthless. Peter was flabbergasted, and did not cease to praise her beauty, her captivating manners, elegant appearance, and cooking skills whenever they entertained guests. He did, however, find that she worked too long hours, and he blamed the demands of her job for her breakdown. He himself was not such a high flyer, and he experienced less stress as a result. When I examined her existential crisis further, it appeared she had undergone several operations in order to fulfil Peter's wishes even more. She had had a breast enhancement and a nose-job, her eyelids had been lifted, and her teeth had been perfected, all in the course of two years. Peter now demanded lipo-suction of her thighs, which he considered to be somewhat fat. He had already made some enquiries and found that it was possible. Ella had resisted openly for the first time ever, and said that she did not want any more tweaking done on her body. Peter did not let up, and pressed on about the surgery. The conflict ended in their first row ever, in which Peter had slapped her.

I can remember my abhorrence at hearing this story, and did not really know how to deal with it at the time. I could not understand Ella's willingness to let this all happen to her and I felt a strong aversion to Peter for treating her as an object. Ella went into a downward spiral of depression and was admitted to hospital. I lost contact. Later, after learning more about gender theory and the connection it has with psychopathology, and after being educated in the treatment of violence in love relationships, I thought about these two young people now and then. This case had it all: reduc-ing women to objects, so they do not feel they have a right to exist and cannot build any self-esteem, and the focus of men on achieve-ment, which in turn leads to their "dehumanizing" and becoming fearful when their wives reach a higher point on the career ladder, resulting in the downward spiral in which they both get caught up, which leads to escalation and violence. I would have dealt with it differently now.

In 1976, I started relation therapy for couples who experienced a broad variety of problems. I educated myself both at home and abroad, and became more and more experienced in working with this complex matter. However, some cases got me nowhere. An almost palpable tension hovered in the consultation room and it was difficult to build a work relationship, which, in most cases, worked like a charm. No real contact came about, and I felt relieved when the couples did not turn up after a while.

In May 1991, I took part in the International Women's Confer-ence about systemic therapy, held in Copenhagen. Systemic vio-lence was one of the major subjects, especially violence committed by men against women in heterosexual relationships and the conse-quences thereof. The majority of speakers who talked about this subject hailed from the USA. They were more advanced both in the theory-shaping regarding violence and in the development of methods for handling violence. Afterwards, I came to the shocking realization of how little I had actually mentioned the subject of violence during the course of an interview, and that this could explain a number of unsatisfying lapses in therapies. Of course, the subject of violence was mentioned, but only in the vaguest of terms ("a smack is handed out in any relationship") and always in relation to other problems which needed do be dealt with. Post May 1991, I drastically changed my modes of thought and work method with regard to working with violence between partners. I studied the thesis of Römkens (1989), which showed that, in the Netherlands, about one in five women have to deal with some form of physical violence by their male partner. I realized that these numbers would probably be much higher with the couples who came into therapy. This, in turn, motivated me to ask couples very specific questions about the several expressions of violence. Even with couples whom I had treated for some time, violence appeared to be common practice without it ever being discussed properly in therapy. I started to work with clients on taking responsibility for breaking escalations before touching problematic issues. After all, a safe work relationship was impossible when talking about difficult issues could lead to new escalations at home. Slowly but surely, I gathered experience in working with couples where violent behaviour occurs. I found support in Goldner, Penn, Sheinberg, and Walker's paper, "Love and violence: gender paradoxes in volatile attachments" (1990), and later I found similarities in the work of Martine Groen, who had specialized in working with issues of violence for much longer. Together, we developed a theoretic framework in which we were able to understand the violence between men and women and which offers handles for therapeutic treatment with these couples. This chapter is a reflection on that subject.

When Goldner, at the beginning of 1997, had submitted her most recent publication (Goldner, 1997) and came to Haarlem in April 1997 to give a workshop in the Lorentzhuis, a centre for systemic therapy, education, and consultancy, it transpired that her work and our work had progressed in the same direction. It is possible that you will encounter ideas in this chapter that correspond to the ideas of Goldner. All three of us were pleasantly surprised that, on both sides of the Atlantic, the same modules were being developed. We are very happy to credit Virginia Goldner with all honours that are due to her as a pioneer in this field. She has inspired us in order to develop the treatment that we will describe next.

A head-start in the consultation room

Harry enters first. Broadly built, he has tattoos on his arm, and wears tight-fitting jeans and a white T-shirt. Bianca follows him silently; she is slim, and also dressed in tight jeans and a white T-shirt. They sit down. I tell them something about the practice in which they have landed and my position there. Subsequently, I sign them up. This reveals their age, where they live, what they do for a living, or whether they are unemployed, if they have any children and, if so, how many and of which parent, who referred them, and what kind of medical insurance they have. This offers an abundance of information about their social status and their circumstances. Sometimes an admission form, where the names of the partners as well as their children are taken down, shows four different last names and the complex context of a remarried family is revealed at once. Therapists in institutions, who have to delegate the handling of this paperwork to office staff, do miss the opportunity to gather this relevant information at first hand. After all, this information forms the social fabric that binds all therapeutic sessions.

Harry is twenty-two and Bianca is twenty. They live in an upstairs flat in an old quarter of Haarlem. They have no children. He is a cab-driver, she is a check-out girl at a supermarket, but she is on sick leave because she started to make too many mistakes brought on by frequent headaches.

Subsequently I explain the procedure relating to the fees and their own contribution (€ 15.00 per session). An open discussion follows as to whether this could be a problem. Openly discussing the finances surrounding the therapy is essential. It creates an ambience of transparency where everything is open to discussion. Furthermore, it emphasizes the fact that therapy costs money. If people have financial difficulties, it will come out in the open immediately. In our practice, a lack of money does not translate into withholding therapy from people who cannot afford their own contribution. In emergencies, we find one solution or another.

In Harry and Bianca's case the fee is no object. I explain what a first interview entails.

Therapist	"As I already mentioned on the phone this interview will last for an hour and a half tops. I want to know about the problems that made you come here. I would like to hear it from both of you. You can each tell me your own story and you do not have to agree with each other. At the end of the interview I will summarize both your problems and we will draw up a plan for the therapy. Who wants to start? Tell me, what has brought you here?"

Harry: "They say I'm in the wrong, but that's not how I see it. I am here because she wants me to and because she says there's no hope for us."

Therapist: "Could you tell me about the things that bother you and which you would like to change?"

Harry: "I don't see any problems; she just has to stop moaning about me doing everything wrong."

Therapist: "I heard you twice already about being accused of handling everything the wrong way. That must bother you. Do you get cross when someone says you do things wrong?"

Harry: "Yes, of course I get angry when someone bugs me all the time."

Therapist: "I would like to understand you properly; can you give me an example? When was the last time you got cross?"

Harry glances at Bianca, who stares at the floor.

Harry: "This morning. I had some trouble getting out of bed. My shift ended at three in the morning. She called me every five minutes to get out of bed because we had this appointment. And when I finally did get out of bed, she just wouldn't let up. I can't stand that. She knows that very well."

Therapist: "So, you got cross, and what happens when you get cross?"

Harry: "Well, she knows very well that she has to stop when I get angry."

Therapist: In what way do you get angry? Do you yell, do you say spiteful things, or do you say nothing at all, do you give her a shove, do you hit . . . What is it that you do when you really get mad?"

Harry glances at Bianca again who looks back, more alert this time.

Harry: "Now it all boils down to my anger, but that is caused by something, we were both supposed to tell our side of the story; she can have her turn now and tell everything that is bugging her."

Therapist: "I do want to hear both your stories. Thankfully, we have plenty of time for that, but I would like to get on with this first. In what way do you get mad? Do you stick to words or do you hit as well?"

Harry: "I slap her now and then, but she had it coming."

Within five minutes we are talking about violence. In our experience, rather then avoiding it, it offers people some relief. They themselves know very well that their conflicts get out of hand regularly, and that leaves them deeply ashamed most of the time. If it does not come out in the open in the first interview, a tension will be present. They will constantly be wondering when "it" will come out.

Working with the issues on violence has also changed my ideas about how to conduct a first interview. I used to think that one had to take time to get acquainted with one's clients and to get more familiar with their surroundings, that one should make them feel at ease, that one had to ask about everyday things before touching on their problems. I have stopped doing that. In my experience, it is much better to use the tension that people bring into a first meeting and to involve oneself by listening properly to their problems. After all, they are not here to discuss their hobbies. Getting the violence out in the open quickly is not always this easy. At times, resistance is much stronger, and one pussyfoots around for a long time. Asking specific questions proves to be the best strategy. We ask each partner about their concrete actions. When the man is violent against the woman we ask him how often, in what situation, how serious, if the violence leads to physical wounds, and so on. We do not question the woman about the violent actions of her partner. This would force her into the position of "betraying" her husband, and this could prove to be dangerous for her. Maybe she had to promise beforehand not to mention the violence. Any information the wife offers is often coloured by fear, which results in playing down the violence. Asking the man specific questions, in general, offers more transparent information. Asking the woman about her actions is also important, her part in the escalations. Does she chase him? Does she paralyse? When? Where? And so on.

Therapist: "Bianca, I hear Harry explain that he has the feeling that he cannot do anything good in your eyes, then he gets extremely frustrated and explodes. What do you do when you get angry?"

Bianca: (looking at the ground) I do say something, I say the wrong things and then he gets angry."

Harry: "Now you see! She admits, she says stupid things, I never do good, I cannot stand that."

Therapist: Then you say harsh things to each other and then things get out of hand . . ."

I make violence the focal point if it does occur. I also explain why.

Therapist: "I would like to share something with you. Scolding and hitting happens in a lot of relationships. Just as in your case. You are not an exception to the rule. I do, however, have a problem. I think that scolding, threatening, intimidating, hitting, shoving, kicking, and other forms of violence are not the way to solve problems. Mostly, they only magnify any problems that people may have. It renders your relationship unsafe, so you can no longer enjoy each other's company, and makes the therapy unsafe as well. We cannot discuss things when there is a serious possibility that things will escalate at home, maybe because of the topics we discussed during the session. I find it too unsafe as well. I cannot conduct my work in a proper manner when I constantly have to worry about things getting out of hand in your home and whether Bianca is at risk. We will have to find a way to resolve the problem so that she will not get hit any more at home. I have worked with a lot of couples where the husbands hit their wives. Also with women who hit their men, mothers who hit children, or adolescents who hit their parents. I have come to the conclusion that in most cases these are not bad people. They themselves find it awful not to be able to control their anger. They are ashamed that they sometimes let things get out of hand. I also know that something can be done about it in order to cease the scolding and hitting. I would like to work on that first. We can start the therapy after that and then we can discuss all the things that cause problems in your relationship. This precedes the therapy. Would you like to work on such a programme?"

In some cases, couples quickly agree to this proposition. Often, they have tried to stop the beatings. Women attempt this by avoiding situations that might bring about an escalation, while men try by promising afterwards to do better next time. They often feel guilty and are determined not to hit again. Despondency surrounds this issue, precisely because it often goes wrong again. The fact that the therapist proposes that something can be done about it and that he/she can help, offers hope. It is a well-known fact that creating hope for the better is one of the strongest working factors to positively influence the success of therapy. Sometimes, people come into our practice for therapy precisely because they have issues with violence within their relationship and they are aware that we are specialized in handling this. In those cases, they willingly go ahead with a programme to end the violence because that is what they came for in the first place. In some cases, it takes much more effort. Cultural differences play a part in this.

With Harry and Bianca it went like this:

Harry: "I find it hard being painted as a violent wife-beating caricature, because that is not me at all. I do not like to hit and I have not done it that much in my lifetime. I am not the type who hits easily. Only when I am provoked to the hilt . . . and she is very good at that. Long ago, at school something similar happened. There was this boy who kept on teasing me because my dad worked as a refuse collector. He put up others against me about me smelling bad and stuff. I gave him the hiding of his life. The teasing stopped at once. After that they knew not to mess with me. As far as I know, nothing like that has ever happened again. I am not a fighter. But with her . . . I don't know. She can be so . . . and then I lose myself. She doesn't let up. She always keeps on nagging, about everything. I just lose control. If only she would stop moaning, everything would be fine."

Therapist: "I understand that things happen which test you to the limit, we can discuss that. But I want to start with working with you both on creating safety in the home. When you feel safe together we can discuss difficult things and find solutions without the fear of escalations and explosions. Will you work with me on this?"

Harry: "I think you are as good as Bianca in getting your own way, but OK, if that's what it takes . . . I'm here now, it wears me down too . . . tell me what to do."

Therapist: "Bianca, do you agree that the violence between you is a problem and that we have to work on stopping it first?"

Bianca, full of tears: "Yes, I am always scared, I wanted to leave him, but I was afraid to, and yet he can be so gentle . . . I often said that I would not take it anymore, he promised me so many times that it would not happen again . . . I am not sure it will work."

Therapist: "It's understandable that you have doubts, but do you agree to go ahead with the programme to increase safety, because you have to do your bit too?"

Bianca: "Tell me what to do."

I prefer to negotiate with the husband first and only then ask for the wife's co-operation. Men are often less motivated for therapy. When a husband willingly co-operates with the programme he acknowledges his violent behaviour and is prepared to take responsibility for it. That is vital for the programme to succeed. However, it will only work with the spouse's co-operation, when she is willing to take her responsibility for her part in the escalations, and if they pull together in order to stop the violence.

Sometimes, it may take much more effort to convince husbands and wives to collaborate with a programme: for example, if they are in agreement that it (i.e., the violence) is not a major problem and they choose to talk about other subjects. In such cases, I put my dilemma to them. "You have come here to ask me to help you and you want to discuss important issues in your relationship, but neither of you wants to apply yourself to a programme that can put an end to the violence within your relationship. That does not work for me, because I can only do my job within a safe framework. I would like to get on with the programme. I do not wish to send you away; we have a dilemma which I cannot solve just like that."

By making the problem a mutual one, it is often possible to make a start with the programme. The fact that they only do it as a favour to me in order to get into therapy with me does not bother me in the least. If putting an end to the violence works out well, they will be motivated into exploring new avenues themselves. In the most extreme cases, this does not work out at all. Some husbands refuse point-blank to take any responsibility.

> *Patrick*: "I don't agree. It is her problem after all. She knows exactly how to get me all riled up. Sometimes that's precisely what she's aiming for. Take that vegetarian nonsense of hers. I need meat as she knows very well, and still she tries to feed me that crap. Or she doesn't get any beer because she thinks I drink too much, so I am left without any. It just makes me howling mad. I work hard and I need it. She has to take that into account. If she doesn't, she's asking for trouble. As long as she co-operates, everything is fine."

Patrick kept this up. I will not start the couple therapy then. Therapy is only possible if the perpetrator of violence is willing to take responsibility for his behaviour. If this does not work, the therapist has to try other ways, such as the path of social control, where the safety of the wife and any children is paramount. It is advisable to inform the GP of your findings. You could advise the wife to take refuge in a women's shelter for the sake of her own safety and that of her children, or to move to a safe place. Another possible action would be informing the police when demonstrable violence has occurred. A report to the police can lead to excluding the man from the house for ten days or longer.

It is common knowledge that violence often goes hand-in-hand with alcohol and drug abuse. If this is the case, our approach is not immediately feasible. The therapy programme demands some level of self-control of the participants. Serious alcohol or drug abuse can affect this in such a manner that therapy is not an option. We are not talking about a few beers here, but about serious abuse. With some couples, escalations only happen together with excessive drinking. A referral to addiction care is then the best option.

Because we want to concentrate on couples we can work with in an ambulant setting, we do not elaborate on this.

Sometimes, it becomes clear that both partners use violence.

Peter: "Jacqueline attacks me more often than the other way round. She just charges at me. I am only defending myself."

Jacqueline (fierce): "Yes, but I'm the one who ends up with bruised ribs, a contused wrist or a leg covered in bruises."

Peter   (threatening): "You know very well how that came about, I would shut up about that if I were you, you shouldn't try to stop me if I want to leave and it wasn't my fault that you fell in such an awkward way against that cupboard. I just shoved you aside."

Therapist: "I can tell you two are matched good and proper. You both fight. There is one big difference though. You are bigger, heavier-built, and stronger than Jacqueline; she is more at risk with you than you with her. Are you ever really scared of Jacqueline's attacks on you? What I mean is, do you really feel you're in danger when she attacks you?"

Peter: "No, not really, no, but I don't take any crap from her."

Therapist: "Jacqueline, are you scared of Peter when he attacks you? Do you feel that you are in danger?"

Jacqueline (softly): "Yes, of course, and it shows. I really have to be cautious with him. He is right though; I am not a goody two-shoes myself, especially when it's almost that time of the month again. I can be very unruly then."

Therapist: "Peter are you at times afraid of Jacqueline?"

Peter: "Yes, of her sharp tongue, she can humiliate me till I get mad."

Here, focusing on safety first is crucial; both have to co-operate on this target first and be willing to take responsibility to change their own behaviour.

The agreement

If approval has been given for a programme to work on ending the violence, I elaborate further:

Therapist: "I want to explain to you how this works. First I would like to hear an example. Take the one you mentioned before. It all went pear-shaped this morning. How exactly? Bianca, would you like to start?"

Bianca: "Well, he was still asleep because he had a late shift. We had to be here at ten o'clock. I didn't want to be late; I can't stand being late, so I rose early. That's when I started to fret. Let's not wake him too early or he will get cross, but I shouldn't wake him too late because he needs time to wake up properly and get out of bed. I was also a bit intimidated about coming here, so I wasn't really at my best. I made some coffee and went upstairs at half eight with a cuppa. He was pissed off, it was way too early. I went downstairs again, coffee in hand. Nerves made me spill some coffee on my T-shirt. Naturally I was cross with myself. I entered the room to get a clean one. He thought I'd come to call him again, but that wasn't so. I tried to explain about the coffee and all that, but he only got more worked up about it and told me to shut-the-fuck-up. I started to cry and that really got him going, and he said that I was intent on showing that he was always in the wrong, that it was exactly what I was aiming for, but that wasn't true . . ." (cries).

Harry: "But you were nagging at me endlessly about getting out of bed, that I needed plenty of time to have a shower and stuff and that you had already made some coffee and that you were up and ready . . . it just got on my nerves."

Therapist: "If I understand correctly, you started to hit her when she started to cry."

Harry: "That is right, yes, I can't stand her crying, especially because we had to come here and all the blame would be put on me. Well, that worked out really nice, didn't it? I was right all along."

Therapist: "What I would like to know is: when did you, Bianca, know that it would all go wrong? You are the one who has more experience in all this; you knew at a given moment that it would all go wrong. How did it come about this time?"

Bianca: "When I entered the room again for the clean T-shirt and he didn't want to listen. I tried to explain, but he didn't listen at all, yes, that's when I knew . . . here we go again. But I couldn't stop it, however hard I tried to calm him down, it only got worse."

Therapist: "That is enlightening. I will elaborate more on this later, but first Harry. When did you sense it all went wrong, that you lost your self-control?"

Harry: "It wasn't like that at all; I was having a nice sleep and got cross at her for waking me so godforsaken early. When she entered the room again . . . I don't know . . . I really can't recall want happened . . . I don't know what I said or did . . . she just has to stop, say nothing, leave me in peace . . ."

Women can often pinpoint the exact moment when things go wrong; they know they will get hurt, but are incapable of effectively stopping the process. They are, however, highly trained in catching any signals and they try to anticipate accordingly. Women often feel responsible for preventing the violence from ever happening. Römkens (1991) has described it well, and calls this phenomenon "projection and internalizing of responsibility and guilt". In our example, Bianca tells how she had already been planning a favourable strategy long before the actual wake-up call, in order to minimize the chance of an escalation.

Men mostly say that they have no control over it, that they started to see red, or that they are overwhelmed by a wave of anger. Goldner and her colleagues (1990) describe how, for men, violence can be both an expression (and experience) of power and of help-lessness.

I often use a metaphor which seems to strike a chord with men.

Therapist: "I notice that you find it hard to recognize when things go wrong. I want to tell you something. When I was a child, I used to love to play in the sea. I was only allowed to go knee-high into the water and I didn't like that at all. My mother had explained to me about the dangers of the undertow that can sweep you away if you venture too far into the water. Of course, I tried it now and then. I ventured further and further out into the sea and noticed that it became increasingly difficult to walk back to the beach. One day, I wandered too far into the water and it was true: the undertow pulled me along, however hard I tried to fight it. Luckily, a strong man saw it all and was able to get to me in time.

Compare this to your anger. First, you start to get cross. You can still go back, but if you venture further it becomes harder and harder, until you have passed the point of no return, the anger has overwhelmed you, and it all goes wrong. I want to explore how we can make the first move and the programme is all about not venturing further than knee-high, so you will always be able to return.

Harry: "Okay, I understand. You are right, you know, I know things go wrong at some point but I cannot go back. That pisses me off even more, the fact that I am beyond the point of no return. I get even angrier with her for getting me in such a state that things really do go wrong."

Therapist: "I'm glad you recognize it; now we can explore up to which point you can go so that you will only go knee-deep. Can you pinpoint at what moment you were up to your knees?"

Harry: "Well, that is kind of difficult. I was sleeping peacefully, I didn't feel like waking up and coming here, I felt I was being coerced by her. It immediately went wrong when she woke me up, she acts like . . . with the coffee and such . . . I start feeling guilty at once, I can't stand that . . . I have barely opened my eyes and I am in the wrong again . . . that feeling . . . it gets me mad straight away . . . maybe way beyond my knees."

We can see how Harry uses the metaphor to reflect upon his own behaviour and the interaction between himself and Bianca. He mentions a couple of important issues which we can work on later in the therapy. It is true that women who are being abused behave, due to the effects of trauma, in a manner that triggers the violent behaviour in men even more. Both feel powerless to cut through this circle. Be that as it may, I do maintain that the situation has to be deemed safe before the therapy can commence and these important issues can be discussed.

Therapist: "You mention some important issues which we will follow up later, when the therapy has commenced. Now that we know how things work with you both, I will explain the anti-violence programme first. In fact, it is quite simple, the key-word being: "time-out". Time-out means that you cease all interaction between the two of you for a while. The one who proposes the time-out either leaves the room, the house, or, in case you are outside, goes in another direction. If one of you asks for a time-out, the other has to oblige. That is the deal. It is very important. By bailing out of the situation you can prevent yourself from being swept away by the under-tow. That is why it is so important that you both recognize the first signs of danger. I suspect that you, Bianca, know them only too well, and that you, Harry, if you pay proper attention, will indeed recognize when you are up to your knees in it."

Harry: "For me, I'm sure I've done it a hundred times before, she wants to keep on talking and I just want to leave. If I walk out of the door, she tries to hold me, she wants to have it all out with me, but I can't, and then if she tries to stop me from walking out I shove her aside or hit her. I find this a rather good proposition; it doesn't strike me as being that hard."

Bianca: "I don't like this at all, he's the one who always leaves, I don't agree with all this, you are giving him a get-out-of-jail-free card; he can just say "time-out" and he will be as free as a bird. I really do mind him leaving every time I try to talk."

When I first started this work the same reaction, which occurred more than once, threw me off balance. But, through the years, it dawned on me that it is precisely on this threshold that the most awful fights happen. Women are often more verbally gifted than their male partners and want to discuss matters. Subsequently, men feel pressured and are confronted with their inability to express themselves about emotional subjects. They cannot deal with this superiority of their wives, and walking out is a way to regain power. It is understandable that women turn against this because, for a while at least, they can feel empowered through discussion. I have taken note of the importance of not letting this complexity lead me astray and to leave it alone until a later stage.

Therapist: "I understand that you don't like it if Harry walks out when you are having a conversation. But your safety is at risk here, and that makes a time-out vital. You can both ask for a time-out. So, when you feel things are going the wrong way, you too can say, "time-out". I would like to add something important though. The one who asks for the time-out has to re-establish contact. So, Harry, if you are the one who asks for time-out and you have left, you are also the one who has to come home, go to Bianca, and re-establish contact by saying something to her. You yourself know best when you have calmed down sufficiently and if you are capable of being nice to her again. The same goes for you, Bianca. If you ask for a time-out, Harry has to agree. You decide when you want to go and talk to him again. If you both have kept your distance for a while, often it will take a turn for the better. With a lot of couples I have found that it does work, provided you stick to it. Are there any questions or is everything clear?"

Harry: "So, take this morning for instance; I should have said 'time-out' as soon as she woke me."

Therapist: "Yes, that is exactly right."

Harry: "I would have got out of bed later and I would have gone to Bianca to come here."

Bianca: "Yes, but he would have slept until ten o'clock and we would have been too late for this appointment."

Therapist: "I would rather have that than another escalation; your safety is the important issue at hand."

Bianca: "OK, so he would say: 'time-out' and I would have to walk around with a coffee-stained T-shirt because I am not allowed to enter the room until 'Sir' is ready to show himself."

Therapist: "I can imagine it being an annoyance for you, but from where I am standing your safety seems to be more important."

It has often struck me that women do not comply easily with the proposal, even though it concerns their own safety and the breakdown of violence. We have a hypothesis about this phenomenon. A woman said, "I would rather get beaten than him leaving me." Obviously, the beating is seen as some form of contact. There is a fear that there will be nothing left once the beatings have stopped, that you will be ignored. After all, the opposite to love is not hate, but indifference. Whatever arguments are put forward, it is paramount to insist on a time-out programme, to discuss any possible pitfalls, and to eliminate these where possible.

We learnt to ask how clients can make the time-out programme a failure. The top ten strategies clients mention is as follows.

- One partner telling the other one to take a time out. "I can see you are agitated now, you have to take a time-out as the therapist said." (One has to take the responsibility oneself to take a time out.)
- Using the time-out in the power struggle. Taking a time-out as soon as you do not like something.
- Going to the pub during a time-out.
- Going to family or friends that side with you against your partner.
- Starting the same problematic discussion directly after the time-out.
- Preventing the partner from taking a time-out.
- Not focusing on calming down during a time-out.
- Staying away for a long time without sending any message.
- The one who stayed at home leaves during the time-out without leaving any information.
- Waiting much too long before taking a time-out.

Clients often are very good in thinking about situations in which they could fail the programme. In talking about these situations we often laugh, and the clients become aware of their motivation. They can let the programme fail, that is easy; they can also let it work; that is a difficult job.

If there are no further questions, one has to ask very specifically if they are willing to co-operate.

Therapist: "Now that everything has been clarified, I want to ask you again, Harry: 'Are you willing to participate?'"

Harry: "Yes, I am."

Therapist: "You too, Bianca?"

Bianca: "Me too."

Therapist: "Then I would like to see you both at the same time next week, and, Harry, if you do succeed in not hitting, shoving or ... you know what I'm talking about, then the therapy will commence. If you did succumb to beating, I want you to call me and tell me about it, if I am not available you can leave a message, you only have to say that things have got out of hand again and I will know enough."

At the beginning of the therapy I will see a couple every week. When the violence has ceased, I will see them less frequently, say, once every two to three weeks, and this will later on be brought back to once every month. In most cases, we will have completed a series of fifteen sessions before we finish. I do not explain why I want Harry to call me once things have gone wrong. I leave that for now. If it happens straight after the first session, I can possibly arrange to see them sooner. If it happens later, I will be prepared for the second session being used again for discussing the programme of ending the violence. Furthermore, having to call me would act as an additional restraint.

Harry: "... and then it almost went wrong and I thought: Jesus, I will have to call her again, it suddenly sprung to mind, well: I'd rather walk out."

In most cases this intervention has immediate effect, but sometimes it has to be repeated and it is important to discuss what went wrong and where it went wrong. If the violence has not ended after three sessions, I will not continue in the same manner; one has to discuss some other way of time-out. I ask if they could split for a short time; maybe one of them can stay with family or friends. In those cases, therapy remains possible if both husband and wife wish to maintain their relationship. Safety for partners and children stays central before therapy can commence. Sometimes, breaking up can be a better solution, if one of the two does not want to continue their relationship. With that, I am touching on a different subject: divorce processes. We do not cover that in this book.

When the therapy commences

One often succeeds in not hitting in the first week. This immediate success acts as an important layer of trust in the therapy, the therapist, and in each other. The therapist will, of course, express a lot of appreciation about the success. If it did not work out, it is important to find out what exactly went wrong. In Harry and Bianca's case, it turned out to be successful in the first week and afterwards hitting occurred only once, later on in the therapy. Every time a setback occurs, the therapy is halted and the time-out programme is discussed again. Very annoying, but important, nevertheless. No other subjects will be discussed in such a session and therefore it can be a very short session indeed. As soon as the violence is under control, the therapy can recommence. Some couples are happy once they have found a way to end the violence. We always try to motivate them into continuing the therapy, in order to achieve a better understanding of the complex dynamics of their male–female relationship and reduce the chances of any setbacks. In most cases we succeed in motivating them to doing so. If not, it is important to leave the door ajar, to offer them a chance to come back. Owing to the initial success, they will take up that offer more readily.

Once the therapy proper can commence, we try to tell a story together in order to make the problems in the relationship more comprehensible and to create more space for love.

Often clients are stuck in the interpretation of events in their own story, which is gridlocked and which encloses them and their surroundings in limited positions. This interpretation is created within their social status and their own personal history. In therapy, we all tell a new story together, a story that creates space.

In working with couples where the husband uses physical violence against his wife we have developed some kind of framework in which our clients can tell their own story. Within this framework we describe the dynamics between women and men which result in violence at certain stages. It has transpired that clients could recognize themselves in this description of their process. On the basis of these data, we have described *a downward spiral of violence* in which each different stage can be identified. This downward spiral can be seen as a metaphor; it is an account that enables us to give meaning to the interaction between men and women where violence occurs, making use of the many theories that have been written about men and women in our culture. While we have noticed that, for example, African, Bosnian, Serbian, and Turkish people might recognize much in our account, we do base it mainly on Western culture. This does not mean that we underestimate in any way the importance of cultural background and environment. If we work with couples from other cultures, we are open to their stories and invite them to try to mould our descriptions into their situation. This approach is respectful, and prevents clients from other cultures from being pigeon-holed, which does not exactly do justice to any differences.

As a matter of fact, we are often confronted with the remark that hitting is sometimes taken for granted in other cultures and that there are even women who think that their husband does not love them any more if he stops beating them. We maintain our point of departure that violence is not a proper solution for any problem, a personal stance which should hold always and anywhere, as far as we are concerned. If people want to continue the beatings as part of their culture, we do not want to work with them and they will have to find others who do accept it.

We replicate the spiral below, and we will subsequently discuss the different stages, one at the time, along with the appropriate labels. Harry and Bianca will reappear several times, so you will be able to follow their story throughout the therapy. At times, other couples will be discussed. When we describe the different phases, one will notice that the interactions we describe are recognizable in many male–female couples, not solely in couples where physical violence has become part of this interaction. Goldner (1997) states that, with couples where violence occurs, the male–female patterns are magnified as such. She expects us to learn much about male–female interactions in general if we can fathom the processes between men and women where violence has become part of the interaction. We agree with her on this. Our downward spiral of violence is a description of often recurring processes between men and women. The men and women in our cases have become trapped, even though they have often tried to free themselves of their own accord. Violent eruptions can simultaneously be attempts to free oneself from the entanglement, even though it has an opposite effect.

The spiral of violence we explain here is connected to the situation where the male violence is attacking, defending, and physical, and the female violence is mainly guilt inducing. The two imply and amplify each other. As we mentioned earlier, women also attack men, and in gay and lesbian couples violent escalations happen as often as in heterosexual couples.

Adaptations of the spiral (Figure 1) can be made for these situations.

1st Stage

The Romantic Ideal

13th Stage
Total dysfunctioning on all levels of the partner system.

2nd Stage
Cracks appear in the ideal, awareness of differences.

12th Stage
Growing fear within the husband of losing connection. Attempts to re-establish the contact by increase of control: more violence. Splitting the violent actions from the self.

3rd Stage
The wife starts a discussion about the relationship and makes criticisms.

11th Stage
Growing isolation and "freezing" of the wife. Alienation from her own body, feelings, and thoughts. Symptoms of dissociation and splitting of parts of the self. Restricted awareness.

4th Stage
The husband repudiates and reacts scared–defensive.

5th Stage
The wife feels responsible and saves the relationship.

10th Stage
The withdrawing behaviour of his wife conjures up fear in the husband and leads to more aggression. Feelings of betrayal and bereavement about the loss of the romantic ideal.

6th Stage
Relaxation in the husband, restoration of the romantic myth.

9th Stage
The wife falls silent, loses contact and becomes isolated. Feelings of betrayal and bereavement about the loss of the romantic ideal.

7th Stage
The wife becomes increasingly frustrated and experiences veiled anger

8th Stage
The husband becomes increasingly frustrated and starts using physical violence

Figure 1. Downward spiral of violence with couples.

First stage: the romantic ideal

In spite of the divorce rates, the romantic expectations which young people have about the love of their life are still alive and kicking. However, some of the common expectations offer less and less hold. Most people nowadays lack a clear symbolic order which prescribes how husbands and wives, fathers and mothers, and children ought to behave. The current ideal of equality is not compatible with everyday life. Lonely Hearts advertisements and websites show that men are still looking for younger, less educated women, and that women are looking for slightly older men with a similar educational background. Lower educated young men and highly educated women are having difficulty in finding the right partner (Meulenbelt, 1990). In addition to this, men often do not know what is expected of them: "a sensitive macho"—what *is* that, what are the requirements? Despite all these confusions at all levels, the romantic expectation still holds firm. "Some day I will meet someone for whom I will be the most prized, who acknowledges my merits, who can give me what I need and to whom I can give what she/he needs." This is precisely what people are looking for in romantic love. Willy (1975) describes in his book about partner relationships how people select each other on the basis of their own unsolved conflicts.

For this purpose he employs a psychoanalytical frame of thought. In his opinion, young people will choose a partner whom they expect to give them what they have lacked so far: for example, appreciation, love, care, or power. Around these themes, relationship patterns will develop which, in the long run, will become rigid. Willy calls such a pattern a collusion. People who lacked care as a child will find themselves attracted to someone who can give them this care or someone who may actually need their care. More often than not, the other will have the same basic conflict, which will lead to a relationship in which the one wants to be the other's "saviour". Willy calls this an oral collusion.

Johnson (2004) connects violent behaviour with the attachment theory. Her premise is that people are looking for a safe attachment in a couple relationship. That means that they need to know and experience that the other is there for them when they feel stressed and threatened. We can detect these longings when we listen carefully to the romantic expectations that people have.

To achieve more insight into the first stages of the relationship, it is important to examine the very beginning. How did they meet, what attracted them to each other, how did the first meetings go? This information will clarify much about later problems. Often, this information will lead to further examining both their backgrounds and into developing a genogram. A genogram is a kind of family-tree in which three generations of the family lines are drawn, the births and deaths, occupations, relations, break-ups, and every other important event. An example of such a genogram can be seen in Chapter Eight. When we develop a genogram with the clients, we learn more about their childhood and what they have learnt from their families about men and women and the relationships between them.

Let us see how this transpired with Harry and Bianca.

After I had complimented Harry and Bianca, and especially Harry, on the fact that they have succeeded in avoiding violence, I propose that therapy can commence now. I explain the importance of preventing violence from happening again and that the therapy will try to create more space for the positive sides of their relationship in order for them to enjoy each other's company more. In order not to fall into the same trap, where the romantic ideal is placed centre stage again, we state adamantly that this does not mean that they will be on cloud nine from now on, and that they will not find everything they need in each other, but that it will be much more pleasant from now on.

Therapist: "I would like to start at the beginning. How did the two of you meet?"

Bianca (laughing): Through my brother, he was friendly with my brother. I was only thirteen at the time; I hadn't a clue. Later on I copped on that he liked me there and then. He asked me to go out with him, but I wasn't allowed to. I thought it amazing, my big brother's friend who paid so much attention to me."

Harry: "She was a grand girl, always laughing, ahem, always cheerful, that's what attracted me to her."

Therapist: When did your relationship really take off? How did it come about?"

Harry: "Her brother threw a party to celebrate a job offer, she came too and that was it."

Bianca: "I saw him standing there, a real babe [they both laugh], when we were dancing together . . . it was out of this world, I was head over heels in love."

Harry: "I already expected her to be there, I was looking forward to it, I had lost contact for a while. I was curious about how she had turned out, exactly as I thought she would. I figured . . . I want her, I went straight for her."

Therapist: "So you were strongly attracted to each other. You are both telling me that each of you found the other attractive. You also tell me, Harry, that you fell for her cheerfulness, long before. Are there any other aspects that you found attractive?"

Bianca: "The fact that he was so strong, so muscular, I liked that, but it also gave me a sense of security: [I thought] 'Nothing can ever happen to me while I'm with him . . .' [adds softly], Just goes to show . . ."

Harry: "She was so . . . you said it already . . . so cheerful, her eyes . . . I never see that any more."

While talking about the beginning, they both realize what they have lost. Instantly responding to this is a pitfall. More information is needed about the beginning. If it covers a time when they were in love, and this applies to most cases, then talking about this period will conjure up a positive ambience.

We also hear that she fell for his strength and that he fell for her cheerfulness; this provides information about any possible lack they might have experienced in their lives. Sometimes attraction is associated with want, sometimes even with similarity and recognition, as demonstrated in the following information from Sanne and Pierre.

Sanne: "I recognized it instantly in him; he is just as hurt as I am. I will console him good."

Pierre: "She looked gorgeous, self-assured, representative, and with a lot of guts. That one's a proper match, I thought, she has her eye on the prize too, proper arm-candy."

Often the source of the problems is embedded in these accounts about attraction, too:

"She is not as cheerful as she pretended to be."

"He is not as caring and protective as he seemed."

"He doesn't need comforting any more and he doesn't comfort me either; he only hurts me by withdrawing."

"She looks haggard now, that's not what I opted for; it's not what I had wanted."

Mastenbroek (1995) conducted a research into the indications and development of violence against women in relationships. She extensively portrays the early stages of these relationships in which the romantic expectations are embedded:

"He was always there for me, he would always do anything for me; he'd take care of everything. Like: 'Are you comfortable there and wouldn't it be much nicer over here. This is way better.' Or propping up a cushion against my back. Things like that." [p. 37]

Mastenbroek shows how this overwhelming attention already involves border-crossing behaviour and could easily spill over into controlling and isolating. In her examples, these men show sexually dominant behaviour. Once the relationship has been established, these men tend to withdraw once more, thus leaving the woman with the responsibility of maintaining the relationship. Mastenbroek focuses on the consequences of male behaviour for women; she does not engage with the combined action between them. This is exactly the field that we are exploring. In the initial phase, the vast influence of what we have come to call "gender information" is already clear, as we have described in Chapter One.

Back to Harry and Bianca. After they have told me about how they met and what attracted them to each other, we try to connect this to their experiences as children.

Therapist: "Harry, you repeatedly told me that you found Bianca's cheerfulness very attractive, that she had a twinkle in her eyes. Can you tell me why that was so important to you?"

Harry: "Well, I just do. I don't like all that morose stuff."

Therapist: "Why, have you experienced it before?"

Harry: "Well, yes, my mother, she was forever miserable, always complaining and nagging. I was fed up with it."

Therapist: "I would like to hear more about that. I want to make a genogram of the family that you were born into. I will explain what it is. Bianca, the same goes for you. I will ask you questions about your family as well. I'll do this in order for us all to come to a better understanding of what both your backgrounds look like, how you two have come to a grinding halt, but also how the situation can be improved."

Next, I explain what a genogram entails. While developing the genogram, we encounter much relevant information. We précis the information about Harry and Bianca here for you.

Harry is the eldest in a family of three boys. His father was an alcoholic and abandoned the family when Harry was eleven and his youngest brother three years old. The brother second to Harry was nine. From a young age his mother depended on Harry. She complained to him about his father, who wasted all the money on drink and who never had two pennies to rub together. At the age of seven, Harry had to go to the pub to talk his dad into coming home. His mother was proud of him. After his father left, she involved him even more in her life. He got mixed messages all the time. On the one hand he was told that men are worthless, free-loaders who were not to be trusted; on the other hand, she gave *him* the sense of being truly worthwhile, the centre of her life. When Harry was fourteen his mother found a boyfriend and everything changed. All of a sudden he was no longer the centre of attention. He could not get along with this boyfriend at all. He thought that Harry did not need to meddle in everything and that he had to find his own way. At first, Harry had helped to raise his brothers and now he was no longer allowed to. His mother turned on him, too, and took sides with her boyfriend. "You are their brother, not their father." His two younger siblings took to this like ducks to water and rebelled against him. He became increasingly isolated and was cast in the role of scapegoat. At fifteen, he hardly bothered to come home at all. He left school at an early age and went from one job to the next. He roamed the streets or lounged about in a snooker joint. "You resemble your dad more and more," his mother said. At the time, he hung out with Bianca's brother. That is how they first met. Bianca had already told us how she looked up to him and how she enjoyed the attention that he bestowed on her; a girl who could recognize his merits, a girl who was glad to be with him.

We are of the opinion that the symbolic mending of the man's first love, the love he has for his mother, often influences the choice of a female partner. Much has been written about the influence of the fact that women and men are raised mainly by women (Chodorow, 1980; Meulenbelt, 1984; Olivier, 1993; van Lawick & Sanders, 1994). Harry became aware that he could earn and keep the love of his mother on the one hand by acting forcefully: by protecting his mother, by collecting his father from the pub, by helping to raise his brothers, etc., however, on the other hand, he was not supposed to resemble a man because men were worthless. Obviously, this is clearly a case of conflicting gender formation. To top it off, he had to go through the painful experience of being traded in for another man, just like that. This fear of being traded in when he is no longer needed had a significant influence on this relationship with Bianca. His statement: "I had barely opened my eyes and already I have to feel guilty, I'm already in the wrong, I can't stand that", speaks volumes.

I would like to emphasize here that examining Harry's history does not mean in any way that he cannot be held responsible for his violent behaviour. Although we understand more about him and his behaviour, this does not mean that we excuse his behaviour. These two, understanding and excusing, are often confused. In our work we do not excuse violent behaviour, but we want to understand the dynamic of it. As Goldner puts it poignantly in a workshop she presented in Amsterdam in July 1995, "Understandable doesn't make it excusable". With this in the back of our mind, it is possible for us to listen to the accounts, be empathic, and at the same time stay focused on the fact that the violence has to stop.

Bianca grew up as the daughter in a family of two; she has a brother two years her elder. Her father worked as a mechanic in a big garage and her mother worked as a housekeeper for other families. She was the apple of her father's eye and "a ray of sunshine in the home" for her mother. She could get along very well with her brother. She tells me that she had a wonderful childhood, with no worries; there were always friends about, and hers was not a strict home. She was not a very good pupil but not a bad one either. After primary school, she passed an administrative course at a vocational school, got a typing qualification, and started working for a company. She did not like the work at all and could not handle the constant pressure put on her to perform. She enjoyed being a check-out girl at a supermarket much more, where she and her colleagues got along well. Until she started living with Harry, she led an untroubled existence. If ever there were any setbacks, either her father or mother would solve them. At school and in society she was under the protection of her big brother. She expected life to continue as it had before; including Harry. The problems arose when Harry started to become possessive, when she could not make him happy quite as easily, and when he got cross with her.

When we take a look at Bianca's gender formation, we can see that she has associated her identity with "making the other happy" and "being protected". She speaks about how she chose Harry because of his strong presence. She was obviously looking for a partner who could take over the role of protector which her father and brother had played. In exchange for that, she would make him happy, just as she had always managed to do with her father. The fact that her parents were not too pleased with Harry because he did not have a proper education, no regular income and, to add insult to injury, did not have "the right family background", did not bother her in the least. They moved in together after only three months, still in love and excited about making their own home together, choosing furniture, buying a nice bed, etc. She was convinced that she could make him happy and that everything would fall into place for him. These romantic expectations fit the female gender formation: *she* will make him happy, "mould" him into the "perfect man" he really is deep-down. A real breeding ground for desperate conflicts . . .

Second stage: cracks appear in the ideal, awareness of differences

We will further describe the downward spiral in more general terms. Thankfully, Harry and Bianca had not yet arrived at the last stages of the downward spiral; if that had been the case, therapy would have been impossible. Another kind of help would be needed then, and one would have to intervene in order to break down the hopeless situation.

Whenever possible, examples will be given for the different phases, but I would like to emphasize that what follows now is a compilation of the many accounts we have heard from women and men.

At a given moment the new situation for the young couple will prove to be less rosy than it was before. Harry wants her to be there when he comes home. He gets mad if she goes to her mother when he sleeps in after a late shift. Bianca misses her father, mother, and brother and is not as happy as she thought she would be. Harry discovers that he does not mean the world to Bianca after all, and that she sometimes needs her parents, her brother, and her friends too, that she can be homesick at times, and that she is not cheerful all of the time, but that she can be moody and sad as well. Sanne discovers that Pierre does not always need comforting and Pierre finds that Sanne cannot always "see through him" and that she will know his every need, even though he has not asked for it. Arjan discovers that Marina is not always as self-assured, but that she can be insecure and timid as well. Marina finds that Arjan does not love her unconditionally. Cracks start to appear in the romantic ideal.

Third stage: the wife starts a discussion about the relationship and passes comments

Generally speaking, women can discuss their feelings much more easily than men and they often feel more responsible for maintaning a sound relationship. This again is gender formation. Bianca decides to express her discontent. She says that she is not too pleased about him getting worked up about the fact that she goes to her mother or to a friend and that she cannot be with him all of the time; after all, she has a life of her own. She would like to discuss this with him.

Yet another example, that of a highly educated, well-off couple, goes like this:

Sanne: "I don't like you slouching in front of the telly night after night, I can never talk to you, we never go out any more;

we look like an elderly couple that have nothing to
share with one another. I think we should do something
about it."

Or, in Marina's case:

"I cannot live my life looking like I've just left the beauty parlour
all of the time. I cannot look like I've stepped out of the pages of
Marie Claire when I have had a full working day. I just would like
to be allowed to be tired at home, to be a couch-potato; I cannot be
myself around you."

This openness and these comments are often not understood as a
constructive way of maintaining a sound relationship.

Fourth stage: the husband repudiates and
reacts in scared–defensive mode

Harry is being criticized and he cannot deal with it. With his
mother, such comments meant loss of love and eventually being
traded in. Add to that his male pride being hurt. He does not want
her to set the rules at home, he is afraid that if he lets her, he will
be lost. A lot of men consider this to be a spectre: a man being under
his wife's thumb, a man who is seen as a laughing-stock by other
men and who loses his freedom, in short: a man whose masculinity
has been taken away.

So, Harry does not react with understanding and openness, but
with repudiation and slander.

"Will you stop moaning; you could go to your mother dearest or
those friends of yours while I'm at work, you don't really need to
do that while I'm home, now do you? If I get out of bed after a late
shift, I just want my cuppa, is that asking too much?"

Arjan's answer to Sanne is altogether different:

"If you don't like it; you know where the door is."

But the same thing is played out here too. Sanne feels responsible
for keeping the relationship sound and gives voice to her dismay.

Arjan feels threatened and responds offensively and dismissively. As does Pierre:

> "Where do you get all this nonsense? I don't want you to dump your fatigue on me, thank you very much, you can do that elsewhere, I don't want such a hag at home. You wouldn't want to catch me slouching about like a tired old sack of potatoes, now would you?"

Nothing is resolved.

Fifth stage: the wife feels responsible and saves the relationship

In general, women have learnt that they are responsible for the pleasant atmosphere at home and that they have to give the one with whom they share their lives a sense of well-being.

In the examples of Bianca and Harry, Sanne and Arjan, Marina and Pierre, it is the women who attempt a rescue.

> Bianca: "No, of course it isn't too much to ask, you're right, I could simply go over to them while you're at work, shall I make us a cuppa, just forget about me saying anything."

> Sanne: "But I have no intention of leaving you, sweetheart, I just want us to be happy together, I didn't mean it that way, you know that I'm really crazy about you, I just don't want you to be unhappy."

> Marina: "Sorry about that, I'm not in good form today, I didn't sleep all that well either. Tell you what; I'll have a nice bath, get dressed up to the nines and take you out to dinner, how about that?"

In all examples given, the woman concedes and demonstrates the required conduct in order to save the relationship. With that, she at once denies herself her own needs and focuses on the needs of her male partner. Women often tell us that they thought that was how it is supposed to be. Bianca speaks about how she genuinely thought that he was right and that she could go out whenever he was at work, that she should not be so selfish. Sanne spoke about feeling guilty immediately once he said that she could go any time she did not like the way things are, and she also thought that she was a right sourpuss, that she should be content with a man who is at home, and that he had the right to relax and do nothing. Marina, too, takes his stance about the situation and tries to be the wife that he wants her to be. We can see how women tend to not only suppress their own needs, but abandon their own assessment of the situation and their relationship as well. Put in this manner, power lies with the one who gives meaning and who can impose this on to another. In the examples at hand, the power of the man is once again restored; *his* meaning-giving is being regarded as of higher ranking than hers. Acknowledging masculine power by endorsing his convictions forms a part of gender formation. We often encounter it and it can go very far: for example, when a violent husband defines his wife as a psychiatric patient. A dentist once said about his wife, who was fifteen years younger and whom he abused, "She is genuinely depressed, or manic, or schizophrenic, whatever, there is definitely something wrong with her, what she does is really out there."

This statement was accompanied by examples of her weird behaviour: sometimes, she would lock herself in her room as soon as he came home and she would not speak to him for weeks on end. She would lie in her bed and would refuse to see anyone, not even her children. These periods of withdrawal and silence would always follow a serious row in which she would scream and get so worked up that he had no choice but to seize her heavy-handedly in order to calm her down. At first his wife resisted being labelled "insane". She said, "I'm unhappy." Only after he succeeded in convincing her mother and a couple of friends of his definition of the relationship, so that they themselves would pronounce her to be ripe for a mental institution, would she allow herself to be convinced of the same and pronounce herself to be "insane". As a result of her short stay in a psychiatric ward of a general hospital, the couple was referred to me, and this gave her the chance to express her definition of the situation once again: "I'm unhappy." This provided a tool for putting an end to his abusive behaviour, followed by intensive relationship therapy. These people were already trapped a long way further along the downward spiral of violence.

Before they got to that stage, there were many situations in which the wife tried to rescue the situation by attempting to appease the husband. Such rescue attempts are not without their rewards, but do not resolve the underlying problems.

Sixth stage: relaxation in the husband, restoration of the romantic myth

Due to the wife's rescue attempt, the husband can relax once more. His mind is put at ease. She does listen to him after all, he feels worthy again, and he can rely on her love for him. This conjures up affectionate and devoted behaviour in the husband, which in turn makes them very happy for a while. They both feel that they were not mistaken about each other after all. They think: this truly is the one, and all the cracks are papered over once again. More often than not, all this is accompanied by a reconciliation ritual: a beautiful present, going out for a meal, or wonderful lovemaking. For a while, anyway, the romantic myth is restored once more. Stages One to Six can be repeated over and over again. The conflicts can have different sources, but the process will be more or less the same.

Many couples are able to find solutions. They are able to make adaptations and compromises and can let go of romantic illusions. There, violence will not occur.

Some couples only get caught in the downward spiral of violence with the arrival of children. Children demand totally different abilities and responsibilities. A *status quo* can be tipped out of balance with the arrival of children, old childhood conflicts of the partners themselves can surface, thus rendering solutions, which would have worked before, useless. Naturally, he will say that she has changed after the birth of their first child and vice versa. Often men feel robbed of their "rightful" place:

> "Every scrap of your attention suddenly went to the baby; it was just like I didn't exist any more. Whenever we were having a cuddle and the baby would make a sound, you were gone in a flash. I ended up at the bottom of the list. You became such an earth-mother."

Women often see the same situation in a different light:

> "You were way less caring then. When I was pregnant you were still endearing, but after the baby was born, you were never home, your work became ever more important and, to add insult to injury, you started an affair; is it any wonder that I felt neglected?"

Again, gender formation plays a significant role. Furthermore, the division of work and care undergo radical changes after the birth of a child (Meulenbelt, 1997, pp. 114–115).

Although, in this case, the entanglement in the downward spiral takes place much later, all stages can be recognized from there on.

When no adaptations to the new situation are found, frustrations grow. Men tend to look for compensations in the outside world; they stay longer at work or in the pub and at home they hide behind the computer or television. Women suffer more explicitly about the relational difficulties; they want to reach their man and start to ask for his attention more and more, often in a negative way.

Seventh stage: the wife becomes increasingly frustrated and experiences veiled anger

Women who continuously suppress their own needs and take on the definitions of their husbands instead of giving their own meaning to situations will become increasingly frustrated. Their anger will start to lead an undercover life, because women have never properly learned how to express it in a direct manner. We all know them: the discontented, nagging wives, always going on about insignificant physical discomforts and forever complaining about everything and everybody, the all-American "ever nagging housewife". When a relationship therapist encounters such a wife and is unable to see what triggers this behaviour, the wife will often irritate her/him, with the result that she will be described as passive–aggressive, with a malfunctioning aggression regulation; in short, the therapist can understand only too well how the husband might lose control once in a while.

Bianca was heading in the same direction. She became increasingly dissatisfied; she was suffering from regular headaches and back pains, she could no longer handle working behind the till, she no longer wanted to make love because she felt out of sorts, and she started to suffer from depressive bouts.

Whenever she did get out of bed, she would complain about the mess that Harry made, about the laundry that would not dry properly, about rowdy neighbours, and a lot more. Many couple histories show the same pattern. Slowly but surely the tension at home will gather, women tend to complain more and more, men feel attacked and start to defend, attacking and defending mechanisms lead to escalations, with violence as a consequence.

Eighth stage: the husband becomes increasingly frustrated and starts to be more violent

Here, the power of the husband changes into helplessness. The complaints and unhappiness of his wife make him feel guilty and as if he is a loser; she gives him a sense of not quite making the grade and of always being in the wrong. This is what men repeat time and again: "I never seem to do anything right any more, however hard I try I seem to get it wrong all the time." They feel helpless. In Harry's case, the process that he had gone through already with his mother is repeated.

> "Whatever I did, it wasn't good enough. Whenever I was quiet, she would say. 'You're so quiet', and when I did talk, she would say, 'I am so tired.' Whenever I wanted to make love, she had back pains, and if I kept my distance for a while, she would say, 'Don't you love me any more?' It's enough to drive anyone round the bend."

> *Therapist*: "And when you finally did hurt Bianca, how did it come about?"

> *Harry*: "That was the time that I had walked out, I just couldn't take it any more, had a beer somewhere, just the one. When I came home, she said that my mother was right after all, that I really was starting to resemble my dad. Well, then I just saw red and I shoved her good. She fell against the telly and her jaw was all black and blue, I felt so awful. I was deeply ashamed, I thought, I will never let this happen again— that's what I thought anyway . . ."

This account was told at a later stage in therapy (during the third session) and it is striking how Harry claims responsibility for his own violent ways. It is still "I saw red", but he also says "*I* shoved *her*." This change in the use of language is a sign that Harry has started to define and experience the situation differently. He describes himself as an active person in his own right and not as a victim of an impossible wife. When a husband uses violence against his wife for the first time, it will conjure up so much shame that he will split this behaviour from himself and will externalize it. "I'm not doing this myself, she makes me to do it." In this way, the active source is located outside the husband himself, and that is a significant factor in the continuation of the violence. In order to control the violence, he needs to control her, change her attitude, not his own behaviour. This meaning-giving gives rise to violence and new ways of control. In therapies, it is paramount to be alert to any changes in the use of language.

In certain forms of therapy, for example, directive therapy, it is common practice to outline sentences such as "I shoved her". Clients are actively encouraged to change passive sentences into active sentences. For myself, I prefer not to outline, but to let change happen through dialogue. In claiming responsibility for their own behaviour, clients, in their own accounts of what has happened, will show that a process of change has been set in motion.

Once violence has been used, the chances of repetition increase, despite the adamant intention of the husband not to. The fact that he blames his wife for driving him over the edge is an additional source of anger. It is only in exceptional cases that violence will be used only once, usually because it is so frightening that no repeat will ever take place. However, a single occurrence of violence used by a husband against his wife can have far-reaching consequences. A fundamental trust has been breached; she will have to tread carefully around him. Goldner gave a striking example during her workshop of a husband who had beaten up his wife, just the one time, around Christmas. Afterwards, whenever they had an argument he needed only to say, "Remember Christmas" to get her under his control once more. Among other things, you can always recognize women who have repeatedly suffered from physical violence by their constant alertness when they are in close proximity to their husbands. They seem constantly to assess whether they are in danger. This is also the case with Bianca who, as already described, keeps a close eye on Harry when laden subjects are talked about. This alertness leads to women "scanning" their husbands as soon as he walks in the door; how does he look, how tense is he, can I ask him that question that has been bugging me for days, or should I leave it for now? Women choose to do anything to pacify their husbands first, so that they themselves can ask for whatever they really want later on. This could easily be interpreted as "manipulation", which is part of the gender forma-tion of the female. If you are in danger, you have to tread carefully in order to achieve anything at all. Because manipulative behaviour by women often irritates men and is seen as guilt-inducing, the wife and husband will get further entangled in the downward spiral.

Often, sexual violence will be used at this stage. In most cases, the sexual needs of women will often vanish because of continuing stress, but not in all cases. Sexual contact can be seen as a compen-sation for the suffering. It is the only manner in which intimacy can be experienced. Women say, for example, "In bed he can be so sweet again, attentive and gentle, that's so nice, it gives me a chance to forget about it all." And men say, "She will be sweet all over again, I still can make her happy in bed, especially after we had a row, I can sense her forgiving me." In most cases it does not work out that way, and the bed becomes one of the battlegrounds. Withholding sex can be a way for women to punish their husbands. It is hard to make love to a man who hurts you at other times. A lot of men feel abject rejection when they are denied sex; it hits them right where they feel connected to their own body and with which they feel bonded. Moreover, they see it as an assault on their masculinity, on their own existence, if they are not allowed to have sex with their own wife. Even now, a wife, especially regarding sex, is seen as a "property" to which a husband is entitled. This is in keeping with the dominant opinion that men need to have sex, that something will go very wrong if men cannot get rid of their sperm now and again (Goldner, 1997). Because both male and female believe this to be true, sex becomes the ground where terrible fighting takes place. The fact that all people, women included, of course, need to be caressed and cherished gets ever more pushed into the background. When there are children, women can enjoy their cuddles. Men feel even more shut out, which in turn could lead to anger and forced sexual contact: rape. That the female partner will lie underneath him, stiff as a plank, and does not seem to feel anything (except rejection or disgust) leaves men in rage and despair. Ever since the sexual revolution, women *must* enjoy the sexual intercourse they have with men; if they do not, they rob the man of proof of his masculinity, proof that he "performs well".

When violence and sexual violence have become a part of the relationship, the desperation in both husband and wife will increase exponentially, even though each will see it differently.

Children

If there are children involved, they often are in tune with what goes on between the parents. Martine Groen will elaborate on this in Chapter Nine. It is advisable to invite the children to therapy at least once, to assess how they are doing. Are they being involved in the rows? Are they being abused themselves? Are they getting hurt, or is their development in any danger? Once a proper work relationship has been established with the parents, one will always succeed in seeing the children, with or without their parents present. Talking to the children without their parents has the advantage that they can talk freely, but has its downsides, too: it could put them through a conflict of loyalties and magnify their feelings of guilt. Moreover, children could be burdened by their parents with all kinds of instructions about what they can and what they cannot say. This could trap children in a corner.

That is why we prefer to see children with their parents present. It could prove beneficial when parents hear their children talk about climbing into each other's beds, shivering with fear, when their parents are fighting, or hearing the children tell about how they themselves feel guilty. Children often think that they are to blame for the fighting because they have been too rowdy, because they have forgotten to run an errand, because they did not do their best, etc. Sometimes, parents confirm these fears by saying that they are having a row because the child is determined to harass its parents.

Children can express themselves eloquently about how responsible they feel themselves, how they will try anything to prevent the parents from fighting: for example, by making a mess, by throwing something, or by actually placing themselves between the parents and telling them they have to stop fighting. It is important to assure the children that they are not to blame and to explain that the parents are undergoing therapy because their father does not want to hit their mother any more and that they both think that they have to solve their problems. Of course, it is preferable if parents are able to explain this to their children themselves, but sometimes the explanation the therapist offers may be helpful.

The "dispelling of blame" with children is one of the most important therapeutic interventions. If children have not mastered speech yet, or are too young to grasp any explanations, it is still a good idea to invite them to a session in order to see how they cope and how the parents handle their children. If there is any concern, further examination might take place, through the GP, for example.

Ninth stage: the wife falls silent, loses contact, and becomes isolated. Feelings of betrayal and bereavement about the loss of the romantic ideal

Once this stage is reached, the consequences of trauma become truly visible. These consequences will lead to more desperate acts and in turn lead to an ever-descending spiral. Women are increasingly ashamed about their deplorable situation. They no longer dare to contact their family and avoid chance meetings in the streets. They often have injuries to hide and walk about timidly. They also feel ashamed with their friends and make up lies about their injuries. Everything is aimed at avoiding another outburst of violence, which leads to a restricted awareness. Apart from this never-ending struggle to survive from one day to the next, and avoiding painful and shame-inducing interactions with the partner and the outside world, there is an all-consuming sense of betrayal, the sense that the man of their choice has pretended to be different altogether throughout their courtship. "Dr Jekyll" turns out to be "Mr Hyde". That beautiful tree-trunk that is supposed to support you turns into an awesome crocodile (Dahl, 1978). They feel as if they are caught in a trap, and now they cannot get out and they must have missed the real prince, who surely must be out there somewhere. The romantic ideal is not dismissed, but simply regarded as a missed opportunity. Whatever was promised to them as a little girl is withheld from them, and that triggers a sense of mourning for the loss of cherished illusions. This process of bereavement actually has started long before this, when the cracks appear in the ideal and she chooses denial: "I will turn him into the prince that he truly is, even though it may not seem to be so for now". Once the notion sinks in that it is not going to work out after all, a sense of betrayal, of despondency, and sadness about the loss will predominate. Consequently, withdrawing behaviour and physical malaise will set in. This mourning process is not something that women go through exclusively.

Tenth stage: the withdrawing behaviour of the wife conjures up fear in the husband and leads to more aggression. Feelings of betrayal and bereavement about the loss of the romantic ideal

As I have stated before, men hope to find the loving relationship that they had established with their mothers in their first years, with their wives. Chodorow (1978) describes how painful the process is for men in our culture (though not solely in ours) to detach themselves from the bond with their mother once they have to develop their identity as men and are forced to turn to a distant and emotionally absent father. They feel forsaken. The bond with their father does not measure up to the intimacy they have felt with their mother. Boys can find themselves in a phase of loneliness, which they compensate for by acting as a tough guy. This behaviour often results in appreciative comments. When they fall in love, the longing for the former loving bond with the first woman in their life is rekindled. The new woman will always be there for them, she will not abandon them. The fear of yet another loss and the pain that comes with it might resurface when the man is threatened with losing his wife. This is the case when she actually says she wants to leave, but also when she becomes emotionally distant, when she is, as it were, "no longer present". The husband tries to hold on to his wife by strengthening his control over her, which results in a further increase of violence. Moreover, he, too, feels betrayed, feels that she has made out to be someone she is not, that she has pretended to be a bubbly girl but turns out to be this grumpy woman. She used to make him feel that everything he did is perfect, but now he cannot do anything right. He, too, mourns the loss of the romantic ideal, and feels the poorer now that he can no longer make her happy. But by trying "to bring her in from the cold" by means of violence, he only makes matters worse.

Eleventh stage: growing isolation and "freezing" of the wife. Alienation from her own body, feelings, and thoughts. Symptoms of disassociation and splitting of parts of the self. Restricted awareness

The symptoms of trauma take the upper hand. There is no longer a sense of betrayal and mourning; all that is left is listless survival. All symptoms of a "post traumatic stress disorder" are present. In the case of sexual violence, the woman "transcends her body" and lets everything wash over her; she no longer feels anything, it is not her body. She no longer knows what to think or feel, the only thing that occupies her thoughts is how she can get through another day without too many bruises. She is no longer able to properly think about other solutions, like how to get out of this situation. Her whole world is reduced to this.

We come across this far-reaching restricted awareness among people who find themselves in life-threatening situations: one is aware only of the immediate surroundings and all thoughts orbit around it. "Where do I get a loaf of bread today?" might be a thought that keeps spinning round and round for hours. It goes without saying that at this stage relationship therapy is useless. Another kind of help is needed then.

Twelfth stage: growing fear within the husband of losing connection. Attempts to re-establish the contact by increase of control: more violence. Splitting the violent actions from the self

As we have described earlier, there is a growing fear within the man of losing the bond. The more she withdraws and "is no longer present", the more he tries to win her back by violent means. The man, too, becomes alienated from his own body, feelings, and thoughts. His awareness, too, becomes restricted. He splits his own violent behaviour from his self-image and lays the responsibility on her impossible behaviour, with which she rejects him and shuts him out. He, too, feels ashamed, and is preoccupied as to how to keep the deplorable situation at home a secret. His thoughts, too, are caught in the situation in which he finds himself trapped. He sees no other way than to try to turn the tide by using the same violent methods over and over again.

Thirteenth stage: total dysfunctioning on all levels of the partner system

Once this stage is reached, the signals can no longer be hidden from the outside world. Although family, neighbours, the GP, shopkeepers, acquaintances from school, and others have suspected for a long time that something is not quite right, there comes a time when caring for overtakes the fear of butting into somebody's private affairs. For example, the neighbours call the police when they hear the next-door neighbour's wife screaming once again. A charge is brought, and assistance for the victim begins.

Women first need help in order for them to retrieve their own thoughts, feelings, and physical sensations once more, and to take them seriously. This healing process, which can lift disassociation, is a painful, difficult, and maybe a slow process that can take a long time. We encounter these women in the psychiatric field. They might have a history of sexual abuse in their childhood, but they might also have suffered prolonged abuse by their husband. As the treatment of these women does not fall into the scope of our practice, we will not elaborate on this matter.

The flip-side of the coin goes for men. Through prolonged abusing of their wife, they, too, have become detached from their own body, feelings, and thoughts. First, they will have to be persuaded to take responsibility for their own violent behaviour. This reclaiming of a part of oneself that has been split off is a painful, difficult, and slow process as well. In some cases, couples are unwilling to let go, even after prolonged abuse; they meet each other for company. Relationship therapy can, however, start only if both accept the responsibility to work on safety and stopping violent behaviour.

Summary

Our previous accounts about the downward spiral of violence do not do justice to the many individual stories we have heard. It is not that men are only able to express their anger; thankfully, there are also men who come out with their grief, openly show their fears, and are able to express their feelings of love. Not all women turn to nagging and developing physical complaints when they are frustrated and angry; some women can express their anger very well and are more than capable of standing up for themselves. Some women are abusive towards their husbands, and some men can gracefully handle a "no" from their spouse regarding sex.

On the basis of the accounts that we have heard, we have developed a spiral which, as I stated before in this chapter, can be regarded as a useful metaphor. Every case is a variant on the same theme. The spiral must be regarded as a framework that enables us to understand a specific case history, and not be mistaken for a description of "the reality" between men and women.

We have become accustomed to presenting the spiral, as depicted on page 45, in the consultation room and to showing it to the couples we work with. They seem to be able to recognize the patterns without any difficulty. Education and schooling do not seem to matter in this regard. They can recount their story properly with the help of the circle, and it seems to put their minds at ease to know that they are not alone in this.

One more remark regarding children: from the ninth stage we have not mentioned any possible children. However, what we have described at the eighth stage applies equally to any subsequent stages. If children witness serious violence, they themselves develop symptoms which are just as grave as undergoing the abuse themselves. Martine Groen will elaborate on this in Chapter Nine. When children witness violence, they often become victims, too. We are not talking about incest here, because that is a different issue altogether, about which a lot has been published (Draijer, 1988; Lamers-Winkelman, 2000; Sheinberg & Fraenkel, 2001).

We would like to emphasize again the importance of not losing sight of the children, because the next generation may trigger new downward spirals of violence. The sooner one works on "liberating" them, preferably while maintaining the bond they have with their parents, the better.

Bianca and Harry

Thankfully, Bianca and Harry did not have children yet and they came into therapy in time. There had been some violent incidents (sexual as well), but there were no severe traumatic symptoms as yet, which could make ambulant therapy difficult.

I would like to mention an interesting development: after the second session, during which Harry could proudly announce that he had not used his fists and where we could investigate his past, it surfaced that Harry had been to see his father. This is his account:

> "We were talking about my father then, and I thought, I'm going to ask him about him leaving, did he already have that girlfriend then? And why didn't he look me up in all those years, not once? It kept bugging me, so I thought, you know what, I'll go to him right now. When I arrived there, they were in the middle of a huge row, they didn't even notice me. My father dragged her straight across the room by her hair. I could see it all through the window. At first I wanted to take off, but I didn't. I went inside and said: 'Cut it out, the both of you. This isn't what either of you want and something can be done about it. You too should go to van Lawick'".

This resulted in a meeting with Harry's father and his second wife. I managed to build a proper work relationship with them, too, and this resulted in something different altogether. At a birthday party where the whole family had gathered, there was talk about me and consequently about the violence of men against women. "We both agree", Harry's father said, "that violence is not the answer. We are going to keep an eye on each other." That was the best present I could ever wished for. Something remarkable had happened here. In a network where violence was regarded as "the norm" and had been for generations, the secrecy was breached and the definition of the violence changed from "being a solution to a problem" into "this is not the answer". However, Harry's father did not want any further sessions; the thought that he needed a woman's help under- mined his masculinity too much for his liking. He said, "It is great that my son is doing it, but it is not my thing. We will manage just fine by ourselves."

Three months later, Harry's mother came in with her second husband. I did sessions with them as well.

I am not naïve enough to think that this change is going to last. I definitely plan to ask how everything went at some later stage.

This brings me to my final remark. At the start of this chapter, I stated the importance of planning the first sessions at short inter- vals, in order to maximize the chance that no hitting will occur between the first and the second session. Once violence has ceased and the therapy has started, the therapy does not differ that much from other relationship therapies, the only distinction being the emphasis on violence, repeatedly asking whether is has occurred and discussing its consequences.

Once the therapy has reached its final stages, we found that it is advisable to leave more time between the last couple of sessions. For example, if the frequency was once a fortnight, it is first changed to once a month, and subsequently into once every three months and once every six months. The fact that an appointment has been made for another session, even though it will not take place for another six months, seems to support the positive development and prevents a rapid relapse into the downward spiral of violence.

The explanation of the spiral of violence, as mentioned above, stems from the first publication of this book in 1998 (van Lawick & Groen, 1998). At that time, we supposed that violent behaviour most of the time is expressed by men against women. Now we recognize better the part the female plays in escalations, and we also recognize better escalations that can take place in other family relationships that follow a certain pattern. We still think that under- standing gender formation of behaviour is crucial, but we have also created a more general form of the spiral of violence that can be adapted to different relationships.

Phase 1   Romantic ideals and illusions.
Phase 2   Ruptures in the romantic expectations caused by disap- pointments.

Phase 3   Trying to repair the ruptures by correcting and changing the behaviour of the other, maybe with violence.

Phase 4   Corrections do not lead to the wished-for change, but are interpreted by the other as attack and reproach, which leads to defensive behaviour of the other or counter attacks. Escalations start.

Phase 5   Escalations form new and more serious ruptures in romantic ideals and illusions.

Phase 6   Feeling of betrayal and mourning the loss of the romantic expectations.

Phase 7   Growing uncertainty about the relationship, withdrawal, fear of abandonment, increasing dysfunctional patterns. More escalations and violence.

This more general spiral is a useful frame to understand how violence can occur in love relationships. Also, parents can start with romantic expectations of their children that they should be nice, sociable, intelligent, good-looking, and so on. When children do not meet this picture, parents often start to think that something went wrong and they try to change the child's behaviour in order to fit the picture. As a consequence, the child starts to withdraw or oppose the parents. Frustrations grow. Escalations start.

A core premise in our work is that many problems start when people cling to illusions like the idea that we can change the world and people to conform to our wishes. Sorrow has to disappear through medication or therapy, a silent introvert child has to become extravert and sociable through medication or other interventions, wild children have to become quiet, partners have to become self-assertive, emotional, and so on. Our cultural context is full of promises; all problems can be taken away by (mental) health care. These illusions stimulate violence because they do not invite people to accept the frustrations and the tragedies of life. Accepting the tragedies of life means enduring frustrations and reverses, and not blaming causes outside oneself, such as a wrong partner, child, or parent. Alon and Omer state clearly that holding to romantic illusions leads to demonization; accepting the tragedy of life goes against demonization (Alon & Omer, 2006).

CHAPTER FOUR

From ill-behaviour to relational behaviour

Justine van Lawick

*Systemic psychotherapy regarding physical
violence within relationships*

This chapter is a sequel to Chapter Three. The time-out programme depicted therein is summarized briefly here. Subsequently, the effectiveness is analysed. The time-out programme seems to work as a regulating programme in which clients learn to calm themselves in situations that conjure up fierce emotions. The time-out programme is not a miracle cure for violence, but a tool for clients to learn to calm themselves, which in turn will lead to increased self-control. It can easily be mastered to break through escalations; not only does it prevent physical violence, but it can also be used to prevent psychological violence. Clients feel more empowered through self-control than through intimidating and humiliating the spouse. This creates a foundation on which the development of reflection can be built. When the capacity to calm and control oneself merges with the capacity to reflect, violent behaviour will be channelled into relational behaviour. Recent publications about attachment, attitude, and neurobiological processes cast a new light on the effectiveness of this model.

In the therapeutic process, the time-out programme and therapeutic sessions seem to interchange constantly. Learning to reflect and calm oneself in a number of topical situations is a central theme in these sessions. The circular interview that has been developed within system therapy seems to stimulate and enlarge the reflective capacity of clients and, through this, contributes in a positive and effective way to the desired change.

What makes the time-out programme a workable programme?

Using the time-out programme seems to be an effective tool that allows users to focus on violence as a "life-ruining factor" that puts a strain on all concerned and that has to be addressed in order to proceed.

"Violence destroys all you hold dear" is an appealing catchphrase. In this sense, this model connects neatly to the method of externalizing the problem, as developed by White and Epston (1990). Nobody will be blamed. Everybody will be made equally responsible for doing their utmost to gain control over "violence as a life-ruining factor". Men, in general, hold their spouse or circumstances responsible for the violence: "If she didn't nag all the time, there would be no need for me to hit her". Without blaming anybody or trying to figure out who is right, I will explain that the main focus should be for the man to control himself and not to let circumstances, such as a nagging spouse or whining children, an employer's undeserved reproaches, the mood of the stock-market, etc., get the better of him,.

Leaving, if you feel the other party is taunting and provoking you, acquires an entirely different meaning: it is not a sign of weakness but a sign of strength not to let yourself get needled by others and to have self-control. Initially, this programme was aimed at preventing physical violence, but now this has been widened to cover cracking down on escalations in order to prevent physical and psychological damage. This addresses behaviour such as criticizing, scolding, humiliating, shaming, financially controlling, or socially isolating the other party, together with a broad spectrum of physical acts, such as preventing the other party from leaving the room, locking them up, shaking, pushing, hitting, punching, choking them, hitting their head against a wall, throwing them on to the floor or down the stairs, kicking them, or any combination of this kind of cruel behaviour. As the time-out programme teaches its clients to recognize the accumulation of tension at an early stage, and subsequently to take action to calm oneself, this in turn can prevent psychological and physical harm. Reports of battered women show that harm caused by psychological violence some-times has more far-reaching consequences than physical violence. A client expressed herself as follows, "I can forget the beatings, but what he said while he was doing it keeps haunting me."

If the programme is a success, it creates a foundation on which therapeutic counselling can focus more on relational and other issues. Experience shows that outbursts of violence can recur. It is advisable to focus solely on the violent behaviour at the next session. What happened exactly, could a time-out have taken place, and why did it fail? A sense of acceptance is imperative: "As I told you before, it usually crops up again. This is quite common. For now, we have to examine thoroughly and strategically how it all went pear-shaped and how to avoid this in the future".

Often, it will seem like starting all over again. Both are ashamed that the conflicts escalated again, that one of them or both exploded; they feel like a failure and want to blame the other. It is not his fault that it all got out of hand; it is because of the impossible, humiliat-ing and tormenting behaviour of his wife or his adolescent son. It was not her fault, but his withdrawing and ignoring her that made her explode.

The therapist has to be patient and go through the same motions again. Once more it is about creating a non-accusing atmosphere in which the time-out programme is detached from the essence of the conflicts. One discusses at which stage physical tensions and heart-beat increased, why the opportunity of a time-out had not been seized, and how it can be taken in a similar situation. Only when this is clear can a new appointment be made for a more substan-tial consultation.

The symbolic order

The theory on the symbolic order casts light on the workability of the time-out programme. The concept of symbolic order springs from the anthropologist Lévi-Strauss. Lacan developed the importance of the symbolic order for the psyche even further (Schokker & Schokker, 2000). Lacan's symbolic order is a linguistic order that regulates our society, comprising social regulations and rituals that make a society feasible. Our behaviour is regulated by it in detail. The symbolic order is characterized by maintaining ritualistic exchanges that confirm the social order. If somebody asks how you are doing, the expected answer is "I'm fine", not an elaboration on everything and anything that goes on in your life. The symbolic order is, by definition, impersonal, and has to do with certain roles that have to be fulfilled in order to preserve the social order. A judge becomes a judge by putting on his robe; he voices the law there and then, his personality is not relevant. The same goes for a policeman or teacher, but also for a father and mother. Of course, parents can be looked upon as unique beings with their own personality and history. Lacan, however, emphasizes the function of parenthood detached from the person. The acceptance of parental authority is essential for regulating the social order within a family. Lacan elaborates on this in his reformulating of the Oedipus complex. He states that the child, by accepting "the law of the father", learns how to structure and limit his pleasures and not to become submerged in the longing for the mother. The law of the father (also known as the name of the father) does by no means coincide with an actual father; it is a symbolic function. It is, in fact, possible for a biological father to be present in such a way in a family that the symbolic father is actually absent. According to Lacan, the corruption of power is the denial of the symbolic mandate. It is confusing the person with the role he plays. If you hold a position of power in the symbolic order, people do what you tell them to do and that is when you start to believe in your own power. At that point, the function cannot be implemented properly, because the person and the function are one and the same, the necessary distance and reflection are lacking. This seems to be the case with political figures who do not see their position as an honourable mandate of society, but as a personal merit and a personal right. Populism is the consequence.

The same goes for violent men and women who cannot control their violent impulses. In families and relationships in which there is too much chaos and a lack of boundaries, it is important to shape the function of the law of the father in a Lacanian sense by inviting one to determine boundaries and to take responsibility through self-control, with the time-out programme, for instance.

The time-out programme addresses people to their function, rather than to their personality. It is possible that they are personally deeply wounded by another person, but, in their position as partner or parent, they have to keep their self-control. The time-out programme detaches the function from the person, so to speak. Failing this, at times, the assistance of the police will be needed to restore the function and to offer protection.

Within this structure, it is possible to set reflection in motion, and this is an essential step towards a more fundamental change.

An eruption of violence is always preceded by a building-up phase. The parties involved are not always aware of this building-up. At times, the anger seems to come out of nowhere.

Ricardo comes home and sees his wife, Angela, carrying a heavy ladder. He lunges at her, wrenches the ladder violently from her, causing her to fall backwards and hurt her head. Ricardo calls her a filthy whore and kicks her for good measure.

At first glance nothing has preceded this outburst. As I unravel this scene with Ricardo and Angela, the following unfolds.

Angela and Ricardo have been in a relationship for five years. Both are of Antillean origin. After a miscarriage, Angela is pregnant again. They have a lot of conflicts that usually start with Angela criticizing her husband. He does not earn enough, he drinks too much, gambles, is jealous, and only has sex on his mind. Ricardo sees Angela as the love of his life and will do anything to keep her. He is jealous by nature and is anxious that she sleeps around. He works in construction, mostly finishes work around 4 p.m., and regularly frequents his usual pub on his way home, where he hangs around for too long and drinks a lot. If he has drunk away a lot of money, he likes to try to earn it back by playing the slot machine, and subsequently loses more money. This also happened that same afternoon.

On his way home Ricardo feels guilty. He is late. In his mind, he can hear Angela's ranting: "You haven't got two pennies to rub together, you booze away all the money you earn, are you supposed to be a dad, a fine example you make, I'm better off by myself . . ." He even starts to defend himself: "Nothing I ever do is good enough for you, I work don't I, I just gave you the new pair of stockings you wanted. You ought to work a bit harder yourself, you're the one who's lazy . . ." Gradually, he convinces himself that he is right and that his wife does not have the right to fly of the handle like that. She humiliates him in front of his neighbours. She will surely dump him, so she can sleep with that neighbour from a few houses down the road. He's not going to put up with it any longer . . . Because of these internal monologues Ricardo gets more and more excited and tense.

Angela is at home and waits for Ricardo. He is late. Her sister and mother are expected to call later that evening and they were supposed to hang the new curtains for the occasion. Angela gets more and more agitated. "That bastard is late again, I suppose he'll booze and gamble away all his money. He's totally useless. He forgets me and even forgets the baby. He doesn't look after us. My mother is right: men are all losers who give you nothing but grief. I will have to do it all by myself, again."

When he comes home, he sees her dragging the ladder and then things get out of hand. He suddenly realizes that he had promised to hang the new curtains before the arrival of her mother and sister. It completely slipped his mind. "She only does that to show me what a loser I am", he thinks. "She wants to show her mother and sister that she can do it all by herself and that men are indeed as useless as her mother always says."

These interpretations and the tension he had already created on his way home form the run-up to the attack on Angela, who, after all, did humiliate him and makes him feel bad about himself. He wrenches the ladder from her hands, causing her to fall backwards. Her frightened eyes and her screaming enrage him even more; he calls her a filthy whore and kicks her.

Angela is surprised and frightened by the fierceness of the attack and retreats into herself.

With the training of the time-out programme, such incidents will be unravelled extensively. Step by step, the possibility of avoiding the escalation will be examined and the moment identified when this was not possible any more.

Learning to notice physical signs makes it possible to create an awareness of the anger build-up. In Ricardo's case, this started during the day at the construction site where his employer was short with him for not being quick enough with renewing a windowpane. He leaves all fired up, and wants to relax with a beer before going home. In the pub he adds even more tension when he realizes that he is late, has had too much to drink and wasted too much money. He feels he failed in his function as a breadwinner, protector, and future father.

He transfers the shame and guilt he feels about his failures into anger towards his wife, who always makes him feel bad. This anger and the violence cause him to fail even more in his function as a partner. The time-out programme can teach him to calm himself before entering his home. By walking past the pub, for instance, or by leaving there sooner, or by going for a walk and calling ahead to say that he is sorry that he is late. In the next phase, it is useful to examine where his addictive-related behaviour stems from and how to handle it.

In Angela's case, I give thought to her behaviour and safety. In what way can she take responsibility for her actions and her own safety? Angela can reflect on the effect of her continuing criticism and humiliation of Ricardo. She also could have felt that her tension grew and that her heartbeat accelerated when Ricardo came home late. She could have asked her mother and sister to come earlier and help her, or she could have left a note and gone to her mother and sister instead.

The repetitive going over of such incidents helps clients to master the time-out programme. It is a challenge for clients to prac-tise self-control as a sign of strength and good will.

The time-out programme offers a clear boundary through which stability has a level chance and chaos does not reign. In Lacanian terms (Schokker & Schokker, 2000), one can posit that a clear symbolic order is lacking in violent relationships and that the programme helps to put this right. It is, by the way, important not to confuse this symbolic order with the functions caused by social-ization. A lot of studies into socialization of men in patriarchal soci-eties show that men see their wives as their property, that a man is entitled to be cared for by his wife, including sex, that he can control his wife and punish her if she does not fulfil his expecta-tions. It is exactly these expectations that legitimize violence within relationships (Bancroft & Silverman, 2002).

In this respect, it is interesting to read the study by Gilmore, an anthropologist who studied the meaning of "manliness" in Western and non-Western cultures (Gilmore, 1994). He concluded that in almost every culture masculinity is a status one should earn through exhibiting certain abilities. Worldwide, these abilities can be classified in three categories: (1) a man should achieve sexually and produce offspring, (2) a man must be a good breadwinner, and (3) a man must protect the ones who depend on him. There is a connection between the social context and the harshness with which these demands are being put on men. The harsher the conditions, through lack of life resources or the privations of war, the harsher the demands put on men. In our affluent Western world, these demands on "real men" can be more flexible and there is space for individual variations. But these demands, too, are part of male and female expectations.

In the aforementioned example, Ricardo felt that he failed, being a bad breadwinner and not protecting his wife and future child properly. His wife and family tackle him on these functions.

Women's liberation and youth emancipation have made different varieties of family life feasible in which equality is the keynote. However, if this is done without social regulations and rituals that make living together possible, then chaos will arise. Violence is one of the symptoms this chaos generates. In the intimacy of a family, a time-out programme can be applied as a social regulation and as a ritual that brings structure to living together. Within this structure, it is possible to engage in psychotherapeutic treatment.

The importance of calming

Another important aspect of the time-out programme is that clients learn to calm themselves and others before things get out of hand. Gottman (1999) regards calming oneself and the other as one of the most important qualities of a successful partner relationship. This can be classified under what he calls "repair actions". Gottman has done research into partner relationships for over twenty-five years. Happy couples, too, know conflicts, often about the same reccurring topics. Happy couples, however, are much more successful in repairing than unhappy couples. Repairing can consist of verbal and non-verbal actions, such as mollifying words, saying you are sorry, comforting, stroking, and also calming oneself by leaving the room before a conflict gets out of hand. Restoring contact after leaving the room increases the success rate of repairing.

It is interesting that, within the research about the development of attachment patterns between parent and child, the importance of repair actions after a misunderstanding or conflict has been underpinned (Siegel, 2001).

An additional safety valve regarding the time-out programme seems to be my request to call me, should things get out of hand. The couple can make an advanced appointment during which they can analyse why the time-out did not work, in all tranquillity. Several times, I have been told by men that they were on the verge of lashing out when they suddenly remembered my request to call me. This thought helped them to regulate themselves.

Apparently, the voice of a therapist can be needed at times to successfully carry out a calming action. In a report on a workshop with Tom Andersen (Delpeut, 2002), a good example of the above is given: Andersen is in consultation with a very violent man who uses his fists. Andersen asks the man what the fist would like to say. The fist wants to stop the other one from behaving in a certain manner. Andersen calls this voice "the voice of the man's angry part", and asks for "the voice of the man's safe part". He invites the man to listen to "the voice of the safe part" in future confrontations. Typically, the man manages to control himself more, but he links his own changing behaviour to Andersen's voice that kept ringing in his ears. Andersen acts as the temporary, significantly safe parental figure assisting the man in calming and regulating himself. Only then the parental figure can be internalized and an own internal voice created. The capacity to calm oneself becomes part of the self.

Biological processes

In the process of an escalation, blood pressure, muscle tension, heartbeat, and respiration speed up and stress hormones build up in the blood. By thoroughly going over the physical perceptions that are linked to the increase of tension, a client can be taught to break through the build-up of tension. One can say that violence occurs when the more primitive parts of the brain are stimulated. I often explain that stress "dumbs you down". Build-up tension affects the full use of the brain, which is why rigid thinking patterns take over. With rigid thinking patterns, solving conflicts is no longer possible. The primitive brain only "knows" three functions: fight, flight, or freeze. Behaviour stemming from these functions leads to violence. Only if a calming action reignites the full use of the brain can one reflect and find non-violent solutions.

Reflection, mentalizing, and the reflective self-function

An exciting and informative discussion is taking place at the forum where psychoanalytical thinkers, attachment theoreticians, and neurobiologists meet and talk to one another. I would like to see systemic psychotherapists take part in this dialogue, because I am convinced that we can learn a lot from all these theoreticians, but that we, too, can contribute some important elements. In this chapter, I focus on clarifying the dynamics of violent behaviour. The fact is that, in recent literature, violent behaviour has been associated with the inability to reflect.

First, I will discuss a few general theoretic concepts which were recently developed within this context. I refer to the English (Fonagy, 2001; Siegel, 2001) and Dutch (Gomperts, 2000; Nicolai, 2001a,b; Van Gael, 2002) publications in which these theories are elaborated at length.

The point of departure is the development of the psyche of a human being at the interface between human relations and the unfolding structure of the brain. A child is born with a certain genetic programme that compels it to attach itself to its main carers, the attachment figures; the brain is destined to connect with other brains, so to speak. In interaction with these attachment figures, a child develops basic patterns for the association with others, so-called internal work models. These attachment patterns can be determined through the Adult Attachment Interview (George, Kaplan, & Main, 1996).

Ainsworth, Blehar, Waters, and Wall (1978), among others, researched these attachment patterns with children by putting them in a situation where they were left by the parent for a short while: the "strange situation" test. Several different patterns are recognizable. Sixty per cent of the children appear to be attached safely, 40%

unsafely. Fifteen per cent of these children develop an avoidance pattern and retreat into themselves, 15% of the children become preoccupied with parental attention, cannot be alone, and compellingly look for the constant attendance of the parent, 10% have a disorganized pattern and subsequently a fierce, unpredictable manner of response.

How do these patterns develop themselves? The focus in this process is the co-operation between the parent and the child; it is about sharing emotions in a fine-tuned relationship. In this co-operation, the parent tries to give meaning to the signs of the baby and the baby learns to adjust itself to the behaviour of the parent. Stern (1985) describes this as "attunement".

Communication with attachment figures is crucial for the development of a positive self-image. Within these communications, the child learns to give meaning to its own emotions and to regulate them. The focus of the self as a self with an in-tune other forms the foundation of the ability to feel connected to others and care for others.

Coherent to this, basic circuits develop in the brain, which are connected to vital mental processes: the capacity to take part in interpersonal communication, the generation and regulation of emotions, the development of the autobiographical self-image, and the construction of a "self-narrative", the capacity to detect and understand the mind/psyche of others, and the development of an ability to practise well-considered, reflective, and moral behaviour.

The capacity to see oneself and others as human beings, whose behaviour is steered by feelings, desires, and cognitions, develops within a safe attachment relationship with a parental figure. This can be either the father or mother, but it can also be another involved adult. The capacity to reflect on inner tribulations of oneself and others starts its development in the first couple of months after birth, within the affectionate and fine-tuned interaction between baby and main carer. An eight-month-old baby can already feel the emotional state of the parent and tune itself into it. The baby is a participating person in the attachment process.

When the development of the capacity to mentalize goes well, a six-year-old is capable of thinking about what somebody else thinks about a third person's thoughts. A six-year-old can also think about what somebody else thinks of what he is thinking himself. If this development continues, a twelve-year-old will reflect on an internal psychic reality and a sense of subjectivity. Such a child acknowledges the existence of different points of view, feelings, and longings. The reflective function develops strongly until the mid twenties, but can develop also later in life.

The developed internal work models often have an important impact on later life. An example: if a six-month-old baby laughs while his father tosses him into the air, the father might say, "You like flying through the air, huh?", and if the baby subsequently starts to cry when his father, in all his enthusiasm, tosses him up too high, too roughly, he might say, "Oh, that was really foolish of me, that was too high, huh, that's scary, come into my arms".

A father who has been humiliated himself, shamed and criticized often by his own father, would give another interpretation: "Cry baby, don't be such a wuss, come on, I'll catch you, you shouldn't cry, you think I'd let you fall". If the mother, in turn, starts to react in a panicky way, pulls the baby out of father's hands and gives him a furious look, the father might yell, "I'm doing it all wrong again, you know what's best for the little prince, but I'll tell you something, you'll turn him into a wuss, he has to toughen up a bit".

In this way, the small child is confronted with a hard-to-grasp succession of fun, pain at the big tough hands of the father and the rough tossing about, the fear of his father's angry voice, anger and panic coming from his mother, and subsequently the tension and yelling between the parents. Experiences of fun, well-being, and being connected are mixed with experiences of fear, pain, confusion, and panic. If a small child, during his first years of childhood, is regularly confronted by the main adult carers with such unpredictable, frightening, swiftly changing emotional reactions, it will not learn to integrate and regulate its own emotional reactions. The mentalization will not be set in motion.

Why is this mentalizing so important and how does this relate to, for example, the problem of violence? Mentalization is connected to self-awareness, social and moral consciousness and with affect and impulse regulation. Through the awareness of one's own psychic reality and that of others, caring for the other can be possible without losing one's autonomy. Mentalization appears to expand the resilience of children and adults. Shocking experiences can be handled better.

Of course, every baby experiences situations in which parental figures are not properly in tune with the baby's needs. The repair phase is important to restore contact. In the previous example, the father could say to his wife, "I'm sorry, I actually went too far, I had so much fun tossing him into the air that I didn't pay attention any more", or the mother could say, "I saw you both having so much fun, but when I heard crying I thought you had dropped him. I scare easily at times, I'm sorry". The parents can hug each other and hug the child together. The contact is restored. Babies, too, can learn to adjust themselves to their parents and learn how to connect again once things get out of hand.

In this process of looking and finding one another, adding meaning, misunderstanding each other, and finding each other again, an attachment pattern will emerge. The quality of the parent–child relationship becomes part of the implicit memory. Somebody who has been known and treated as a precious and loved human being develops a self-image that fits the profile. A child that is made to feel a burden, inconsolable and incomprehensible, or even as an evil creature, develops a self-image of being hopeless, troublesome, bad, and worthless.

A reflective capacity that has been developed in the first years of childhood through learning processes in interaction with parental figures appears to offer strong protection against shocking experiences. It increases the mental resilience.

Van Ijzendoorn (2002) recently published research about the children of victims of the Second World War Holocaust. In this again, determination does not offer a proper point of departure. With the majority of the studied people, no transference of trauma seems to have taken place. On this note, the hypothesis of second-generation victims and the transference of trauma seems to be up in the air again. Many parents appear to protect their children against the transference of their own traumas by living future-bound and being in tune with the needs of the child. Especially when they were safely attached themselves, their resilience during and after the war stayed strong and they had the capacity to mentalize, which, in turn, they can set in motion in their child. The feasibility of managing to hold on to that resilience even after going through such heinous experiences offers hope.

Going back to the violent adults, it seems to be a good point to suppose that these people have not learned to reflect, to regulate and calm themselves. Van Gael (2002) gives a detailed account of how we can picture this process. If a baby is faced with neglect and abuse, the development of the mentalizing ability is halted. The child cannot picture itself with its own inner world and that of the carers. After all, the image the carers offer is so hostile, threatening, and destructive that it is impossible for the child to incorporate this into the self-image it will create. The cruel, disqualifying, hostile, and unpredictable other must be kept outside the self-image. The child protects itself by staying unaware of the malicious mental state of the other and by not thinking about it. The child cuts itself off from the mental representation of the other within itself. No empathic and reflective ability can be created if this process is kept up in relation to others.

Empathy, being in tune/sympathizing with the other can be seen as a forerunner of the reflective ability. When these persons mature, they are incapable of seeing the other, in intimate relationships, as a thinking, feeling, and longing creature. They take their own mental images of the other as a point of reference and these images are often rigid by nature. The image of the other is hostile and experienced as real. No definite awareness has been developed of the effect of their own behaviour on the perception and behaviour of the other. This can result in cruel and merciless behaviour. The ability to identify with the other has not been developed; subsequently, no empathy for the other arises. Fonagy, Moran, and Target (1993) call it "mindless aggression". Focusing on the body and on physical violence are also signs of a lack of mentalization: thoughts, desires, and feelings are not seen as a state of mind, but are directly transferred into physical acts. There is a lack of symbolic representations, which in turn translates every emotional arousal into physically action-guided strategies that precede the capacity for mentalization.

Given that there is no integration between the state of mind and subsequent behaviour, and that behaviour is not regarded as steered through a state of mind, the behaviour is disowned; one does not bear any responsibility. This removes any restraint on violent behaviour that is present with mentalized individuals. Because images have no symbolic "pretend" quality, the image of the other is seen as real, a state of mind cannot be seen as differing from reality. The lack of inner mental representations will be the cause of a sense of emptiness and emotional isolation. Gomperts (2000) sees a direct link between destructive behaviour in adolescents and an undeveloped or damaged mentalizing capacity.

The behaviour of these people is steered more often through impulses from the lower regions of the brain and not through the more complex state of reflection and self-organization that requires the co-operation of both halves of the brain. Response patterns do not develop as flexible patterns, but as rigid ones. Emotions escalate rapidly, hostile images gain the upper hand, and reflective actions become impossible. Minimal provocation can bring about an excessive emotional reaction in which inner turmoil, fear, panic, and strong feelings of shame and humiliation gain the upper hand. In such a state, an individual can regress into infantile anger and aggressive, intimidating, and violent behaviour. I have given an example of this in Ricardo's behaviour.

It is important to research whether the theory of attachment and mentalizing can be used as a tool to widen the area of therapeutic possibilities.

Possibilities of treatment

Are all relational violence problems treatable through psychotherapy and especially by systemic psychotherapy? I have struggled with this question for a long time. In my experience, there are few human beings who like to hit, who enjoy it and feel empowered by it. A more usual pattern is a man or woman who is ashamed of the violent behaviour, feels powerless, and gladly transfers any responsibility for his violent behaviour on to his partner. The same goes for parents who hit their child. They, too, often feel guilt-ridden, ashamed, and powerless, and lay the blame for their violent behaviour on the misbehaviour of their child instead of on themselves.

In only a few cases did I encounter a client who was not ashamed of his violent behaviour and who did not wish to reflect on the impact it had on his spouse and children.

Jacobson and Gottman (1998a,b) distinguish in their work two types of violent men. Type 1 has, in the course of rising conflicts

with violent eruptions, a lowered heart rate, low adrenalin production, prefers the use of a knife or another weapon to his own fists,
behaves violently towards the spouse, but also towards friends,
other family members, colleagues, and people out on the street, and
is, in conflicts, intimidating, humiliating, and threatening from the
start. Type 2 men have an increased heart rate, high adrenalin
production during a conflict, prefer using their fists instead of a
weapon, are not violent outside the intimacy of a relationship, and
have a slow build-up of anger. Type 1 men stimulate independent
behaviour of their wife and get angered by controlling behaviour of
the spouse. Type 2 men, on the contrary, want to isolate and own
their wives, are jealous and suspicious by nature, and have a strong
fear of abandonment.

In their long clinical experience, Type 1 men are likely to be
unable to change through psychotherapy. Within the psychiatric
diagnostic this is known as psychopathic. One may presume that
these men have not known an intimate and safe attachment relationship in which they might have developed their reflective ability. The initial ability at birth was insufficiently stimulated and
developed. The neural networks can be extinguished according to
the principle "use it or lose it". It seems, however, possible to stimulate and develop this function at a later stage in life, unless the
brain of a person is damaged through birth defects or from an accident or toxic poisons (among which is protracted substance abuse).
There can possibly be a defect at birth. Are there any references to
this supposition? Given that these men are highly dangerous and
impulsive, that they take no responsibility and know no shame,
trying to create a suitable context in an ambulant setting for treatment will not work, as these men do not want to engage initially in
a work relationship with the therapist. A forensic context appears
to be imperative. In the report of Janssen (2002), regarding trends in
forensic psychiatry, is detailed how security and control can create
a context for a more fundamental treatment of this group of clients.

This is, of course, a rather crude form of classification. Even so,
the distinction between Type 1 and Type 2 has helped me in my
decision sometimes not to engage in treatment, but to refer to a
forensic context. This applies men and women. The most important
criteria are that a work relationship cannot be established, that the
clients do not take responsibility for their behaviour, do not really

want to co-operate with a time-out programme, and know no shame. If I confront them with their responsibilities, they turn their intimidating behaviour towards me.

With the group of violent people who are categorized under Type 2, it is possible to start an ambulant therapy, even if the relational physical and psychological violence can be, at times, severe. Within this group there is also great variety, and researching and mapping of the unique problems of each case is important. However, there are similarities between these clients. Their sense of shame indicates some mentalization, but this ability must have been damaged in relational provocations. With these people, it seems as if the impulses connected to the more primitive parts of the brain have the upper hand in interactive situations. Dutton Golant, and Pijnaker (2000) studied the psychological backgrounds of violent men and found some recurring characteristics. These men mostly had a father who criticized, shamed, and humiliated them as a child. They often developed a disorganized attachment pattern with the mother, because the mother was both a beacon of security and of fear, especially if they themselves, with their son as a witness, were abused by the father. These men were often abused by their father during childhood. The fact that being witness to violence between parents damages children and stunts the development of the reflective function is addressed in Chapter Nine by Martine Groen and has been detailed by several authors (Dijkstra, 2000).

The reflective function and circular questions

Psychotherapy is one of the ways that can lead to developing an underdeveloped or stunted mentalizing ability. In psychoanalytical publications, the emphasis lies on creating a safe transference relationship between client and therapist in which the client can become aware of the mental processes within him/herself and of an inner world of the therapist as well.

Within systemic psychotherapy, this ability is stimulated and developed by means of other methods. The method of the circular interview was developed because systemic therapists are interested in relationships, in the way in which these relationships are presented in the minds of individuals, and in the manner in which this influences and steers their behaviour. Questions were developed that generate information about relationships and representations of relationships. Tomm (1987, 1988) developed a schedule of circular questions in which reflective questions are allotted an important position.

It occurred to me that the use of the circular interview stimulates the mentalizing ability of family members during the time I studied how mentalization, or the reflective function, is measured with adults. Fonagy and Target (1997) developed a scale that is applied to parts of the Adult Attachment Interview developed by George, Kaplan, and Main (1996). This scale appears to be reliable, and the coherence with the attachment modus is high (75%). In other words, the reflective function can predict the attachment curve reasonably accurately. A high reflective function is linked to a safe attachment. The measured mentalizing ability appears to be independent of schooling, social–economical status, and verbal intelligence. The questions used by the researchers to measure the reflective function are, almost without exception, circular questions. I will give an example. At the end of an interview one is asked, "If you have a one-year-old child, how would you feel about leaving it behind?", and "Do you think you would be worried about your child?", and "If you were granted three wishes for your child in twenty years' time, what would you wish for?" These are the questions that we all know well as future-bound, hypothetical, reflective, circular questions.

Fonagy argues that the essence of mentalizing composes a human awareness of one's own feelings, thoughts, motives, and desires, but also of the feelings, desires, thoughts, and motives of the other. It is exactly this function that is evoked and stimulated by the circular interview. One could regard the circular questions as an effective way to stimulate the reflective ability in a non-accusing, accepting, and inviting manner. Precisely because partners, or parents and children, and possibly important others, are involved in the interview in systemic psychotherapy, the mentalizing ability of all those present is stimulated and possibly expanded, which, in turn, might change the interaction outside the therapeutic environment. After all, through circular questions, information changes hands about the inner world of all involved, about their thoughts, feelings, desires, and motives but also their thoughts about the

feelings of others and those of third parties, and about the relationships between those others and third parties. This information will
be available to all those attending the session, and through this they
are more aware not only of their own inner world, but also of the
inner world of others.

This is exactly what mentalizing implies. Just as in individual
therapy mentalization is set in motion by constantly reworking the
therapeutic relation in the here and now, in family therapy it is a
constant invitation to a dialogue between all present inner worlds.
A dialogue is especially stimulated between the as yet unheard
inner voices. In a family in which a father beats his son, the question can be put to him: "How would you like to be remembered by
your son?" This question invites the father to reflect on his current
behaviour, his desired behaviour, the current behaviour of his son,
the future life of his son, their current relationship, and their future
relationship. The mother, too, can be asked the question: "How do
you think your husband would like your son to remember him as
a father?" These seem complicated questions, but experience shows
that an answer will always follow. Often, in this case, "Somebody
he can rely on, who supports him, who shows him the way".
Exploring the current turmoil in the perspective of the father's own
desired father image in a setting of tranquillity seems to bring about
a change effectively.

Another recent example is that of a daughter with endlessly
arguing parents who made a very serious attempt to commit
suicide. I formed the opinion that the suicide attempt was an action
by the daughter to connect the parents and to stop them fighting
their endless fights. I asked the following question: "Suppose you
had managed to kill yourself, do you think your parents would
quarrel more or less?" Her unexpected answer was that her parents
would probably finally split up and would be liberated, because
they both said they could not split up because of her. In the next
counselling session, the shocked parents were able to openly
discuss the possibility of a divorce, the consequences, doubts, and
possibilities.

In another family session in which a son was suicidal, the
mother said, "My child, it is your own life, you have to decide for
yourself", at which the therapist asked the sister, "What do you
think your mother is actually saying and how do you think your

brother will interpret her message?" The sister stated that she thought her brother would think he is irrelevant, that he might as well not exist, but that she thought that this was not what her mother wanted to say. The mother broke down in tears and talked about her attempts to give her children free reign, after her own experiences with rigid, oppressive, and authoritarian parents.

When the wife of a violent man in couple therapy tells of how scared she often is of her husband, the therapist can ask, "Do you want to have a wife who is afraid of you?", and, after the man has remarked curtly that of course that is not the way he would like it to be, the therapist can ask, "Suppose you yourself can see to it that your wife would be less scared, what kind of things would you say and do, without feeling a total wuss?" There are countless examples of circular, reflective questions that can stimulate and expand the mentalizing ability of the attending clients.

Tomm (1994) has developed this method even further by interviewing the initialized other in couple therapy. His point is as follows. When people meet for the first time, they form an impression of the feelings, experiences, and thoughts of the other person. Along with these interpretations one's own personality and history, and the internal work models as well, play a significant role. These impressions lead to knowledge about the other person, which is often not tested, but taken as factual. Our relational behaviour is based on these"truths" created by ourselves. Although these impressions can be very accurate at times, there will always be differences with the perceptions of the partner. By interviewing the other in the presence of the partner, misunderstandings can surface and be analysed. He starts with simple questions: "How did she feel about coming here today?", followed by positive questions, "What does she admire in you, what does she like in particular?", followed by more sensitive questions such as "What troubles her mostly, what scares her, what does she criticize in you as a father?", etc. A condition for the circular interview, as well as for interviewing the internalized other, is that all those attending must feel safe in the therapeutic context. This is probably why systemic psychotherapists are adept at positively labelling and creating an open and safe environment in which voices can be heard, including those voices of the inner world of attendees that were silenced.

The reflective capacity and the narrative approach

Another criterion on which the reflective capacity is measured is the construction of a coherent self-narrative. Within systemic psychotherapy. the narrative approach is highly developed. One of the founders of this approach, Bateson (1972), argued that with a theory we can explain everything if we want to. The constructivists reworked this point in their proposition that people create their own truths through the theory they support, and that, in turn, guides their perception. Feminist thinkers and social construction-ists have made the point that these theories are also defined by the social–cultural context. Thinking in narratives as an arrangement of the reality that steers human behaviour is very familiar to systemic psychotherapists.

In systemic psychotherapy, all is focused on jointly creating a coherent narrative about the reality and history of clients that breaches rigid and destructive patterns and makes it possible to create and support more flexible patterns. Memories are recalled in a story that we tell about ourselves, to others, but to ourselves as well. The Adult Attachment Interview is composed of semi-struc-tured questions that invite someone to reflect about their own memories, especially memories about the relationship with parents and other attachment figures. With the analysis of the results of the interview, special attention is given to the structure and coherence of the story.

In systemic psychotherapy, clients are also invited to give their account of the history of their relationships. They then convey their own interpretations of the relationship's history, the representation of the relationship in their mind, and hear those of the partner and other family members. By bringing the different representations into the open, the narratives are made flexible, through which they can offer more ways to change. More coherence can also be offered in the stories, because information is added and sometimes corrected. Attachment research has concluded that painful experi-ences have a less decisive role in future relationships if they are embodied in a coherent narrative. In psychotherapy, too, clients are stimulated to form a coherent narrative about their history through which they can tell a coherent autobiographical story. This makes them less trapped in the incoherent and often destructive stories about themselves and their experiences. Dallos (2002) calls this a "narrative attachment therapy".

My clinical work with this problem shows that learning and practising the time-out programme does not take a lot of time: often one session suffices to reap the first successes. This increases confidence, and the psychotherapy can commence. As I said before, the time-out programme will take centre-stage after each violent incident. This, too, does not need to take up too much time. Psychotherapy that tries to develop the mentalizing abilities of those involved through circular questions and a narrative approach needs more time. I have learnt to take this time, because the long-term effects are better. This often means contact for several years, frequent at the beginning (that is to say, on a weekly basis), and at a less frequent rate later, the total amount of sessions varying from forty to eighty. The lion's share of the sessions is held with both partners present. Then there are those that include the children, or sessions with the children only, and individual sessions with the wife and, more often, with the husband, which are by now part of a routine.

To summarize briefly, in order to work with violence issues within families it is imperative to create a structure first, for example, by means of a time-out programme. After that, the reflective ability of all involved can be addressed and possibly developed. The circular interview is a powerful tool to stimulate this reflective ability, the mentalizing, of clients. The point of reference herein is a narrative approach. Because of this, clients can learn to regulate their emotions and impulses better, which makes it more feasible for them to create a more positive and coherent self-image. This is the foundation for being aware of emotions, cognitions, and desires in others, and this awakened consciousness aids them to develop a social and moral awareness.

CHAPTER FIVE

Escalation and de-escalation

Justine van Lawick

Introduction

In Chapters Three and Four, we discussed violent escalations which can take place between partners. We can always link these escalations to certain frustrations within human relationships, which are the same all over the world. In this chapter, we explore where these frustrations come from and how they can lead to escalations. We find that clients profit from a schematic description of this process. In this chapter, we also address escalating and de-escalating language and behaviour.

Frustration as an instigator of violence

When asked what kind of frustration can provoke violent behaviour, all over the world four clusters of "instigators" of violence emerge. Cluster A relates to *iniquity*: injustice, betrayal (such as cheating), or a vulnerable person (child) or animal being maltreated. Cluster B concerns *disrespect*: violent behaviour, attacks, name-calling, bullying, humiliation, disqualifying, unwanted physical contact, and, in traffic, tailgating, being cut up by other drivers. Cluster C relates to *neglect*: not getting attention, being misjudged, ignored, not being seen, heard, understood; being abandoned. Cluster D concerns *powerlessness*: resistance, opposition, not being able to do what you want to do, being wrongly accused, bureaucracy, victim behaviour, authoritarian behaviour.

These categories do overlap, but the classification turned out to be recognizable. The frustration, which leads to violent behaviour within families, falls within the scope of the categories. As many women as men mention Cluster A and B, Cluster C is mentioned more often by women, and D more often by men.

All these "instigators" of violence are intensified by substance abuse, such as alcohol and drugs, and also by stress factors such as exhaustion, too much work-related pressure, financial problems, bad housing, noise, illness, and other life issues.

Everyone knows these frustrating situations and everyone knows the tendency towards acting violent, including therapists. A therapist who is saying, "I know the feeling that you want to call names or hit something, I'm not better than you", is able to work with violence. Therapists who are saying, "I'm better than you, I don't know this feeling, I'm too civilized or it's too scary", will not be able to make contact with the clients who are struggling with violent behaviour and cannot work with them.

From frustration to escalation

When people are getting frustrated they can try to do something about it. They can walk away and calm down, or they can stay in the same situation and the frustration will grow bigger and bigger. This can lead to escalation, shown schematically in Figure 2.

When quarrels within families escalate, we explain this on the basis of the diagram (Figure 2). This explanation is clarifying and not accusing. It also shows why distancing yourself and calming down is necessary if you want to break through an escalation.

It starts with a source of frustration, which irritates. When this frustration develops or grows, irritation transforms into anger and later into rage, and finally people cross a line. Several expressions refer to this process: "going too far", "going off the rails" or "step-

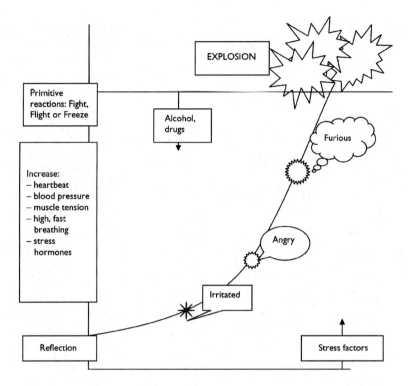

Figure 2.   From frustration to escalation.

ping out of line". Every culture and language has got similar expressions concerning this condition.

When the level of stress keeps rising, the body will reach an alarm phase: blood pressure, heartbeat, tension of the muscles, and stress hormones increase. Respiration is high, fast, and shallow. In the brain, reflection is hindered and primitive parts of the brain are being activated. In the primitive brain, three functions dominate: fight, flight, or freeze.

The other becomes an enemy; an enemy you want to attack or escape, or one who paralyses you with fear. In the fight mode, the other is being attacked with words and physical action. Solution-aimed behaviour and reflection is, in this state of mind, not possible. Stress makes you dumb. Because of that you harm the other. Often, when you calm down, it is incomprehensible that you can hurt and harm someone like that.

Only when the organism calms down can conversations, reflection, and solution-focused behaviour become possible again.

Factors of stress, like debts, bad housing, discrimination, relationship problems, illnesses, problems with children, and social issues lead to the irritation phase as the starting point. Because of this, escalations occur faster and more often. Substance abuse (alcohol, drugs, and some medications) lower the explosion line.

In families where stress factors and substance abuse are high, the area where they can reach a good and solution-focused interaction is seriously affected. Not only do they need to learn how to take some distance and how to calm down, but also conversations with therapists should concern the known stress factors and how they can be reduced in order to avoid relapse.

Personality problems with rigid cognitions about relationships also contribute to faster escalations, as discussed in Chapter Four. Rigid cognitions about male–female relationships, which derive from cultural and social ideas, are an important factor, too.

Naturally, explanations of the process of escalations lead to the notion of taking time-out to calm down. All the persons concerned have to practise calming down, both the person who is leaving the room and those staying behind.

Treating the addictions is necessary if you want to prevent future recidivism.

Regarding violence against children, we want to make clear that the responsibilities are different for parents and children. Parents seem to benefit when they become aware of ascending stress levels and practise "the postponed reaction" after calming down. Of course, parents cannot expect a child to take time-out; they have to take the responsibility themselves to do something to calm down.

Escalating and de-escalating communication

During the process of escalation, the reflective communication is being hindered. More and more, the other becomes an "enemy" one wants to conquer. This process starts because one wants to convince the other that one is right. One does not listen, but tries to persuade the other. Objections of the other are seen as reproach. Everything becomes attack and defence. When no one wins, more and more techniques of persuasion are used: raising of the voice, involving others (it's not only me, your sister and the neighbours all agree), generalizing (you're the one who always forgets something, first, five years ago, our wedding day, then your mother's birthday, or, I hear you, I cannot do anything good for you), the communication becomes more and more black and white, all or nothing, always or never. The other becomes a caricature with no nuances, an enemy. Because both do not listen well, nobody feels heard or acknowledged. Both conclude that the other does not *want* to understand.

These conversations lead to increasing frustration and to escalations, as described above.

In many different ways, therapists stimulate de-escalating communication. The characteristics of this are to listen carefully and try to understand the other. Because of this, questions arise about what exactly the other means. Now the other feels taken seriously, heard, acknowledged. The conversation focuses on the here and now and does not stray from the subject. The one who asks questions not only tries to understand the other, but also tries to empathize with the other. It does not mean one has to agree with the other. It is a possibility that one understands the other's point of view, but still thinks differently. The roles alternate, and the one who has spoken tries to understand the other. The result could be: "we agree that we don't agree".

The acceptance of different points of view turns out to be crucial in handling conflicts. It prevents black and white thinking and focuses more on nuances and toning down. This also means people should be willing to compromise.

This way, the other remains a person you can disagree with. He or she does not become an enemy who wants to conquer you, or who wants to force you in thinking the same.

De-escalating and mentalizing

Chapter Four addressed the importance of mentalizing. Apparently, we can link de-escalating processes directly to the idea of mentalizing. A person who can see the other as a seperate human being with desires, intentions, feelings, and thoughts, and that these can differ from his own inner world, can use de-escalating communication properly. For more on this subject, see Chapter Four.

It will not come as a surprise that a lot of people who frequently find themselves in violent escalations did not develop the ability to reflect and mentalize well. Nevertheless, practising de-escalating communication in therapy sessions can help the person improve.

Together with my clients, I try to collect examples of quarrels that went out of control. In a table, on the left, we write down statements that provoked escalations. Together, we think about the things they could have said or done to prevent these escalations from happening again. On the right, we write the results down. When the therapeutic relationship is good, people actually enjoy finding solutions and ways to change their behaviour.

CHAPTER SIX

Violence in families of various cultural backgrounds

Martine Groen

Introduction

The Dutch philosopher, poet, penal and international law expert, Afshin Ellian, wrote in the daily paper *de Volkskrant*,

> It is utter nonsense to weigh cultural background as a factor in determining appropriate legal sanctions. If [you] do, you imply that minorities are exotic pets. That is rather patronizing. Does a Kurdish man who kills his unfaithful spouse have a right to milder punishment? No, because we do not condone it when people take the law into their own hands in the Netherlands. [17 February, 2001]

There are about 3.1 million immigrants and migrants in the Netherlands, comprising almost one fifth of the Dutch population. Half of these are of non-Western descent. The criteria used for determining one's immigrant status are either one's place of birth, or the place of birth of either parent. According to these criteria, children who have been born here are no longer considered immigrants (former minister Van Boxtel).

The four largest groups of non-Western immigrants in the Netherlands are Moroccans, Turks, Surinamese, and Antilleans. Another substantial, but smaller, group consists of Chinese immigrants. The latter group has been living in the Netherlands for a longer period of time. Motives to immigrate to the Netherlands have varied. Most Turks and Moroccans initially moved here on the explicit request of the Dutch government and manufacturing industries, in order to work here. The Surinamese moved here in large numbers just before Surinam gained its independence from the Netherlands, as they were able then to retain Dutch citizenship. Antilleans are still considered overseas citizens (members of empire, or, in Dutch, *rijksgenoten*). As such, they are legally entitled to various degrees of citizenship rights. However, the situation is complex and differs per island. According to a report by the Dutch Bureau of Statistics (CBS) printed in the Dutch newspaper *NRC* on 9 January 2007, it appears that the bureau expects the number of immigrants to rise by an additional 1.6 million. The expected growth can be partially accounted for by the number of immigrants from other EU countries, and by future children of immigrants already residing in the Netherlands. The highest numbers of new inhabitants are expected to be of Chinese, Afghan, Iraqi, and Iranian descent.

In Amsterdam and Rotterdam, some 35% of the population has a background other than Dutch; in Utrecht it is about 21%. In recent years, there has been a striking shift of residential choices by immigrant populations in the Netherlands. Many Surinamese have moved to Almere. Turks are to be found primarily in the largest cities mentioned above, and also in cities with an industrial history, such as Enschede, Schiedam, and Zaandam. Historically, since their arrival in the Netherlands, Antilleans have been predominantly located in Rotterdam. Also, refugees from various regions and countries have sought and sometimes found residence in all parts of the country, often arriving there severely traumatized.

In a chapter such as this, it is difficult not to generalize. Cultures are complex and have many layers, yet it is worth attempting to sketch general outlines. This chapter is structured in such a manner that specific characteristics of migrant groups are dealt with within those broad descriptions. Primarily, several cultural contexts will be discussed, considering both continuity and differences between various groups.

A question of significance is whether violent behaviour differs between the various cultural groups in Dutch society (including the indigenous Dutch population), and how such differences can affect our ways of dealing with the issue. A specific group will receive specific attention: the refugee population.

One of the cultural characteristics of several non-Western groups is the so-called "we-cultures", wherein other rules are observed than in most western families. This does not imply, however, that there is no such thing as Western we-cultures. Generalizing remains a hazardous activity.

The most important mechanisms reviewed in this chapter are inclusion and exclusion mechanisms. Exclusion takes place within as well as between societal groups, and it remains of utmost importance to understand who is excluded and why, when, and to what effect. How are individuals or groups pinpointed; by what means is personal or collective honour created or violated, and under what circumstances does this lead to violent behaviour?

Intercultural conflicts

What defines violent behaviour and what type of violence is deemed unacceptable are questions answered differently in each culture. In many cultures, corporal punishment is a customary procedure in the education process. Physical violence against women can also be considered a normal procedure, for instance, as women and children can, to a greater or a lesser degree, be seen as male property in patriarchal societies. Of course, the Qur'an does not state that beating women is acceptable, just as no other texts do. The problem must be examined in traditions that are often reproduced in family clans over the course of generations. An overview research conducted on behalf of the United Nations and resulting in the Arab Human Development Report (2002–2004, by various Arab authors), presents information on twenty-two member states of the Arab League with a combined population of some 280 million people. Four issues are highlighted specifically: political freedom, economic growth, education and knowledge, and the societal position of women. All four separate but intertwined pictures look rather grim in this part of the world. If we compare these

(Arabic) Islamic countries to those where other religions are dominant, this is the region where political freedoms are most curtailed. Regarding women's rights and issues, only black African countries show a marginally worse dynamic. One out of every two Arab women is unable to read or write (Enzensberger, 2006, p. 34). Literacy is one of the important means of gaining power and control over one's life. Arab women have been denied access to this on a structural scale.

By way of family reunion, many women and children from Arab League nations have come to Europe. The patriarchal modes of conduct that existed in the country of origin are often transplanted to the new environment. The designated roles for men, women, and children are, in such cases, sharply etched into a hierarchical family structure. Each family member is expected to contribute to the family clan, as individual interests are considered of lesser importance than the good of the family as a whole.

Both Hindustani and Arab Islamic families adhere to such norms and behaviour. Of course, there are differences in the ways these rules are interpreted. In the city, different adaptations are made than in rural surroundings. Yet, family relations remain of central importance, and most often it is clear who can command respect, who decides in affairs of money or marriage, and who inherits what. Heritage is preferentially arranged in such a manner as to benefit the oldest son, representing the paternal lineage. Girls inherit less, and women even less again. The division is dependent on tradition, rather than the rule of law. Women have less say, yet they are of great importance to the family unit. For women in Moroccan culture, it is important to register their assigned share on paper, as they will have no right to demand ownership otherwise. Moroccan personal and family law are construed on different grounds altogether; spouses do not enjoy any form of equality before the law. This does not imply that women do not have rights at all. The logic of patrilineal descent behind these laws does not provide a woman with an individual identity, although she does have a set position within the social fabric made up of the lines between the men in her group: her father, her guardian, her brothers, and later on her husband and perhaps her sons.

The Italian poet, Cesare Pavese, voices the situation thus:

"And women don't count in this family.
I mean that our women stay home
and bring us into the world and say nothing"

("Ancestors", translated by Geoffrey Brock)

The Turkish legal system is based on the Western model, wherein men and women are, by and large, equal before the law. This does not mean that the roles of culture and tradition cannot be decisive in shaping the way choices are made.

Divorce, especially when initiated by the woman, is often seen as shameful for the family unless very explicit reasons can be put forth. Such "good" reasons are strictly bounded; a woman is not an autonomous individual, but a part of a family. In addition, a divorced woman has a slighter chance of remarriage than a divorced man.

> Mrs A is still young, thirty-seven years old, a religious person with three daughters, the eldest eighteen. Her ex-husband left her four years ago, for a woman with whom he secretly, for his ex-wife at least, had two children. The divorce was difficult and no alimony has been set or agreed upon. The family lives in poverty, solely dependent on the social benefits of Mrs A. She has cut off ties with her family-in-law, since her mother-in-law severely abused her on the grounds that she would not have been a good wife for her son. The daughters have no contact with their father any more. The eldest wants to go out, but her mother does not let her. She does not want to be made an outcast again. They live in an area where many single Turkish mothers live, and everyone keeps a keen eye on each other. She is afraid she will be excluded from the social sphere if she does not adhere to the norms of the Turkish community in their neighbourhood. A divorced woman had better adapt.

It is permitted for men to marry non-Islamic women, but not vice versa. For women, divorce is complicated, even after abuse. Often, a woman will lose her rights in the country she came from, and sometimes that includes the rights over her children. This depends on the country of origin: in Morocco this is not the case. In Algeria it is, and in Iran and Iraq it may or may not be the case in individual examples.

These differences in cultural traditions and laws result in difficulties for Dutch relief work, especially when two different legal systems are involved, (e.g., Dutch and Moroccan). It has implications when the social worker asks questions about such family systems. One barrier to asking third parties for help is shame—for men even more so than for women. This is a question of honour.

> A woman from Surinam marries in the Netherlands. The marriage is arranged. She is a Hindustani and he is from India. She is from a lower caste than he is. The families have set a dowry. But, in the end, after the marriage has taken place, he is not satisfied. He begins to physically abuse her, severely and regularly. She studies but does not dare to move herself any more. She is ashamed, and she knows that if she informs her mother or grandmother they will say that it is her husband's right to beat her, and that she is not an angel herself, either. She begins to isolate herself. She should go to college, but starts to miss classes regularly, because of the bruises. Besides, he is not too happy with her studying at all, as she should be helping him build his business. Finally, she runs away and goes into hiding at a friend's house.

> The shame brought upon both families is what weighs heaviest on her. How can you ever make up for such trouble? She feels hopeless, and her physician has to prescribe her antidepressants.

The position of women in Hindustani culture is not equal to that of men. If a woman is raped by a family member, she cannot report it. She would be cast out, for this would bring disgrace to the family.

Creole family relations are very different, even though here also the importance of the individual is considered secondary to that of the family as a whole. Creole culture is characterized by a patriarchal as well as a matriarchal tradition, the latter finding its origin in slavery. Men were transported to distant plantations to be put to work, which made women fully responsible for raising the children. They were then dependent on other women and family members for survival. This has brought a more matriarchal culture into being, with networks of women making decisions, large and small, together.

Most immigrants in the Netherlands come from "we-cultures", which aim primarily at maintaining family ties and group focus before individual focus. Modes prescribed generations ago are still of key importance to the way the family reacts to violent behaviour.

The system of social work is designed to offer individual assistance, aimed at the empowerment of one person, most often a woman. Women enter the social care system more easily than men do. In several ways, this situation runs contrary to the problems faced by migrant families. As individual interests are of secondary importance in we-cultures, empowering individuals might, in those families, disturb the situation even more rather than helping those involved to deal with the violence they are confronted with. A hierarchical patriarchal family system calls for another method than we are used to in regular social or psychological care work.

It may be tempting to follow the Dutch model of social or psychological work, as both social workers and psychologists are confronted with transitions from more traditional family cultures to individual relations between people. One of the most important aspects of such transitions is the erosion of unequal power relations. In this process, language is a defining element: for instance, when children start translating for their parents. Moroccan or Turkish women who have divorced in the Netherlands and remarry a man from their country of origin speak Dutch, and move freely in Dutch society, while their husbands are dependent on them and might feel isolated. On the other hand, there are also women who come to the Netherlands without speaking the language. They may end up even more isolated.

The Utrecht police department has collected many declarations filed by predominantly Moroccan women taken from their villages and housed in the Netherlands in high-rise apartments, isolated, with small children and broken promises of a bright future that would lie ahead. If beating commences, these women are entirely dependent on their husbands; they have no legal status and no means of income. They are cut off from all sources of power or means to stand up for their rights. Ironically, powerlessness and frustration are often related to occurrences of domestic violence.

Most migrant families become entangled in a maze between two cultures. Rules, codes, and rituals are under severe pressure. Either they will be strictly reinforced, or a vacuum emerges where they succumb, without a suitable alternative to replace them. Such situations can be the root of a violent chain of events.

In 1979, researchers Dobash and Dobash described how greater equality between partners leads to fewer conflicts, as more responsibilities are shared (i.e., children, money, household). The ensuing respect for each other's tasks and judgements results in a lower chance of violent conflict. These results correspond to a comparative cultural study of physical violence within ninety small communities. It seems that such violence does not occur in fifteen of the ninety communities. The following de-escalating factors were pivotal:

● monogamy;
● economic equality between the sexes;
● equal access to divorce for both marriage partners;
● the availability of third parties able to attend to child-care;
● frequent and predictable intervening in marital conflicts by family and neighbours;
● norms that encourage non-violent solutions to conflicts outside the household.

As to interventions by third parties, six were specified as having protective potential within small communities. Only when the abuse is considered excessive will members of the community apply the following interventions:

● direct intervention by family, neighbours, or conflict mediators;
● family or neighbours offer shelter to women;
● public sanctions of husbands by means of gossip, legal sanctions, supernatural sanctions ("supposed"?), or payment of financial compensation
● women divorcing their husbands.
● no interventions at all (Richters, 2000).

Apart from these interventions, other factors contribute greatly: the chance of conflicts resulting in violence increase sevenfold under the influence of poverty, unemployment, and scarcity of suitable housing. Unemployment rates among immigrants and migrant populations are high as opposed to those of indigenous groups. Forty per cent of Turkish and Moroccan youths are unemployed. Children from single parent families often leave school early; up to twice as frequently as do students from families with two adults.

Child abuse

Child abuse is an internationally acknowledged phenomenon, but, in every culture, there is a different understanding of what constitutes or defines child abuse. In some cultures, corporal punishment is part of one's upbringing. Such measures are taken so as to teach the child respect and to obey. A beating is not considered a violent offence against a child, but rather as a pedagogical method. In Europe and the USA, people are dissuaded from using corporal punishment; educational methods that are preferred in these regions focus more on rewarding and encouragement to teach a child certain skills.

Malevolent violence against children is divided into four categories: physical, sexual, and emotional abuse, and negligence. Yet again, these concepts are construed differently in each culture. These differences give rise to problems in the Netherlands. Children growing up in between two cultures can easily lose track of what is and what is not acceptable. Beating children is not commonly accepted here. In families wherein conflicts are resolved violently, it is usual to find that all members of the household become involved in some way or another. Just being witness to violence has enormous consequences for children. From recent research, it appears that children are affected as severely by witnessing violence as they are by being directly subjected to it. Traumatized people tend to repeat the violent behaviour they have had to deal with. This goes for children as well as for adults. Reliving a trauma heightens the physical tension, sparking the re-enactment of the trauma in an attempt to overcome the tension. With children, some specific features can be observed. With every phase in their development, children will react differently to violence. If they cannot find words to express their feelings, effects will be seen in their non-verbal behaviour and in their general development. In boys, tensions are most commonly vented through restless or erratic behaviour, both at home and in school. Too often, their busy behaviour is diagnosed as attention deficit hyperactivity disorder (ADHD) and Ritalin is prescribed as a remedy. Girls will more often become secluded and silent, resulting in a reduced capacity to acquire new skills (see also the chapter on children).

Fortunately, in recent years, the effects of violence on children has drawn considerable attention. There is a proposal before the Dutch administration that research should be conducted into the extent to which violent patterns within the family unit lead to violence on the streets or at school. Especially in the USA, such research has shown that one out of three boys confronted with violence will repeat these patterns both on the streets and in school, as well as in their relationships later on in life.

> "We are full of errors, horrors, whims,
> We, the men, the fathers—another one takes his own life,
> But there is one shame that we will never suffer,
> We will never be a woman, the shadow of another."
>
> Cesare Pavese (*Raster* No. 93, monthly review with poetry)

Culturally, men are encouraged to express themselves violently, even when the emotion expressed is not aggression. To nuance one's feelings is an acquired skill; girls get the chance to do so and boys do not. Expressing fear, sorrow, and pain is needed from the first phases in life onwards. Research shows that cyclical abusers cannot control their anger, cannot voice it verbally, and cannot process it emotionally. The responsibility for the beatings is laid on the other: she is mean; she made me do it. In such moods, they see the woman as a "whore", as somebody who threatens to leave them. Unrecognized shame and alienation often lead to violent outbursts.

Women use violence, too; they throw objects, humiliate and shame the other, but they are generally unable to summon the physical force that men possess. Men do not suffer permanent physical injuries when they are maltreated by women.

Women who are systematically abused will often end up in a vicious circle they cannot escape from any more. This is partially explained by the violent episodes being alternated by periods of love and relative harmony. If the relationship lasts long enough, the abuser will only have to refer to the violence in order to let the anxiety reach its peak level. Regularly, women are too traumatized to stand up to this. This strange loyalty is also referred to as traumatic bonding disorder, or the domestic version of the Stockholm syndrome (named after a bank employee in Stockholm who fell in love with her hostage-taker). In order to survive, the victim will adjust to, and eventually even identify with, the demands of the abusing party. This pattern is reinforced even more if the abuse is unpredictable; the hope that things will turn for the better stays alive. The abuser will do anything to stay on top; all his strategies are aimed at controlling the other. Women are a chain in the cycle of torture in a dysfunctional family. A woman's own need for power and her indirect rage will be redirected to the children; the husband is too strong and her shame will worsen the situation. On the other hand, women in such situations are alert at all times, and their strategies are aimed at their own survival and that of the children.

Frequently, social workers will wearily ask, "Why does she stay with that man, why doesn't she leave him?" Sometimes they will even feel contempt. "That's it, now she has to live with the consequences herself." But things are apparently not that simple. Their relationship is complicated, paradoxical and caught up in the logic of the conflict. The further the woman backs away from the relationship, the greater the tension will be for her to return. The need to regulate the family situation, at least to a certain extent (also known as "homeostasis"), will uphold the *status quo*. Bad memories disappear, and the woman hopes that if she tries even harder, her man may be able to control his moods and violent outbursts. Not just she, but also the other family members, would rather forget than acknowledge that violence belongs to the pattern they find themselves in. They attempt to protect themselves against the sad past and prevent it from resurfacing. The pressure to remain secretive, to uphold the rules that keep the family from disintegration, the shame that would result from speaking out, will often result in a fear of allowing outsiders into the private sphere. Also, women might blame themselves for the violence and feel very dependent on their partners. Children will tend not to invite other children, women to refrain from maintaining friendships with other women, and men will only socialize with other men outside of the house. Once outside, they will often be popular and charming.

Even when women have been divorced for a long time, the desire for their former partner may return.

Mrs X, an Iranian, left her husband two years ago. She had lived for twenty-five years with the man, who abused her and her children severely every six weeks. He has seriously assaulted and sexually abused one of the girls. She describes her ex as a person who emerged from the civil war severely traumatized. She finds excuses for him and denies his responsibility. Even the fact that her daughter has suffered serious physical trauma cannot "cure" her of her desire for him as her hostage-taker. She keeps in touch with him in secret, for which she feels deeply ashamed and guilty.

Method: how to end violence within migrant families

Each health care organization works with procedures to regulate the intake of new clients. Both the normal social work agencies and other first line organizations use standard questionnaires. In these lists, it is not common to enquire thoroughly into sensitive issues such as violence, incest, or rape. A good questionnaire has been developed by Movisie, a centre for gender-specific renewal of care procedures for combating sexual violence, in which sexual violence is dealt with as a separate category. Violence within the family is not on the questionnaire, but separate questions can be inserted.

There is no publicly known procedure to detect violence within the family for personal physicians. Because this profession often comes across the physical traces of domestic violence, it is necessary to research and come up with practical signalling methods. Perhaps, the Movisie questionnaire could be a point of reference. The intake list of the Meldpunt Utrecht does, of course, contain questions on violence, the role of partners, and other important family relations.

In general, and also when women want to escape the violence, it is important to ask about the partner and keep the option of family meetings open. The majority of women will eventually return to their husbands. In that case, it can be necessary to talk with the whole family and to have information on the partner.

The intake

Migrant women, just like other women in the Netherlands, will only seek help when there is already a serious problem. Women and children are regularly the speakers for the problems a family has. Apparently, that is a fact internationally. In most instances, it is difficult to find out what exactly is the issue at stake. Psychosomatic complaints can be a release valve when tensions have risen too high. An intake is a diagnostic instrument, and to find out what the underlying issues are, ingenious ways of questioning are needed. Many layers may need to be unveiled.

To start with, getting in touch at the "point of entry" is important, meaning that the social worker has to appear genuinely interested both verbally and non-verbally. Second, it is important that the client is actively engaged in the conversation. Conversation techniques are *the* instrument to activate the client. Such techniques include asking short questions, half open and closed questions, structuring and summarizing the information so as to be able to make headway with it. Open questions often lead to long answers that can get very emotional. Reflection on feelings can lead to release of emotions, possibly overflowing the actual need for help. Targeted questions offer better results, perhaps with additional suggestive encouragement, as long as it is empathic. During the first conversation, inquiry should be made into the signals mentioned before.

The intake is the moment to make an inventory of issues that may spark conflict. Ask questions to this end, both to the person in need of help and to her (or his) partner. These issues can give vital insights into the family situation even if there is no violence in a specific case. Points to be addressed are as follows.

- The story of the migration, separable from flight for political motives and economic circumstances. There are many sides and consequences to the story of the migration, and women hold different positions then men.
- Money issues. Who earns more; who manages money affairs; what rules have been set for spending money; for whom is money set aside; in whose name has the money been earned; has it been earned in the Netherlands or elsewhere; the inheritance, dowry, and other obligations.
- How much money is sent abroad and who takes care of that? Has this sparked conflict?
- Are there issues of drug or alcohol abuse, problematic gambling, or sedatives?
- Legal status. How did the procedures go; what is whose status; are new family members expected to arrive from abroad?

- Who is dependent on whom with regard to legal status and for welfare money?
- Who carries authority in the family, the mother-in-law, the husband, the wife, grandmother? Who is responsible for child education?
- Sexuality: how many women are members of the household?
- Children. How many? Girls, boys? And their school results?
- Which child assumes authority when an adult man is away? What do those responsibilities entail?
- Employment situations.
- Neighbourhood and social context. What contact is there with neighbours and other networks?
- What issues lead to conflicts?
- How are conflicts fought out? Is there violence?
- Who beats who; how often, how hard, how much, where on the body, and where in the house? Are others present; are children present, and what do they do when they see their mother being beaten up? What is the reaction of the abuser to that? Are they excluded from the conflict or made part of it? How does the fighting end?
- Do people have police records or other legal problems?
- Is there violence or/and rape? If so, what resources does a woman in need have to get herself and the children to safety? Does she take the responsibility she can? Many hints have been developed to point out to women what resources they could put to use.

The issues that might lead to conflict situations may be difficult to talk about. An indirect way of asking questions might be helpful to chart any possible solutions. Feelings of guilt, and especially shame, can inhibit the ability to answer questions. Options to de-block will be dependent on traditions within the family system. Sometimes, a direct and authoritative method will be useful, especially if men have to be helpful in reversing the violent tide in the system.

Shame, rage, and humiliation

Shame is an important feeling for the regulation of social systems. It plays a significant role in child education and in traditional cultures; to humiliate another or to feel shame is a means of keeping the morale of the community intact. Different opinions exist on the differentiation between shame cultures and guilt cultures. One such opinion is that the distinction is misleading. Shame is a basic emotion which has gone underground in cultures wherein guilt has won pre-eminence. In shame cultures, shame is a daily reality, openly used as a means of social control. The virginity of girls and sexuality of women is thus a management problem for the collective. In the West, this is not the case, as the restrictions on sexuality have been internalized during child-care. In shame-regulated societies, sexual desires are curbed by forces outside of the individual. There, the responsibility for the protection of women and the family's honour lies with the men.

By not adjusting to the demands set by the sexual mores, women bring disgrace to the family. This is one of the worst offences in a shame culture. Men feel forced to maintain continual surveillance of women's behaviour and will therefore behave in a stringently dominant way. Divorce is not an option for women, even after prolonged abuse. They would run the imminent risk of excommunication. Abuse, beatings, and rape, but sexual pleasure, too, are topics better not discussed, especially in public. Cultures of shame are cultures of silence. Silence protects the community because shameful episodes might have far-reaching consequences.

In non-Western cultures, emotions are less individually experienced and more directed towards the collective. They refer to processes that mediate between persons, actions, and occurrences. Shame has both a public and a private function. It regulates the moral codes of the community. For women, this means that they are struck by shame repeatedly. Or, as a woman said, "Where do I not find shame? Everything is saturated by it." For men, this code means that they can openly channel their shame into rage. That will only happen when rules are transgressed and alienation occurs on the grounds of which the other can be excluded. This exclusion mechanism does also exist in Western cultures. In the opinion of Sheff (1987), unacknowledged shame and alienation are directly related to rage. In such a culture, shame has to stay hidden. Elias (1978) has described the process of repressing shame by analysing etiquette books from the Middle Ages to the late nineteenth century.

Characteristic of Western culture is the attempt to banish the extremes of human emotion from the public sphere.

> Social survival and success in these societies is, to a certain extent, bound up with a reliable outer skeleton of individual self-control. It should neither be too hard nor too soft. In such societies, there is limited space for furious anger, blind rage or the urge to hit somebody upside the head. Severely agitated people, engulfed by emotions they cannot control, are cases for a mental institution or a jail. Situations of great arousal are considered abnormal, and a dangerous prelude to mob violence. [Elias, quoted in Goudsblom, 1997, p. 156]

In his research, Elias shows that the urge to hide shame has grown increasingly imperative over the centuries. The thresholds for shame have risen and shame has been progressively internalized.

Hitting somebody because of shame is not uncommon. If men hit others, shame is often a pivotal factor. Most men who beat women report that they have been severely humiliated by their father and have an ambivalent relationship to their mother. To be ashamed gives rise to the unbearable pain of humiliation. It seems as though the rug has been pulled from under your feet. Women and men have been socialized to handle shame differently. Women hide and bear the shame in silence. Men become angry and will humiliate others. Women may also vent their shame on their children. This spiral of shame lays the foundation for the spiral of violence.

It is not unusual for men to protect the honour of their family in highly patriarchal family structures. That responsibility can be an entry into involving the perpetrator in the solution of the family's problems. From the way migrant men have been treated after charges were pressed against them, it can be concluded that an authoritative approach can help to change violent family behaviour (Kik & Baars, 2000) Often, men are severely traumatized in their youth and they will blame their partner for their failure. The feeling of inferiority is also a reason to descend into jealousy. Jealousy can be a reason for a man to commence beating, especially as he may be held responsible for protecting the women in his family from unwanted attention from other males.

If a man suspects his wife of looking at another man, it could be a reason to be violent. This can also happen the other way around. A woman can be so jealous because she suspects her husband of having extramarital relations that she will follow him around the house and humiliate him in front of the family. This, in turn, can be grounds for him to beat her. Dutton points out that women should be alarmed when, during the beatings, their husband calls them "whore" or "slut". That means they no longer respect her because they think she is involved in lasciviousness with other men. The man views her as an evil object, not worth any effort. His aggression knows no bounds when he feels humiliated by someone he resents.

> Ahmed comes from a traditional Turkish family and is married to a Dutch woman. The abuse of his wife started during a holiday with his family in Turkey. Dispute had arisen as a result of her clothing. She wore her skirts too short, in their eyes, and communicated too freely with their daughter in the family sphere. He felt jealous, and he found that she had exceeded the rules of female conduct within the family.

> Moreover, the relation with her mother-in-law became increasingly difficult. The abuse grew to such proportions that she escaped after taking up contact with her own family. He later returned to the Netherlands and tried to make up, but did not succeed. Once the border of violence has been crossed, the way back to normality is not an easy one.

Women can also be very jealous and use the tool of humiliation. They can chase their husbands around, but will be less inclined to view them as objects. Moreover, they lack the physical strength to beat a man to the floor. The emotional bond, and the desire to recover that bond, is often predominant in women. If it is no longer an option to repair those ties, male family members are sometimes used to remove any children from a former husband by violent means. Or the ex-spouse is falsely accused in order to prevent divorce or disgrace for the family.

> A Creole Surinamese woman has lived with her husband for a long time. They have two children. He does have a house of his own, but in reality he lives with her. If they go to work, her mother looks after the children. The woman feels that another woman is somehow involved.

She starts an inquiry and finds indications that her suspicions may be true. She pursues the man and humiliates him, especially in the presence of the children and her mother. Her mother chooses her side, and thus the abuse starts. He cannot escape a submissive situation and feels sad and pursued. He is no longer allowed into the house if he cannot justify his absence. His tension bursts out into rage.

The prolonged intake

It is recommended to make a family tree of the whole family to chart patterns of shame and the behavioural rules that families adopt. A number of questions can give indications concerning violent conflict solving.

Each initial interview is an exploring conversation, intended to resolve what issues are in need of special attention. To be able to identify problems, it is important that problems are collected and that, subsequently, an estimate is made of whether and how violence plays a role in the family.

The questions formulated below form a supplement to the issues presented above. In families where shame is a huge obstacle to seeking help, they may prove essential.

- Who in the family is and who isn't ashamed when you speak of the way your husband treats you?
- If he beats you, does he call you "witch", "whore", or "slut"?
- Has he been violent to you before? How frequently? Did those incidents result from specific situations or did they seem to arise out of the blue?
- Did specific circumstances, such as a separation or moments of jealousy, occur to provoke the violence?
- Who stands up for you the most if you are in trouble, and who the least?
- What does your partner do if you have an argument with his mother, who is living with you?
- Who in the family agrees that a husband can beat his wife if he loses face? Who doesn't?
- Do people in your family honour the idea that women are the possessions of husbands, mothers, mothers-in-law, or grandmothers?

- Who in your family agrees that a husband is allowed to punish violently in order to save the honour of the family?
- Have you ever failed to go to work because of the impact of domestic violence?
- If your daughter wanted to enrol for further education, who in the household would encourage her?
- If your partner is agitated because your daughter returns home late, who in the household is the one to calm him down: grandmother, mother, you, or one of the children?
- If that did not help, who is best at describing how the conflict got out of hand?
- If I have understood it properly, the conflicts have worsened since the arrival of his mother in your household. Can you describe the relation between you and your partner before his mother arrived?
- What does your mother-in-law do if your husband leaves the kitchen?
- What do you do if your husband is crying? Does he then become more aggressive in word or in deed?
- Who in the family thinks beatings are a fact of life? Who does not?
- Who thinks children are to be beaten if they do not obey? Who will stand up against that?
- Were there those who wanted to stay with the rest of the family, and those who wanted to go to the Netherlands?
- Who feels homesick for your country of origin, and how do you know?
- Is homesickness a cause for conflicts, and if so, between whom, and how?
- Does your partner regularly have sleep impairments, nightmares, or amnesia?
- Do you hold your husband responsible for his uncontrolled furious outbursts?
- Does your husband use a lot of alcohol or narcotics?
- Does your husband regularly lose his senses out of jealousy or fear of abandonment?
- Has your partner ever told you of his experiences with shame? Has he, in so far as you know, been maltreated by his father?
- Has he told you about beatings or abuse by his mother?

- Does he regularly have mood swings, during which he either glorifies or despises you?
- Do you feel that your husband has two faces: one for the outside world and for his friends and another one at home?
- Does your husband go through a cycle of mounting tension, explosion, and making amends?

Motivating the client: the use of scenarios

If the intake suggests that intervention is called for, an assessment has to be made of the possibility of inviting other family members for a conversation, preferably the partner. The first step in such a conversation is to break the silence and to define violence as a serious family problem, which occurs regularly, but which can be stopped. During such a conversation, it frequently helps to point out the functioning of spirals of violence. The insight into the risks to children's well-being and the consequences for their future can especially help a man to confront family problems.

First scenario: motivate the involvement of the husband

The aim of this scenario is to involve the man in stepping out of the spiral of violence and motivating his willingness to do so.
   Suggestions for in-depth inquiry include the following.

- Is your husband willing to end the violence if he knows how badly the children will be affected if they see him beating you?
- Is it possible that your husband will accept risks within the family to stop the spiral of violence?
- Would pressing charges against him stimulate your partner to solve conflicts in a different way?
- How can your partner be helped without feeling humiliated?
- Who in the family can contribute to motivating your husband to change?
- If both of you were able to cope differently with conflict situations, how would that change your position within the family?
- Does it make sense for someone else, for instance your personal physician, to motivate your husband to make a change?

- What problems cause the most pressure for your partner?
- What is your husband most ashamed of, and who does he have difficulty talking to about these feelings?
- Can you help your husband understand that these questions are a result of your concern about, and fear of, his behaviour?

More questions are feasible in order to motivate the rest of the family, but let us assume in the scenario below that you succeed in involving the partner.

Second scenario: the relationship consultation and the time-out procedure

For the social worker, it is important to build a relationship with the perpetrator of the violence. This means a lot of time will be devoted to counselling him. It is important to explain this point clearly to the woman, so as to prevent disappointment on her side. In the first instance, the aim is not to deal with the content of the conflict situation. The therapy session is aimed at securing safety in the home. If the man is able to describe the occurrences of the arguments, his thoughts and feelings at the time, and how he deploys violence, the care worker can move towards the "time-out contract". To get there, in-depth inquiry and summarizing are important conversational techniques.

A persistent approach to the conversation is especially concerned with getting hold of factual inaccuracies such as:

Where did you stand in the room during the last incident?
Can you give an impression of the situation?
What did she say that made you so angry?
Where were the children during the fight?
What did they do?
What does your husband do that makes you specifically angry?
Do you scream?
Where do you hit, pinch, or kick her: on her head, her shoulders, her legs, or other places?

The main purpose of this conversation is to motivate the couple to face the violence and to turn the tide. This procedure is intended to enable the man to physically experience and put words to the mounting tension. He may literally feel this in the abdomen and the area between the shoulders and the neck.

Experience has shown that initial success is often followed by a setback. This occurrence and its possible consequences need to be discussed.

Zamir, who is originally from Turkey, is married to Mohammed, an Egyptian. She translates books, and her Dutch is better than his. He is employed as an engineer.

The beatings started following an argument concerning the education of his daughter. She is more liberal than he is, and thinks he is over-protective. He says that she does not take account of his principles. Although both respect Islam, their interpretation of its teachings varies considerably. She raises her son differently than him. Neither wants to end the marriage, but it is unclear if it can be preserved.

Social worker: "Welcome. I have already talked to Zamir, and I understand that you want to tell us your side of the story too."

The care worker summarizes what constitutes the conflict according to him, and then verifies it with his wife. Subsequently, both are provided with an explanation of what can expected of the therapy process and why. If all goes well, they can proceed to the time-out procedure. This is a reward for their efforts to explain the domestic violence.

Mohammed: "I would like to clarify why it goes wrong in our household. My impression is that my principles are not respected, and besides she speaks harshly of me. When I come home from work and see my four-year-old daughter walking around naked, that upsets me. But if I comment on it, she will be furious and tell me I'm wrong. At a certain point I feel subdued and lose my senses."

Zamir: "But you start screaming the moment you see her. She starts to cry and then you blame me for it. I cannot stand that. Also, when you get home, I'm already busy getting the kids to sleep. If you'd return earlier on in the evening, you could do that yourself."

Social worker: "At which moment do you begin to feel angry? It is an important question if you want to control your anger. A real husband is able to keep his hands to himself, to control himself. No matter how understandable it can be to be furious, beating is never acceptable. Besides, it is also a crime. So, when do you feel increasing anger?"

Mohammed: "I feel the anger when I can no longer control her flow of words. I cannot express myself then, and feel humiliated and misunderstood."

Social worker: "Where do you first experience this feeling, physically?"

Mohammed thinks for a while and then points to his neck.

Social worker: "What helps you relax in general?"

Mohammed: "Sports, and running."

Social worker: "Could you step out of that situation, and go to the gym?"

Mohammed: "No, that will not do. I'd better go outside for a walk, to run maybe. But then she has to leave me alone and not follow me, because that would really make me very angry."

It is agreed that Mohammed will leave when his neck starts to cramp, and Zamir will not go after him. When Mohammed comes home, he will return to Zamir in a normal manner, and he can decide when they will talk about the issue at a later point in time.

Another therapy appointment is made, and they are reassured that they can come by at any time if they fear a recurrence of the violence. Results are positive for a number of weeks, but then they return because an argument has got out of hand again. Zamir has taken the children and gone into hiding at a friend's place. The social worker praises her for putting the safety of the children first and proceeds to evaluate whether or not she should have left earlier on.

Zamir: "He returns home and I can see he's stressed. He starts an argument about something irrelevant—the laundry basket being full if I recall. I am infuriated and tell him that taking care of the house, my work, and two kids is too much. I can see his face change and I call "Time-out", but I do not leave, and neither does he. The tension mounts and he starts to beat me, in front of the children. I grab my stuff and leave with the children. He just keeps on swearing and telling me I don't have to come back any more."

Mohammed: "This is a bad situation and I certainly don't want her to leave. But I wasn't able to control myself. Always that anger of hers. When she called for the time-out, I hardly noticed it any more because I was too angry."

The situation is further investigated. It appears that Zamir was quite aware that something was wrong when Mohammed entered the house. He explains that he is indeed uncomfortable at work. He is afraid a conflict with a colleague will end up becoming his problem. He is already careful in general, as he is aware that foreigners are an easy scapegoat. He cannot share these problems with Zamir, because he is ashamed and afraid to fail.

A next step is to research what can be done when he is stressed due to situations at work. After a lot of talking, he agrees to take up contact with a brother of Zamir's whom he likes.

Again, agreements are made as to what to do when tensions mount; what she is to do when his face changes; how fast she can end the situation, and what can be done with the children. A list is made of possible sources of help. All interventions are aimed at fostering safety at home and reducing tension.

Some concrete questions that can help to focus on this are:

● What can you do?
● Where will you go?
● Who can you talk to?
● When do you have to get out of there?
● What can you do when tension mounts?
● How do you get yourself and the children to safety?

Third scenario: referring the couple

Once the couple have mastered their tensions and the AMW (Dutch Federation of Social Work) has no direct authority any longer, the clients can be referred back to the Institute for Forensic Psychiatry (De Waag), or to another institute that has signed the care program. This may be helpful, as the couple may not find themselves able to agree upon everything all of a sudden. Especially in a case such as one where the children are not all biologically akin to both parents. Family dynamics can be very complex.

Fourth scenario: time-out because of departure
by woman and children to a shelter

Let us stick with the example of Mohammed and Zamir. Moham-med does want to change, yet the tensions endure. Also, he does not want Zamir to leave him. Like so many men, he is afraid of being abandoned. Panic results, and leads to even more serious abuse. They fail to reduce the problems and, when Mohammed relapses once more, Zamir gives up hope. She does not go to a friend, but decides to leave the house indefinitely. She calls the social work Help Desk.

She does not want any contact with Mohammed for now. She has put up with him for a long time, but has had enough. The situ-ation may look entirely different in a week. Most women want some time to calm down before contact is restored. She is referred to a shelter, or a recovery home. The situation is defined as a long time-out to enable both parties to reflect on the situation and plan ahead. After a number of consultations with Zamir alone, and also with her children, talks with Mohammed are reopened. In De Waag or the Regional Institute for Mental Welfare (RIAGG), the time-out procedure can be practised again. Mohammed could also go to a men's group to learn how to voice his feelings and learn to practise self-control.

Fifth scenario: pressing charges with the police
and coercive treatment

Assume that Zamir presses charges against Mohammed to moti-vate him to get therapy. Mohammed is invited by the police to make a report at the station. An employee of De Waag talks to him and tries to persuade him to accept treatment. If this is a success, he can start a trajectory. The "six-step model" is offered, but legal procedures in hand serve as a means of applying some pressure. The police may also decide to have Mohammed removed from the house. In the scenario above, this is a realistic option.

Alternatively, Zamir could press charges as a means to obtain a divorce, or if she wants to end his constant interference with her new life. Such persistent interference may result from his feelings of loss, which can be unbearable. In such cases, she may be able to impose a restraining order on him. Further care will be needed for Zamir to find relief from post-traumatic stress complaints. The same goes for the children, and for Mohammed too, if he is motivated enough.

Sixth scenario: five motivational conversations
with the woman alone

From working with the accompaniment group, it became clear that social workers are generally more familiar with the treatment of individual women. If violence appears to play a substantial role in the relationship, it is possible to offer the woman five consultations to motivate her to alter the situation. The following steps have been formulated.

1. Make the client responsible for her own safety and that of her children. Educate her on the consequences of long-term exposure to fear, threats, and violence. Together, devise a concrete plan of action. Ask whether she recognizes the symptoms mentioned above. Be very concrete on the subject of violence. Make an inventory of possible sources of help include questions such as the following:

    ● In case you wanted to leave with the children, how would your husband react?
    ● Who be most disgraced, if both of you were to give up?
    ● Which human resources are there, inside and outside the house?
    ● Who in your surrounding is aware of the domestic violence?

2. Enlarge the social network, if possible involve family members.
3. Involve a person with authority, possibly an imam or a family member who has a strong position and does not tolerate abuse. A lawyer can be asked to mediate.
4. Check whether it is possible to create a time-out phase. When can the woman leave and how can she ensure her own safety and that of her children, when temporarily in a shelter?
5. Provide information material on the consequences of flight, both for herself and her children.

6. Supply her with a list of shelters for abused women that provides information on what to take when fleeing.

In general, there is no use in continuing the consultations if the situation remains unchanged. Nevertheless, in some instances, a care worker can decide to stay in touch. This can increase the pressure on the family to act anyway. But it is not recommended to continue the conversation with a woman who is systematically abused. It can even be harmful. To be included in secrets surrounding domestic violence is a questionable practice. Often, it is preferable to develop a strategy with a general practitioner and others, including any family members. This should be communicated to the abused woman who appeals for confidentiality, especially when children are involved.

Of course, shame is often an impediment. This can be overcome by talking about it explicitly. Presenting figures on the occurrence of domestic violence in society may open the discussion.

Parallel responses of social workers

Stress and countertransference

Having to learn precisely how violent arguments occur is no light matter. How and where somebody is hit and if blood was shed are questions that have to be asked in order to assess the family situation correctly. Horror, surrogate shame, fear, and anger are normal responses from social workers to accounts of real life abuse. Social workers frequently working within these circumstances acquire secondary traumatic stress syndromes. In the literature, this is described as a complex array of symptoms, including emotional and cognitive complaints. Avoidance and a feeling of dullness can be the consequence, as well as cynicism and disillusionment. Often, these symptoms have severe effects on the social worker and on other team members. Professions that are confronted with violence must be conducted in a responsible environment. That is only possible when the involved institution takes appropriate measures. Social workers must be trained and supervised continually.

Countertransference is a term derived from psychoanalytic literature. It means that the social worker translates his or her own feelings for the clients into strong antipathies or sympathies. In the case of serious traumatic accounts, social workers can develop all sorts of defence mechanisms, such as denial and suppression.

In consultations with couples, this can be a serious hindrance. In individual conversations, it can also raise resistance to change. In general, these responses originate from unresolved elements of the social worker's life history.

> "I cannot work with perpetrators. I had a spouse myself who abused me. I cannot converse with abusers without becoming furious."

Prejudices

A further complication arises from the fact that social workers import their own prejudices, giving rise to misunderstanding. It is, for example, a prejudice that abuse only occurs in 'antisocial' families.

Additionally, preconceptions concerning Turks, Moroccans, Surinamese, Antilleans, and refugees can interfere with achieving a realistic assessment of the situation at hand. An example of this is the idea that women in Moroccan families are regularly beaten up and that children are treated more harshly than in Surinamese families. Another example of this is that violence occurs less in Dutch families than in Turkish and Moroccan families. Such presuppositions may keep a social worker from delving as deep as is required to get to the bottom of a specific case. Prejudices between different ethnic groups are another example. Dutch, Surinamese, and Moroccan social workers may all have their own true or false images of how other groups function. Such impressions become the basis for decisions they take.

It is important to recognize that racist innuendo and discriminatory behaviour are facts of daily life for all who look different from the average Dutchman. Everyone passes judgement and classifies others. Order is based on norms, values, and rules, and upheld by systems of belief, education, upbringing, and socialization processes. It is a matter of inclusion and exclusion, and we can define racism as the occurrence of exclusion in such dynamics.

"Each day on my journey to work with the public transport, I'll hear a remark or two about the colour of my skin. Sometimes, I hardly notice it, but it can still hurt."

People who are systematically humiliated develop strategies to maintain themselves in Dutch society. Each group has distinct methods, and each "we" implies a "them". To be humiliated often causes aggression. In contacts with social workers, migrants are alert. For refugees, mistrust towards the authorities plays an important role, especially when the authorities in the country of origin have used violence.

To conduct a thorough inquiry into violent situations within households proves difficult for the majority of social workers. These difficulties are added to the general prejudices concerning migrants and refugees. As such, a double denial of the situation at hand can occur, making it even more difficult to stop the violence. This may even lead to more violence. In conclusion, there are several factors for social workers that impede the therapeutic process.

In the next section, we examine which preconceptions play a significant role in hindering the inquiry. Every preconception is followed by information that sheds a different light on it.

Some prejudices social workers may hold or face

Providing information can combat prejudices. Everyone has preconceptions. They are instructive tools to use in distinguishing people. But it remains necessary to know where they come from and how they influence the daily practice of social work. Social workers should know where preconceptions might negatively influence their work and when it is wise to ask the assistance of a colleague.

Prejudice

"What can you do with those men, anyway? You cannot get anywhere with them. I never invite them for a consultation any more, for them it's all about their residence permits in the end. Social work for perpetrators is only for legal men. I do not consult with any illegal partners. They cost money and they extend the waiting lists. The way I deal with it is standard practice."

Information

Men are frequently just as sad because of the violence as the victim is. Social assistance is no legal task, and illegality is no criterion. The question of the residence permits will frequently be part of the power dynamics within the family, and can for that reason alone not be discarded as falling outside the sphere of social work.

Prejudice

All Turkish and Moroccan men beat their wives. It is an integral part of their upbringing. Such is "black pedagogies": obedience is instilled by brute force. These men come to the Netherlands from a patriarchal culture, and consider women as their possessions.

Information

Beating a woman is prohibited by the Qur'an. A man is allowed to slap a disobedient woman with a scarf, but should refrain from hurting her.

Prejudice

Children are beaten more often in migrant families and therefore run a greater risk of emotional and intellectual problems.

Information

Migrant children are dealt with more severely than native Dutch children are. Girls receive more tasks and more discipline. "Educative" slaps are not unusual. Dutch city-dwelling families deal with educational matters differently from those living in the countryside, too, although those differences have narrowed during recent decades. Dutch ideas on child-rearing have changed, and reward is currently a more popular means of education than punishment.

Migrant girls perform better at school than boys do. This could be a flight forward, but the fact remains that they succeed in finishing their education and choosing a professional carrier.

Migrant boys achieve lower results, lower than both migrant girls and native Dutch children. Their starting position is different, of course. In Moroccan law, for instance, boys inherit twice the percentage of their parents' possessions than girls do. They are raised with less structure and more education by example: their fathers serve as an example of male behaviour.

A boy is the pride of a household, and especially the eldest will be held responsible for the protection of the family when their father is gone. They will have to answer for its safety and for the decency of its women.

Prejudice

All Moroccan boys tend towards crime. They are not successful in school and frequently drop out. They hang about on the streets and look up to men with big cars and dubious means of income.

Information

Young Moroccan and Antillean men run a fivefold higher chance of being involved in petty crime than native Dutch young men do. Still, the large majority, of course, is not involved in crime. There is no reason to assume that the group seeking professional social care is overrepresented in crime statistics.

Prejudice

Compared to Dutch and Surinamese women, Moroccan women are submissive and act powerless when beaten.

Information

Disobedience is frequently a reason for Moroccan men to beat women. The woman may be called names, often "whore" or "slut".

Women must obey their men, be a caring wife and mother, and are held responsible for the household. A woman's authority lies inside the home. In the countryside in many countries of origin, women are responsible for everything that happens in and around the home, including cattle if present. Those are clear and respectable tasks. Men ensure the matters outside, have to secure posterity, keep the family safe, and manage money affairs. Such divisions of labour have been observed in many cultures (Gillmore).

In shame cultures, men often have the feeling they cannot trust their women and that for this reason they cannot allow them much autonomy. In general, this task is delegated to the mother of the man, who is often living in the same house.

If the marriage does not work out as expected or hoped for, the woman is often blamed and this may be a cause for abuse.

- Women are blamed for not being able to bear children.
- Women are blamed for only giving birth to daughters.
- Women are blamed if the marriage does not succeed.
- Women are blamed if the marriage is not sexually satisfactory.
- Women are blamed if their spouse dies (Hindustani speak of bad karma).

Prejudice

The arranged marriage is loveless.

Information

The arranged marriage prevails in many migrant families. The aim is generally to enlarge possessions, strengthen family ties, or prevent large religious differences from appearing within the family. For migrants of the second generation, the situation is not quite the same, yet family pressure remains a substantial factor.

It is not unusual to have boys or girls come over for marriage from Morocco or Turkey. Girls are more easily influenced into accepting a marriage partner. Turkish men get their partners from the villages. As their mother is the central figure in the household, she will play a decisive role in the process.

The power imbalance between Turkish men and women is comparable in some respects to the situation in the Netherlands up until the 1950s. There, too, relative equality before the law did not exist until 1958. In such situations, men generally support each other, as do women. Sex roles are strictly separated, both within the household and in the extended family as well as in the wider society.

If these imbalances are disturbed or diminished, tensions and conflicts mount. Violence can increase as community correction subsides. Attempts to hide the abuse from the outside world can also worsen the situation within the home. Second generation migrant women are gradually changing their conception of marriage; however, the pressure of the family and the influence of religion are still undeniable.

Prejudice

Divorce is the wife's fault.

Information

Most divorce conflicts deal (as in society in general), with issues of possession; that is, earning money, possession of a residence permit, and guardianship of the children. The complexity increases when two different legal systems are involved: for example, Dutch and Moroccan law. Moreover, the often negative imagery surrounding a divorcée plays a significant role. In some communities, a divorced woman is compared to a house without a front door, "open to all winds". Divorcées are easy to manipulate. They have little self-esteem and the failed marriage is regarded as their responsibility.

If a woman is divorced, she should no longer accept her ex-husband on her territory. This is a broadly accepted convention. Also, he should not visit the children at the mother's house. That should always happen in public places, or at least with other family members present. For women who live in the Netherlands and who are financially dependent on their former husband, this is a tough issue.

Because a divorced woman without a man is regarded as socially irrelevant, there are often attempts to get her married again. Frequently, family members have a cousin or another friend or relative immigrating for a new marriage. It is unusual for a woman to live on her own.

In Turkish families, the continuation of a marriage is seen as a matter of honour. In case of violent domestic abuse by the partner, divorces can occur, but the woman will, from then on, be seen as unworthy by the man and his family.

For Dutch social workers, it is rather difficult to get insight into the dynamics of cultures that do not accept divorce. Moreover, the economic and psychological dependence of women are interlinked in a complex manner.

In both Turkish and Moroccan families, it is common that the former husband refuses to leave his ex-wife alone. Arguments about keeping in contact are manifold, and may include the children and issues with money or legal documents. Violence frequently occurs when a man is re-entering the house of a woman. Women also have reasons to restore contact with their former husbands. As divorce decreases their social status, they might become isolated, have difficulty with paperwork, economic problems might arise, or they are burdened by having to take care of the children by themselves.

If the former husband and wife are able to regulate the visits outside the house, the relationship between them could de-escalate. If they do not succeed, tensions can resurface. In the following two cases, these complex dynamics are illustrated.

First case

As a rule, a man can beat his wife in his or her own house, but not in the houses of other people. After a long period of violence and abuse, a woman and her children go into hiding. Her ex-husband finds her at her new residence and promises her, with witnesses present, that the beating will not occur any more. Yet, as soon as they are home, the abuses continue since he feels humiliated by her. Again, she flees.

Second case

After many violent escalations and via police intervention, the man is refused entry to the house. Help from an imam was sought, but he confirmed the authority of the husband.

The couple has had counselling, and a number of provisions were made, seemingly to their mutual satisfaction. He comes to collect the children at the proper times, but fails to return them in time. Gradually, she allows him to regain a place in the house. One thing leads to another, he promises to change, and she believes him. Eventually, tension mounts and erupts violently. Their social worker is furious with the woman, and says she should never have allowed the man back in.

We see this countertransference more often in professional social work. Much work has gone into getting a couple back on track and the social worker has devoted a lot of energy to the process, yet his or her efforts seem to be discarded. Feelings of powerlessness and anger result, and are often transferred on to the female client. Everybody working with violent families will recognize these feelings, but they should not be acted upon. Only when social workers try to understand the dynamics, not just of the families concerned but also the ones they are subject to themselves, can professional solutions be achieved.

Prejudice

Sexuality is a taboo for Middle Eastern and Northern African women. They are prudish, and not responsive to sexual experiences. For Caribbean women, the opposite is the case. They are strong and warm-blooded in their sexuality.

Information

Norms and values vary from one culture to another. As to the interdependence between domestic violence and sexuality, a broad division between two cultural models has been made (Mernissi, 1985):

> Societies wherein sexual prohibitions and obligations are internalised during child rearing, as is the case in western societies; and others, where external measures are imposed, often especially upon women, as is symbolised in some societies by the veil they [have to] wear.

A woman's decency is a matter of great concern in Muslim societies; not just for herself, but also for the family. Her honour enables the family to avoid marrying into families they don't want to connect with. Men are responsible for fending off unwanted attention for their women; women are expected to behave piously and not to attract the wrong kind of attention. Merely looking at another man can qualify a woman to be subjected to anger, jealousy, and possibly rage.

Women from the Middle East and Northern Africa cannot generally talk about sexuality in public or with men. It is a subject discussed among female friends or relatives and even then can be considered touchy. For second-generation immigrants, the situation is different, but among them, too, education is still an important task for social workers.

Many, but not all, women from the Caribbean are in a different position altogether. These situations can be much more complex: in some circles men and sexuality are discussed both light-heartedly and seriously, yet in others taboos are severe and comparable to those faced by Turkish and Moroccan women.

Dishonourable women are punished and revenged

Especially in the Turkish community, honour-related violence is still used. A Moroccan woman may be ostracized, but generally it is preferred to achieve some sort of compromise through negotiation. It will also depend on the specific local origin of, and traditions within, the family as to whether a dishonourable woman will be expelled from the community or violently revenged.

Revenge takes place according to certain codes. It will often consist of a violent settlement between men. Women might be severely beaten or killed if they had an affair with another man. Social care organizations in general, and shelters in particular, have to assume that the fear of women in such circumstances is legitimate. Several primarily Turkish women have been killed in the Netherlands in recent years.

In Hindustani families, too, female honour is a topic of debate. As with Turkish and Moroccan families, virginity up until marriage is of the highest importance, and failure to preserve it is not accepted. A woman can be banished from social life, even if she has been raped before marriage.

Women from the Middle East and Northern Africa are raised and disciplined to guard their virginity. It is a matter of family honour. From interviews, it is observed that the women themselves see sex before marriage as disreputable behaviour and indicative of low self-esteem. Women identify strongly with their family tradition, which can serve as a beacon when in need. Their position is compromised if they do not support this code of decency.

A man can return his new bride, and reclaim the dowry if she is not a virgin. There are options to restore the hymen. Such a restoration functions as a release valve for a family problem, yet it allows the myths surrounding virginity to survive. For men, it is considered a virtue to marry as a virgin, but it is not a necessity or even generally expected. The word "virginity" refers to a state expected of women.

Refugees and their special position

Refugees have a distinct position in the Netherlands, as compared to other groups of migrants. They have fled their homes because of violence in their country of origin. Some of them were politically active. Political resistance—via the press, raising a banner, or holding a gun—has put them in harm's way. They have been severely persecuted, tortured, or continuously threatened. The threat of violence—either by a partner or by a government—can be as traumatizing as actually having to undergo it. The victim is virtually held hostage in such a situation. Not just torture or fear of torture, but also violent fantasies stemming from fear and pain can lead to nightmares.

Among refugees, there are many who were threatened because they belong to persecuted ethnic minorities (for example, Serbian Muslims, Kurds, Tamils, Tutsis), because their sexual identity did not fit in with the prevailing norm, or because their ideas about religion or politics differed from the mainstream. In sum, they are people in minority positions, threatened most commonly by brutish governments. Some were able to bring their families with them, and they can also appeal for legal status in some cases. Most, however, have had to leave their families behind.

At the Dutch Ministry of Justice, refugees from over eighty nationalities have been registered. They come from all walks of life, from different religions, ethnic and cultural backgrounds, and from all age groups. In some cases, animosities originating in the country of origin will not cease once they arrive here. From former Yugoslavia, for instance, various opposing factions have been granted asylum in the Netherlands.

The road to attaining legal status is often long and hard. Selection procedures, which all refugees have to go through, are not easy, even before entering the Netherlands, and insecurity about this can last for many years. Situations in refugee camps in the home region vary from uninhabitable to apocalyptic while everyone waits for an invitation from a host country. Governments in host countries often target the "best" refugees: those they expect to be economically viable, or those who will cause fewer problems than others. Those who remain in the camps are at risk of becoming permanent inhabitants of the camp. Because of such insecurities, tensions can run high in the camps, causing severe psychological problems for those involved.

During asylum procedures, employees of the Ministry of Justice will examine the asylum application. Whether or not asylum is granted depends on the same ministry. It is possible to appeal against a negative decision, but that will prolong the procedures enormously. People can collapse under the rigours of such procedures. Having to recount a traumatic past over and over again to civil servants, who may not be inclined to believe you, is unpleasant at least, especially considering that your life might depend on the outcome. Traumatic experiences with government employees in the home country can provide additional insecurities.

All refugees have an individual story. The stories will vary according to their individual survival strategies. They may respond entirely differently to either coercive or voluntary professional care. Definitions of what constitutes a problem and of possible solutions are cultural constructs. Communicating all of these complex dynamics can be very difficult, both for the refugee and for the care worker. It may not always be easy, but it is imperative that this complexity is taken into account, and treated with care in each individual case.

Experiences of violence

Many refugees have suffered violence or repression, often resulting from conflict with the government in their country of origin. They may have been imprisoned, tortured or otherwise abused. Terror, disappearance of family members, exile, and other hardships are almost invariably part of the stories of their flight. The shape of the violence differs. Terror in Latin America is different from civil war in Africa. A number of constants can be observed, however. If a regime tortures its subjects, it is either looking for information or trying to break the integrity of the individuals and communities involved, mentally and physically. Torture is an attempt to instil supreme powerlessness. Often, family members of those directly involved become targets, too, to achieve the aims of the torturer.

Smeulers (1985) estimates that 30% of refugees in the Netherlands have been tortured. Physical torture might consist of systematic beating, kicking, burning, stabbing, whipping, tying up the hands or feet, not treating wounds, and so on. Psychological torture can be sleep deprivation, mock executions, and threatening family members. Impressive accounts have been chronicled (Van der Veer, 1998; Fallaci, 1980).

Sexual violence is extremely humiliating. Besides the physical consequences, the psychological impact is tremendous. Men and women are often dealt with in the same manner. They are raped— sometimes in the presence of family members—or receive electric shocks to their genitals. During flight and in refugee camps, sexual violence can also be a reality.

Such violence is psychologically of a different kind than the violence of the battlefield, suffered by soldiers and other partisans enlisted in armies or involved in guerrilla organizations. As they are not passive victims, the violence is inscribed with different meaning, and is possibly easier to contextualize. However, they will often suffer from shame and feelings of guilt because of what happened in combat, or because of the loss of comrades or family members.

Responsiveness to violence

Each organization has an admissions procedure with questionnaires. Often, questions of violent behaviour in conflicts or sexual violence are excluded. When treating refugees, it is of great importance to ask about experiences of violence. As such, it is highly recommended to include questions on violence in the admission procedure. The following questions can be helpful.

- What caused the conflict in the country of origin?
- What were the personal consequences of the conflict (loss of employment, removal from school or university, etc.)
- Has the client fled or hid?
- Have family members been "disappeared", raped, threatened, or imprisoned? Has the subject been raped or abused at home or on the street? Who were the perpetrators?
- Has the client been arrested, imprisoned, interrogated, or physically or mentally tortured?
- Has the subject experienced sexual violence, at home, on the street, when fleeing, or in prison?
- Did the client leave much behind when fleeing, and what?
- What was the escape route and how long did the trip take?
- Has she or he experienced war?
- Has the subject experienced violence on the run or in the war? Did she or he see family members or other people murdered? Has the client been under fire, for instance by snipers?
- Did the client experience extreme conditions such as hunger, cold, heat, or thirst during flight?
- If violence has taken place, what was the duration?
- Has she or he experienced violence while in the Netherlands?
- If so, were legal charges made?

Apart from the points above, the care worker can ask questions on post traumatic stress disorder. Some of these questions have already been mentioned in the section on signalling.

It is also important to examine whether bodily harm has occurred as a result of abuse or torture. Often, refugees find this difficult to discuss. Guilt and shame may be a considerable burden if the subject has disclosed information on others when being tortured or because excitement was experienced when executing or undergoing violence.

In exile

All refugees have ended relationships out of necessity. Living in exile is, in a certain sense, a continuation of the violence. The violence and the forced departure distinguishes exiles from other migrants. The former group cannot return to their country of origin. The loss of love and respect that someone was accustomed to receive, the loss of status, of language, of reciprocal relationships, all add to the feeling of intrusive uprooting. The involuntary nature of the migration can be a barrier to adapting to the new homeland. The desire to flee and to build a future somewhere else continues to be seen as an attractive alternative.

Often, refugees have intense feelings of nostalgia. They are easily caught in a vicious circle, which can be exacerbated by the time spent in a refugee camp. Past memories, the desire to see family members, the idealization of the scents and the colours of the homeland can instil passivity in the client, leaving urgent problems unsolved. The isolation in refugee life is difficult to escape. Social contacts with the world outside the asylum centre are naturally limited, as are contacts with the Dutch. This situation intensifies the feeling of nostalgia, which can also be reinforced by the cultural dissimilarities with the host country. For instance, Dutch people understand hospitality differently than Chileans or Nigerians.

The extent to which a refugee will and can adapt strongly inter-acts with the way the host country welcomes refugees and migrants in general. They are not always treated with respect and are some-times confronted with xenophobia. For instance, native Dutch people accuse migrants of aiming to profit from the social benefits system. These unpleasant experiences are not conducive to adapt-ing to the new society. Moreover, such collisions often activate trau-matic memories from the past.

Living in exile can make someone reflect on, but also relive, the struggles and conflicts experienced in the country of origin. Friendships from the past are experienced differently in the new homeland. They can disintegrate, even in hindsight. People develop conflicting attitudes towards the future, towards steps that could be taken, and to existing loyalties. The development of new social and emotional relationships can shatter these loyalties and cause feelings of guilt.

Guilt is one of the principal human emotions: it is a complex feeling and originates from various sources. In addition, it is an emotion often concealed behind all kinds of symptoms and behav-iour. Feelings of guilt can surface in survivors of a war, especially when family members are murdered or imprisoned. These feelings are difficult to contextualize and can be especially tough during exile, because the pressure on family relationships and friendships commonly increases.

Pressures on the family

On some points, there are similarities between people living in exile and other migrants. These include:

- the experience of being treated as a foreigner;
- being subjected to racial remarks and small incidents on the street;
- language barriers;
- an increase in internal social surveillance because social units are broken up and thus decreased in size;
- financial dependence on welfare bureaucracies and family members.

Most non-western families are relatively large and strict rules tend to regulate conflicts. These rules differ from those in native Dutch households.

The uncertainty as to whether the refugee can stay in the host country is a burden on the refugee's family. Can the family build a secure future in the host country? Who will obtain a residence permit, and who will not? Can relatives living in precarious situations in the home country come over?

Family reunification can also lead to tension. While fleeing to the host country or in captivity, a man has experienced all sorts of feelings that are difficult to share with his wife, who arrives after him. In the opposite case, if the woman is the one who arrives first and has already arranged all kinds of practicalities, comparable tensions can occur. A certain level of power imbalance is likely to develop. He does not speak the new language and her outward-looking independence in her new existence is incommensurate with their traditional culture. The power is shifted towards the woman, which puts the man in a difficult position.

Where there are children, tensions can rise even further. Children provide the woman with contacts related to school and the neighbourhood, and language barriers are more easily overcome. These factors stimulate her integration process. When a man is unable both to find work and generate an income once he obtains refugee status, the embarrassment increases. She is the primary wage-earner, which conflicts with the traditional culture in which the man is expected to work and maintain contacts with the outer world. Unemployed men can have difficulty finding useful activities outside the house, and this isolation can lead to fierce arguments.

Language barriers and an isolated position in the host country will negatively influence digesting the violence many refugees have dealt with. Especially traumatized men run the risk of resorting to violent solutions. The family tensions, combined with shame over the fact that they are not able to take care of their family, can result in powerless rage. In these circumstances, arguments can easily escalate, especially when the images of the violence experienced in the home country are still present. This can result in abuses of both the wife and the children, running the risk of becoming even more traumatized. Children fantasize about the experiences of their parents. If they have been involved in, or witnesses of, violence, the risk of being traumatized is increased. They live in a battlefield between two cultures, perhaps even more acutely than other migrant children.

It is not uncommon for men to express shame, dissatisfaction, and apathy through being violent. Women, on the other hand, are experts in expressing what and how they feel. They can hound men with accusations, especially when the men are unemployed and do not speak the language of the host country. Also, political differences can initiate verbal and physical conflict, or remind migrants of situations in the home country. These memories can cause feelings of guilt and powerlessness that can, in turn, lead to violent behaviour. In general, couples try to prevent a divorce. The road to refugee status is long and difficult. Finding your way in a strange country can be a bonding experience for the household, but, equally, it can separate a family. While these circumstances are very difficult to cope with, couples are often dedicated to staying together. Sometimes however, a divorce is inevitable. The social worker will have to provide extra support to facilitate this tough decision.

First contact

Properly conducting the first contact with a client is of great importance. In the case of refugees, they might be more suspicious than others, in particular when they have lived in states where the authorities are strict and ruthless. Questions asked by the social workers may be perceived as threatening. It is advisable to explain to the refugee what the status is of the consultation, what will happen to the information afterwards, and what assistance she or he can expect. Clarity on the part of the social worker will simplify expectations, thus assisting in the removal of suspicion.

Misunderstandings cannot always be prevented, but do not necessarily prove problematic if they can be resolved. In the consultation room, three cultures collide. Next to the home and the host country's culture, there is the culture of the social workers and their own language values, expectations, and routine. Social work is probably differently organized in the host country than in the country of origin. In the case of language barriers, an interpreter is recommended. While it will slow down the process, it will be beneficial in the end.

The following questions could be asked during the first therapy session.

- Is there shame attached to asking for social work in your home country?
- Are emotional complaints translated to physical issues?
- How are difficult matters handled there?
- Are questions related to material circumstances tolerable?
- Regarding questions related to psychological matters, who was your first point of reference in your home country? (Often family members are consulted in case of emotional dilemmas.)

This last question provides an opening to talk about relatives who stayed behind, the mutual relationships before and after the flight, where other relatives currently reside, and the present frequency of contact with the family. In some cases, families have spread all across the world and remain in touch via email and telephone.

What are the current threats, what are the expectations for the direct future, and what are existing hindrances?

The first conversation can also be used to inform the client about common conflicts that occur in refugee or migrant families. For those involved, it is reassuring when social workers can signal these matters as well as other issues, such as conflicts of interest between men and women, problems with children, conflicts with other relatives, and tensions that are caused by processing experiences of violence. In addition, the elementary issues of life should be covered, including money, housing, employment, the situation of the children, school, language, and sexuality. Subsequently, it is important to get insight into the extent to which violence is perceived as a solution for conflicts. If it is, the consultation can be similar to that of other migrant families. The social worker should ask whether the man is willing and able to take responsibility for his behaviour.

The next step is to inquire into factual behaviour by asking the following questions.

- What does he do when he is feeling hot tempered?
- What is the immediate cause for such a situation?
- Where does he feel his anger?
- What happens when he loses control?
- Does he know what occurred afterwards?

During the following session, emphasis is put on the role of the woman by asking the following questions:

- How does she contribute to the escalation?
- How do the children respond?
- When does she notice things are getting out of hand?
- What can she do to reach safety?
- How can she avoid a beating for herself and the children?
- Who can she go to?
- Who can she call?
- Where, inside the house, can she take refuge?
- How can she invoke the help of the police, if necessary?

First case

The couple arrives in a tense mood, having been referred by their personal physician. Arguments have escalated severely. Pedro, a

Chilean man, was tortured during the Pinochet regime. After his release from prison, he fled to the Netherlands and obtained refugee status. Adapting here has not been easy. He did not seek help before. His wife, Pherian, is Kurdish. She fled to Sweden as a political refugee and lived there for a number of years before moving to the Netherlands. She is taller than he is.

Pedro and Pherian have a son of four. Pherian also has a daughter who is ten. Both speak Dutch poorly. Her daughter, Nadia, has much more fluency. Pherian complains that he does not physically control his anger during arguments and looks powerless and in need of help. Pedro says that she is strong and violent, too. It appears she hits him in the face, and he stamps on her arms and kicks her in the back. He admits he is stronger and that he fights more strategically. Her attacks remind him of the days he was in prison and tortured. The unpredictable nature of her fury is especially hard on him. He has trouble sleeping. Nightmares make sleeping difficult, and, when his son cries, he hears the echoes of the crying prisoners. Sometimes his fear leads to rage, and at those moments the son is not spared. This vicious circle is not easily broken. He is ashamed to be carved from the same wood as his tormentors. For him, violence serves as a release valve for such memories.

Both partners have been traumatized by their political history. Traumatic memories block their attempts at regaining control of their anger. First, it is important to explain the wide occurrence of domestic violence, and sketch some of the things that can be done about it. Self-control is not easy under such circumstances, but emphasize that it is possible. Both spouses should realize the consequences of domestic violence for the mental development of the children.

In order to motivate the parents, it is useful to draw up several scenarios and their negative consequences for the children. The choice of a specific type of intervention depends on the ability of the parents to adapt their behaviour and overcome the violence. This couple must detach their current conflicts from the processing of the torture. The contract, in combination with the time-out procedure, seems to have a favourable outcome in their case.

Second case

The second case is mainly concerned with traditions and power imbalances. The social contacts and family ties have to be taken into consideration.

Safdia is a refugee from Iran. She has an affair with another Iranian, Nusret. Safdia has finished a course of study, Nusret has not. The disparity of knowledge between the two frustrates Nusret very much and pushes him to abuse her. She was born into a well-known intellectual family and, although the parents still live in Iran, the brothers are scattered around the world. In contrast, Nusret comes from a small farming community, was educated as a teacher, and joined the resistance. Both of them were tortured by the police. They have close ties with the Iranian community in the Netherlands. Safdia and Nusret are pressured to provide assistance to other Iranians in an asylum seekers' centre. They both work hard, tend to forget their own background, and take tensions out on each other.

Nusret is ashamed to admit that arguments between the two get out of hand and does not seem to be willing to say anything when asked about the causes and the progression of the disagreements between him and Safdia. As he regards shame as a painful feeling and is humiliated time and again, why would he care to trust a social worker? But, after a while, he starts talking about how they met and how they both fled Iran. The couple met in the asylum centre. During the conversation, it appears that Nusret and Safdia have not discussed and shared many things with each other. In the course of the consultations, trust increases, and after a while he seems able to talk about how he feels when losing control in a conflict.

Nusret was born into a family where male and female roles are strictly separated. Physical violence is not uncommon to demonstrate who is in control. Women must be obedient and, to a certain extent, Nusret agrees with this concept. On the other hand, he realizes that it is different now, and he is aware of the dissimilar expectation from Nusret. She originates from a progressive family, where women are expected to go to university and be of significance in the world. Her mother is a doctor. The difference in social background resonates through all conflicts. They both find it difficult to share the pain of the tortures and their feelings of homesickness. Nusret understands that beating is counterproductive, but he finds it difficult to let Safdia know that she should take his feelings into account as well.

During the initial session, feelings of guilt and shame prohibit the explicit mentioning of violence. Nusret is the oldest son and has obligations towards his family. His feeling of honour is highly developed. He feels obliged to regularly send money to his family in Iran. He regards the idea that Safdia could possibly leave him as extremely painful and embarrassing. It appears, however, that this couple is able to make compromises. Nusret will leave the house when he feels that his anger is rising, Safdia promised to go to a friend of hers when the situation gets out of hand.

A second step in the admission process could be the drawing of a family tree for both families. Sometimes, this flows automatically: drawing and talking about family relations is often perceived as a relieving activity. Automatically, new information comes up and talking about fleeing is easier when questions are being asked. Such questions could be:

- Where were your family members when you fled?
- What did they do?
- How did they regard your leaving?
- How are conflicts solved in the family? (This question provides insights into the possibilities currently available.)
- What are expectations regarding women and men in your family?
- What is expected of you while you are in exile?
- What do you expect from the future?
- What are the expectations of the community of the country of origin?
- Should the struggle be continued from the host country?
- Are there any other obligations towards your family?
- What is the financial situation of both partners?
- Are there issues related to sexuality?

Only an initial session that takes the specific circumstances of the refugee into account can clarify whether violence is involved or not. If that is the case, the couple must be motivated to try to make appointments.

Most couples are able to understand the need for a time-out phase, to jointly agree to a contract, and make to appointments for the monitoring of conflicts. This will not happen in one visit, but after a few weeks the situation usually settles. Subsequently, steps have to be taken to strengthen support for the relief trajectory for the couple or the family. This is a complex process and it can take some time.

Social assistance in the host country to couples from other cultures is characterized by specific problems: particular cultural backgrounds, family traditions, political experiences, and beliefs can reinforce traumas.

Once a certain level of trust between the social worker and the couple has formed, it can be difficult to refer the couple for further treatment. It is, however, necessary to strictly limit the borders of the social work system. It can be helpful to form a relief network of social workers around one family. Thereby, a solution can be sought on several fronts. Changing "coping strategies" and constructing a healthy understanding of the past (reliving fond memories) are protective factors for a family in a host country. Finding a new balance of power takes time. It is important that a case manager monitors the progress of a family. Otherwise the family is likely to disappear in the web of formal institutions. All sorts of social workers must collaborate, in order to protect the social worker against excessive personal involvement.

Referring

Referring is necessary in cases where the client becomes psychotic or severely depressed, has physical complaints, or medication is needed. However, this does not automatically indicate that the client disappears from the reach of the social worker involved. When a relation of trust has already developed, it might be important for the continuity of the treatment that the relationship is sustained. In a period of crisis, family life can be totally disturbed. Support and structure for the family members are of the utmost importance.

Recommendations for social workers

1. Basic knowledge about immigrant and refugee groups who live in the host country is a prerequisite for quality social work. This includes knowledge of the following aspects:
    - tradition and religions;
    - cultural and political relations;

- socialization processes;
- differences between men and women;
- the cultural meaning of violence within families.

2. Social workers have to know that not all methods are appro-
    priate for all target groups. These methods are mainly focused
    on the treatment of individuals. They are designed to enforce
    the individual strength of the client and depart from the
    idea that the client's boundaries must be respected. These
    assumptions cannot at all times be routinely transferred to
    migrants and refugees. Often, the problems and conflicts these
    groups face are related to the social and political context of
    the family and the country of origin. The cultural background
    of the conflict will most certainly affect the choices the client
    makes during the therapy session. The existence of a group
    identity, for example, can be more important than Western
    social workers will recognize. Strengthening the identity of
    the client can only take place when the group identity is
    considered. The system of social and cultural relationships
    in which the client takes part, as well as the relevant codes
    that apply to those relationships, must be involved in the
    treatment.

3. Abuse and violence can be addressed only if they are explicitly
    part of the treatment. This is only possible when the practi-
    tioners can overcome their reticence. To achieve this, trainings
    for social workers are needed that target both the self-reflection
    of practitioners and develop competences that enable them to
    address and combat violence within families.

4. When institutions are willing to invest in the training of their
    employees, the next step is to create conditions that enable the
    social workers to perform their profession effectively. In addi-
    tion, the following conditions can also prevent psychological
    problems among the personnel:
    - supervision;
    - a reasonable and varied caseload;
    - extra time scheduled after intensive consultations with
      traumatized people;
    - The continual sharing of content and practice with col-
      leagues in the form of lectures and advisory meetings;

- professional development and sharing of expertise;
- training for the management on identifying secondary traumatic stress disorders or symptoms of compassion fatigue among employees.

CHAPTER SEVEN

The coherence between shame and violence

Martine Groen

S hame is an important emotion in couples who use violence during conflicts in their relationship. The abuser—in most cases the male—is ashamed of his deeds, the one who is abused—mostly the female—feels ashamed about what is happening to her. While the often unrecognized sense of shame in the male can lead to new violent eruptions after some time, the shame in the female causes her to retreat into herself and to humiliate herself. This dynamic strengthens the downward spiral of violence with couples (see Chapter Three) and maintains it. Shame is an issue that needs to be dealt with explicitly in therapies with couples who are seeking help regarding violence in the relationship, in order to breach the downward spiral of violence.

In this chapter, we deal with the question of in which manner there is coherence between shame and violence and how this coherence can be treated in therapeutic situations. After investigating the layers of shame and the coherence with shame as a regulating and debilitating emotion, further research is done to find feasible therapeutic interventions to breach the downward spiral of violence. At the end of this chapter, some pitfalls that the therapist may encounter while discussing shame-inducing and violent

episodes during the course of relationship therapy are discussed
briefly.

> The couple have been referred by their GP. The husband and wife are
> tense as they enter. According to her husband and their GP, she is
> suffering from depression. During the assessment session, after thor-
> ough questioning about the highs and lows of the relationship, it
> appears that the situation is more complex. The husband holds a good
> position as a diplomat. His wife and children have followed him every-
> where, for fifteen years to date, relocating to a different place every
> couple of years. The arguments started after the arrival of their first
> child. The wife did not feel capable of anything, inferior to her
> husband, and deeply isolated. After the arguments, in which the hus-
> band humiliated the wife, she retreated into herself emotionally. To the
> outside world, she kept playing the part of the perfect wife and host-
> ess. Her isolation increased after the birth of their second child. She
> started taking medication to get rid of the bad feelings. She blamed her
> husband. He could not do anything right. Out of despair and the need
> to get through to her, he had started to beat her. As a reaction to that,
> she has retreated even more and agrees with him: she is not worth-
> while. He can beat her to death for all she cares; it does not matter to
> her one way or another. He is ashamed about his wife, for what she
> says, for her appearance, which has not improved, and for his own
> outbursts of anger and violence. His wife has started to drink even
> more and is hardly able to maintain the decorum of a diplomat's wife.
> His limits have been reached. During a recent fierce argument, he
> muffled her moaning by pushing a pillow over her face. She almost
> choked to death. They decided to seek help.

When violence is used in a relationship, there is a continuous
breaching of boundaries between the partners and other family
members, where the abuse goes hand in hand with threatening,
intimidating, humiliating, tormenting, and other emotionally hurtful conduct. The violence is embedded in a pattern of exercising
power, which often shows a switch from violent to relatively calm
behaviour. It is precisely this interchange between shameful behaviour and the periods of loving responses which, paradoxically,
enhances the bond with the violent partner.

In the periods after the outburst of violence both partners experience feelings of shame. The husband is ashamed because he was
unable to control himself and the wife is ashamed because she is so

hurt and humiliated and has not been able to prevent the beating. When there are children, both partners will feel ashamed for their children, because they know that the children are suffering. This phase of shame will often be followed by a period of anger, resentment, hidden vengeance of the wife, and uncontrollable anger of the husband. Together, they will once more look for an area where the boundaries can be shifted. Once the beating has commenced, a barrier of safety and trust has been crossed. This appears to fundamentally change the relationship, which makes a repetition more likely.

> "After the second time that it happened, I noticed that I kept on beating and I just couldn't stop myself. Only in hindsight did I realize what had happened and I was ashamed. I felt ashamed about what has happened, but also because I wasn't able to control myself. I feel guilty for what I did to her."

The analysis of the downward spiral of shame and violence shows the partners' (failed) attempts to restore the relationship time and again. After the occurrence of violence, the couple at first tries to put the relationship back on the right track with all of their might and they try to forget, to deny, what has happened.

This joint denial of the violence and the shame unites them. Both partners are keeping each other "hostage", as it were, in this mutual secrecy and denial. It is a dynamic in which the "partners in shame" become ever more trapped and can no longer see a way out.

This downward spiral of shame holds a different meaning for each partner. In most cases, the female partner retreats into herself and internalizes the shame when she is humiliated, when her body is despised, and her identity is shamed. She shows her resentment in a subtle manner: for example, by becoming ill, by complaining about her shamed body. Her feelings of inferiority become the cause of renewed confrontations. She does her utmost to avoid conflict for fear of further injuries. The male, on the contrary, externalizes his shame by means of violent outbursts, for which he lays the cause and blame on her impossible behaviour. He actually sees in her self-humiliation and victimhood a means to humiliate her all over again. She knows how to hurt him and to put her finger right on his sore spots, giving him no chance for rebuttal. This process of mutual humiliation and shaming becomes a downward spiral with an endless repetition of shaming and violence which, in most cases, cannot be breached from the inside.

Shame as an everyday emotion

"To burn with shame", "to die of shame", are everyday expressions which give meaning to the intensity of shame as an emotion. Shame is just as ordinary as any other feelings. Despite this, social studies have not given this emotion the same level of attention that has been given to other emotions. For decades, feelings of shame and guilt have been neglected as a subject. Towards the end of the 1960s, guilt and shame have resurfaced as important moral categories in the practice of raising children. Shame has become a popular subject in scientific thinking and research (Weijers, 2000). There are three fields that are engaged in this matter: anthropology, psychology, and forensic psychiatry.

Cultural-sociological interpretations of shame

According to anthropologists, feeling ashamed is mainly a social phenomenon and highly dependent on the cultural context. Shame plays a significant role in the socialization of the subject, in order to keep the subject on the right track. Herein lies a significant distinction between shame and other emotions; that is to say, shame points towards behaviour, to moral claims and to socio-economic relations. Shame regulates social interactions between people. Therefore, shameful behaviour evokes social exclusion.

There is a difference in the regulation of shame within the socio-cultural context in Western and non-Western cultures. This is clearly manifest in non-Western cultures of shame, wherein shame is linked to, and expressed in, highly diverse orders with respect to men and women. Shame is linked to the social pact that has been made within the extended family (grandparents, uncles, and aunts) and within the cultural community.

In cases that involve couples from non-Western cultures, shame is often the focal point. A woman who hails from Montenegro formulates it as follows: "Shame belittles you, I am afraid to ask anything, it sets me apart from others. I feel watched, for example, when I go to the cinema on my own. The codes of conduct are very strict within this community, especially for women."

Just how strong this feeling of shame can be was confided to me by someone shortly after the war in Kosovo: "I'd rather have a son who is killed, than a daughter who has been raped." A rape conjures up a chain of events with feelings of shame and corresponding actions of vengeance within the extended family. These can have a devastating effect and far-reaching consequences, not only for the girl concerned, but also for the entire community. The virginity of girls and the sexuality of women are entrusted to the male collective.

In Western society the do's and don'ts surrounding sexuality have been internalized during upbringing. In non-Western societies, sexual needs are controlled by external forces. The responsibility for the protection of women and the honour of the extended family lies with the men. By not concurring with the sexual norm, women bring shame on the family. This is one of the most serious offences in a non-Western culture of shame. Men tend to behave more dominantly and are forced to constantly check upon the behaviour of women.

Divorce is not an option for these women, even after long-term abuse. They are at high risk of being shunned. Everything that could be said regarding physical abuse, sexual abuse, and rape, but also sexual pleasure with another person, is left unsaid. One does not talk about it in public. Cultures of shame are cultures of silence. This silence protects the community, because "shaming" incidents can have far-reaching consequences for the social fabric of the community.

In non-Western cultures, emotions are focused on the interactions with others. They are closely tied to the process of mediating between persons, actions, and events. It is, in fact, the inclusion and exclusion of groups. Processes of shame have a public and private function. They regulate the moral codes of the community. For women this entails continuously feeling ashamed. Or, as one woman put it, "Shame is omnipresent. Everything is drenched in shame." For men, this code means that they are allowed to publicly turn their feelings of shame into anger. That is precisely the contrast with Western culture. In this culture, shame has to remain hidden.

Elias (1978) has described this process of suppressing shame through an analysis of books on etiquette from the Middle Ages up to the nineteenth century. According to Elias, the avoidance of expressing emotional extremes is a hallmark of Western culture. Elias writes,

> In these communities social survival and success are, in other words, up to a certain point relying on a well-trusted armour (neither too strong, nor too weak) of individual self-control. In such communities there is relatively no space left for a show of deep emotions, of strong aversion to and dislike of people, never mind raging anger, blind hate or the urge to bash someone's head in. Highly agitated people, in the clutches of emotions they cannot control, are nutcases who are either destined for hospital or prison. Episodes of high anxiety are deemed abnormal and seen as a dangerous preliminary towards violence in a crowd. [Elias, quoted in Goudsblom, 1997, p. 156]

In his study, Elias shows that the hiding of shame has gained in strength through the ages. The thresholds of shame have been raised; it is a matter of an ongoing internalizing of shame. Elias's research holds a unique position within the scientific literature. In general, shame as an emotion that regulates social, moral, and political life is hardly given any attention within this literature. White (1992) says that this lack of research into shame as an emotion is a result of the euro-centrism from which many research models suffer. Perhaps this void in social science might be explained by the fact that shame has been internalized in the consciousness of the individual and thus is not regarded as a social phenomenon. Regardless, shame in Western Europe, too, has its impact on social interactions. In a subtle way, it has found its way from internalizing of the subject into social structures.

Women in both European and non-Western culture suffer more from shame than men. With men, shame manifests itself primarily in anger and aggression. This distinction between men and women can be encountered in psychotherapeutic practice. It would be beneficial if not only psychoanalytical, but also social science focused more on this shift in the processes of shame. The presence in our society of other cultures, where shame is felt in a distinctly different manner, could act as an incentive.

In interesting research into emotions and culture, Wierzbicka (1994) has studied "language, emotions, and the cultural script". She compares the language of Anglo-Americans with that of Poles, and tries to indicate the important meaningful words in these two cultural scripts. Cultures have different attitudes towards feelings. The norms for maintaining and controlling feelings vary, in particular. Furthermore, the strategies change depending on how the emotional communication flows. Anglo-Americans follow scripts in which they are encouraged to feel good in general, and they have mastered strategies to achieve this. Language supports the script in analysing and controlling feelings, in order to prevent someone from feeling down. Within this script, people feel ashamed when things are not going well, when they feel dependent on others, and when they are no longer capable of solving problems of their own accord. In this culture, therapy is an important means to once again become "self-made" and "self-supporting".

Within Polish culture, there is no shame in suffering, in failing. Complaining is a cultural script, inspired by the Yiddish culture and mixed with the indigenous culture. Somebody who feels lost or has failed finds an outlet in complaining and does not have to flee in shame.

At present, the Anglo-American script has spread all over Western Europe. The ideology of individualization is its most terse expression, with side-effects such as a strong focus on narcissistic longing for success, prestige, admiration, and swift fulfilment of desires. Mooij (2002) refers to the dominant image culture in which narcissistic longing prevails. Through the media and the rise of new technology, image has become the rule, as a mirror for personal experience and social beliefs. Language has been rendered inferior to image, and functions only by the grace of images. This change is supported by the rise of new technology, wherein reality is shaped by image. Mooij poses that "such a culture will be characterized by a strong urge to control and result-orientation, without much awareness of the inevitability of failure" (p. 116). In his view these are the hallmarks of a society in which complacency, prestige, control, unity, and totality determine the image. "I know what I want, I make my own decisions." Mooij, following his reasoning through, states that the narcissism of the image culture is marked by a boundless rivalry and competitiveness within human relations. One mirrors one another; there are no distinct boundaries, no acknowledgement to differentiate the subject from the other. Within this process of strife, it is predictable that humiliating and shaming one another may turn out to be a next phase in the collective narcissism. In my experience with warring couples, it appears that the loss of boundaries and respect for the values of the other is an often occurring phenomenon. It is all about the unfulfilled desire for a total unity, searching for a solution of a deeply felt "deficit" that the partners project on to one another.

Psychological views on shame

Psychoanalytical studies point out that shame is hurtful because it questions somebody's identity. This is not the case with guilt. With that, the deed itself is judged. One is able to make up for, or pay off, guilt; it is not so easily done with shame. Where this emotion is concerned, there is a fundamental inadequacy that brings about a sense of failure, of shortcoming. It is the unfulfilled self-image, or the image you perceive others to have of you, that triggers the sense of shame. The self-image is violated. With shame, the self is the centre of scrutiny; with guilt it is not the self, but the deed that is judged negatively.

Lewis (1971) also puts shame centre-stage as a dominant emotion. In the counselling sessions which Lewis has coded, shame appears to play a more significant part than other feelings such as pride, love, anger, sadness, or fear. A striking discovery in Lewis's study is the fact that shame which goes unrecognized and unacknowledged, and which lies within the realms of the subconscious, will often lead to aggression and subsequent feelings of guilt about this aggression. The shame is denied and repressed in order to avoid feeling the pain. This curbed shame will re-emerge in an obsessive shape, in which the charged scene will replay itself in the inner self. This inner self-repetition of the scene is a defence mechanism against the hurtful feelings of humiliation or the sense of being worthless. One can also apply other mechanisms, such as compensation fantasies, and rely on imaginary projects, such as wealth, fame, and power over others, for example. In therapies with men who beat their wives on a regular basis, this non-shame often re-emerges.

THE COHERENCE BETWEEN SHAME AND VIOLENCE   159

The connection between shame and anger has been corrobo-rated by a large-scale study by Tangney and Dearing (2002). People who feel ashamed have a tendency to retreat and avoid situations in which they might again be subjected to the threat of shame. Running away may bring solace, but not for long, because the shame remains. Another flight strategy is the tendency to lay the blame on others and to react with anger and hostility towards them. Within partner relationships, both these reaction patterns are destructive. Both motivations are also components of the down-ward spiral of shame and violence in which relationships run to ground.

Furthermore, the study by Tangney and Dearing shows that guilt is not linked to anger in the same manner as shame is. People who feel guilty stay connected to others and want to make up for their "mistakes". Guilt does not lead straight to a violation of the sense of self-worth, unlike shame. People who are ashamed tend to operate in a more destructive manner than people who lean towards feelings of guilt. Other studies (Lansky, 1987; Tangney, 1991) show that couples where shame plays a major part are more at risk of having rows which will escalate. Lansky assumes that the unity of couples where both partners are sensitive to shame could often have disastrous consequences. Not only do they bring their own vulnerability into the relationship, but also the inability to bond safely and the fear of being judged negatively. There is also a lack of empathetic ability. Relationships wherein shame is a bind-ing factor are characterized by repetitions of rejection and overt humiliation. In these unities, there is a lack of interactions in which the self-image and the image of the other are confirmed and the integrity of the relationship can be maintained.

Men seem to be more sensitive to shame within the context of social standing and women are more sensitive when it comes to the relationship itself. Men are more likely to show flight or offensive behaviour when they feel humiliated, while women tend to try to ease the situation and see to it that the bond stays intact. Further-more, women in general seem to be more bothered about feelings of shame than men. The studies of Tangney and Dearing show that shame in women expresses itself in self-harm, self-contempt, and self-mutilation. This is seldom the case with men, because they project the shame outwards.

Several studies show that men who beat have more shame reactions and have been subjected more to rejection, humiliation, and name-calling, in public and in private, in their youth than others (Dutton, Van Ginkel, & Starzomski, 1995). Shame is a primal reaction in women who have been beaten. They tend to internalize the shame about violent incidents and to blame themselves.

Theoreticians agree that there is a kind of cohesion between shame, attachment, and self-worth. What this cohesion looks like exactly is less clear. According to Tangney and Dearing (2002) being raised where the raising itself is based on shaming will lead to sensibilities of shame in later relationships and subsequently will lead to more outbursts of violence in escalating rows. The analyst Morrison (1989) speaks of a dynamic tension between experiences of the self that are turned outward and experiences that are turned inward, which can make life seem small and insignificant. According to him, shame can be connected to both poles. He wonders if either narcissistic vulnerability may lead to a sense of shame because a child is unable to develop itself independently and autonomously in the outside world, or that shame manifests itself in the inner world because a child is unable to maintain a sense of self-worth within the longing for an important other. In past decades, psychoanalysts such as Kernberg (1975), Kohut (1971), Lewis (1971), and Lansky (1987) too have made the connection between shame, narcissism, and attachment.

Kohut connects shame, expressed in a violent manner, to narcissistic anger, which happens to people, men in particular, who feel threatened within the primal group (family, family unit). The maintaining of self-worth with these men depends upon an unconditional appreciation of the other, who has to affirm this time and again, or by somebody who is constantly present and idealized. An important element in the creation of shame is the manner in which children are given feedback. Vital in this is the look of the other, which will either be encouraging or discouraging. If the look of the parent systematically denies the existence of the child, the child is at the mercy of its own devices.

In Kohut's theory, there is a difference between the idealized image of the mother and that of the father. The mother is more crucial in shaping the self-image of the child in its first year than the father. Once the longing to be treated as a wholly, uniquely beloved human being is satisfied, this, in turn, will add to a stable feeling of self-worth in the child. If that longing is denied on a regular basis, it will create a vulnerable, shame-sensitive self-image. The child continuously feels that it has failed the other. A direct result is the creation of an overly positive self-image to compensate the failing self, often resulting in a narcissistic personality disorder (Morrison, 1989).

In this range of psychoanalytic thought, shame goes hand in hand with not being able to measure up to the standards set as the idealized image by the parents, which are being internalized by the child. The lack of an ideal or a goal is a continuous flow of disappointment about the self and this will create a feeling of inferiority. This feeling is characterized by a sense of emptiness, gloom, or depression, which has to be warded off. With their flight into narcissism, men especially tend to idealize women, to regard them as saints (the mother, the beloved) and put them on a pedestal. The narcissistic anger surfaces once the appreciation is lost, or when the idealized image of the other no longer holds sway. This can be regarded as a defence mechanism of an insufficiently cohesive self against an overwhelming sense of shame. If the spouse subsequently threatens to leave them, this will be taken as a pretext for men to start the beating.

In Kernberg's study (1975) again, shame is linked to protecting and to defending the self-image that is regarded by the other as failing. This author has described the "Jekyll-and-Hyde-mechanism", a division of the good and bad aspects of the self, which is often recognized by women when they describe their husbands. "He is a completely different man to the outside world, charming and great to be with. But once inside he changes, I can often see it in his face alone." This division mechanism is often regarded as one of the most important defence mechanisms of a narcissistic personality structure.

Views on shame from forensic psychiatry

Dutton (1998) studied and followed 700 men in his forensic psychiatric practice, who were all guilty of abuse, the majority of whom he found were suffering from post traumatic stress syndrome. The three recurring elements in the history of men who misbehave as partner abuser (sudden and random grave abuse and humiliation by their father, an unsafe attachment to their mother, being witness of the abuse and humiliation of the mother by the father) are, according to Dutton, not to be regarded as separate entities when it comes to the development of the violent men. They create a breeding ground for future violent behaviour. He links the repetition of violence in trying to solve conflicts to the repetitive behaviour that often occurs with traumatized men. Characteristic of this is a helpless anger, fuelled by an overwhelming fear of being abandoned again, which cannot be controlled. While beating his wife, the man disassociates himself and becomes another, as it were. His wife becomes the one who is not to be trusted, the whore. Dutton considers boys being shamed by their father as one of the major experiences that will result in the repetition of the violence they themselves have suffered. This emotional outburst coincides with the humiliation and shaming of the other, who is seen as the enemy.

As with most psychoanalysts, Dutton's study, too, lacks the socio-cultural context wherein violence is used. Not only does he not name any cultural element within this context and regards the subject as an independent, isolatable unit of experiences, but he also does not make a distinction between women and men, not even when it comes to the process of socialization.

Weijers (2000), who is interested in jurisdiction for the young, does include the cultural context in his discourse about shame and guilt. In his approach, he links the concepts of guilt and shame together. He claims that shame is similar to guilt generated by failure, which is induced when a child does not measure up to its parents' standards. Interesting in his discourse is the meaning of the moral appeal to shame in the raising of children. Weijers frees shame of its destructive effect by attaching the concept of guilt connected with failure to it. He argues that shame, within the context of raising children, is a process in which the trust of the parents is shamed, and this shaming simultaneously holds the key to repairing the bond of trust. The sense of shortcoming is no longer connected to high and unattainable ideals, but is regarded as the effect of shortcoming on an everyday level to which one feels compelled.

From theory into practice

What does the theory hold for the practical work of psychotherapists with families and couples who solve their conflicts through
violence? The naming of shame and the disentanglement of
patterns of shame seem to be the appropriate way to remove the
downward spiral of shame and violence. The violent outbursts will
lessen once the shame and the pain that go with them are allowed
to be felt again. Only then can the defence mechanisms—anger or
disassociation—be neutralized. Acknowledgement, empathy, and
understanding are healing concepts within psychotherapeutic
practice.

The second way is the induction of guilt, the shift from shame
to guilt, and, subsequently, from punishment and atonement. Social
psychologists Tangney and Dearing (2002) are advocates of this
second way, because they presume that shame will lead to violence
sooner than it will to guilt. They have developed programmatic
projects to prevent shaming. Their therapy is based on a cognitive–behavioural approach, and this fits American society like a
glove. It is focused on a swift repair of boundaries and makes
people take responsibility once more by curbing the process of
shaming by means of inductions of guilt.

There are numerous situations which one can think of in the
raising of children where children are being humiliated or bullied
if they do not do something right. Shaming children is pointless,
according to Tangney and Dearing: just address the behaviour that
is expected of them and punish them accordingly, their conclusion
being that people who have been brought up in a culture of shame
tend to solve conflicts in a violent manner more than people who
have been raised in a culture of guilt.

This conclusion is doubtful, to say the least. The researchers
misjudge the meaning that shame has for their studied population.
Their study is related to the USA and shows that shame plays a
major role in that country and that it has a strong impact on
violence in that society. That does not imply that American society
has to be regarded as being based on a culture of shame. Despite
this, they do not—oddly enough—choose to acknowledge this
shame within its own dynamics and combat it from there, but
instead opt to render it innocuous through the long road of some

kind of collective induction of guilt. This kind of pedagogy lacks any guarantee of success.

Another example of the second way is the approach of Weijers (2000). In a study that lasted for four years, Weijers engaged himself with the pedagogic foundations of criminal jurisdiction. In his view, it is all about helping young people to take moral responsibility for their actions. In the development of the child, he sees two ways to make a moral appeal to the perpetrator: to confront him with feelings of guilt and to call upon shame. Within the legal jurisdiction, it is all about the first; within social relations the second comes into play. Both trajectories have their own effects. Based on this, Weijers wonders if there is any point in shaming delinquents or abusers in relationships, as is being experimented with in New Zealand and Australia.

The third way is that of "reintegration of shaming": the reinstatement of social order through shaming. In New Zealand and Australia, experiments have been carried out with this process of shaming to steer young delinquents back on the right track. This method is inspired by the Japanese culture of shame, where crime statistics are very low. With this approach to criminal behaviour, Braithewaite (1989)—the instigator of the method—aims to restore social order. His method has been applied to abusers within the family circle. It appears to have some effect on the perpetrators if the process of shaming is combined with training which deals with controlling aggressive impulses.

Weijers has expressed criticism of these experiments, specifically because of its instrumental character and the use of victims in the treatment of delinquents. Weijers doubts whether the process of shaming, as seen by Braithwaite, will have any effect. He puts more faith in the instrument of atonement by means of moral guilt, as exemplified in "the moral appeal of the judge". As said before, he believes in the concept of guilt and an appeal to the awareness of personal responsibility.

On its own, none of these three ways is capable of breaching the downward spiral of shame. It can probably only be done through a combination of different elements. In my own practice, it emerged that the acknowledgement and awareness of shame forms a vital element in the treatment of partners in violent situations.

With regard to the "reintegration of shaming", Weijers is probably correct in his assumption that this method is not really suitable for Western culture. In Australian practice, it was used mainly on delinquents and abusers of non-Western origin. In the Netherlands, it could be useful in the treatment of migrant families. In many migrant families, the main source of tension is tied in with the collision between the patriarchal laws within their own community and the freedoms that can be enjoyed within Dutch society. In my experience, families play a leading role in the prevention of violent behaviour in non-Western families where shame is regarded as a guiding principle. I look either for someone within the family, or someone from the broader community who has power and is respected and therefore will be able to use shame as a means of confronting the perpetrator with the consequences of his behaviour. How this authority will be implemented depends on the culture and the community.

However, some dilemmas arise here for the therapist. The process of shaming, which is put in motion by the authority figure, can easily end in collective revenge or exclusion. The therapist may find himself in a precarious situation, in which the question needs to be answered as to how to fit the results of such an intervention within his counselling. He is at risk of coming into conflict not only with his own ethics, but with the Dutch law as well.

The shift from shame to guilt

For therapeutic intervention within Western families, I champion a mixed intervention of shame and guilt. The quest with the couple or family has a sequence that runs from shame to guilt, to confession, and, respectively, to punishment, vengeance, atonement, and possibly reconciliation.

The first step to be taken is the naming of the humiliations and injuries and the shame that accompanies it. An inventory has to be made in which manner and form the shame is felt and expressed.

> He: "We had a huge row, I feel bad about it. I lost control. I don't know how to make it up again. (Cries). I feel ashamed about that as well, I'm good for nothing, things aren't that good at work either."

> She: "I'm ashamed to show my face, I feel ashamed because I could not prevent the fight. I lay down on the bed and took a lot of sleeping pills. No, I didn't wanted to kill myself, just didn't want to be around for a while."

This quote shows how heavy the burden of shame weighs on him and how hard it is for him to have lost his self-control. Once this is aired, a confession will help to ease the pain of shame.

The pain of shame runs deep for her as well. She blames herself for not being able to prevent the row and she retreats; she feels ashamed of him, too, but does not express this.

> He: "I cannot bear it when she retreats and closes herself off from me, at first I try to make amends, but if she doesn't react I will get angry again, even though I am aware that it doesn't help. I feel that she is capable of revenge and that frightens me. Then I'm ashamed for being scared and I want to hit her again. I just want her to react. I want her forgiveness."

> She: "I'm afraid to go out. I don't want to have anything to do with you when you're this grumpy and angry. You are so easily provoked. Thanks, but no thanks. I choose a swift exit after such a row."

Once he is able to admit that he feels ashamed and subsequently feels guilty about what he has done, the next step can be taken, in which guilt can be repaid and how this is to be achieved. The next step will be to determine together the nature and scale of the felt guilt. Not just that of the man, because he is the one who has hit the woman and possibly has smashed some things, too, but also that of the woman, even though her guilt may be perceived as much less. With both parties, the role they have played in letting the escalating row get out of hand will be determined. Out of this inventory, we will identify the tasks that will lead towards atonement.

The last step will be to determine the punishment. This is an unusual step within the therapeutic process; nevertheless, it needs to be taken or else guilt will linger on and forgiveness and reconciliation will be rendered impossible (Groen, 2000).

Shame and the therapist: some pitfalls

Apart from the clients, the therapist may find him/herself entangled within the feelings of shame of the couple or family in the consultation room. This can cause a diffuse atmosphere, which can change into a collective disassociation about the violent incidents. This will result in the avoidance of painful subjects. The therapist will no longer ask for further details or facts. During these sessions he/she can be overwhelmed by misplaced feelings of shame. These can be expressed in anger towards the abuser. This form of countertransference has a crippling effect and often goes undetected: studies show that a great number of therapies either stagnate or run into the ground for precisely this reason (Lewis, 1987; Sheff, 1987; Tangney, 1995).

An example: a man tells without any signs of regret or guilt how he has beaten up his pregnant wife, after a long row, and locked her out on the balcony. He describes how he kicked her in the belly. The therapist feels referred pain and anger and hears the anger in his own voice. The perpetrator is aware that his behaviour is unacceptable and becomes defensive. Animosity comes into the equation, and this obstructs the progress of the counselling.

An opposite form of countertransference is when the accounts of clients conjure up feelings of forbidden longings and fantasies within the therapist. The shame connected with the stimulated imagination can be a barrier to asking specific questions or can lead to over-asking, which causes the clients to resist. Violence, fear, and excitement go hand in hand for a lot of people. Perverse images of domination can stir up some primitive feelings. A higher level of excitement is part of experiences with violence, as are feelings of shame about such imagination.

Forms of intervision, or, rather, supervision, are indispensable in working with families and couples where violence is used to resolve conflicts. The context has to be safe in order to talk about such feelings of countertransference. It is, furthermore, wise to organize one's practice in such a way as to alternate violent cases with other problematic cases or activities.

Secondary trauma can be prevented if the psychotherapists, too, get and take time to dwell on the effects the stories have on themselves. Shame is a difficult subject within the therapeutic practice, not only for clients, but for the therapists as well. The paradox of shame is being ashamed about your shame. It is a conflicting process that does not cancel itself out. This paradox does not only manifest itself within the practice, but also in the reflection about that practice, as is done in supervision and intervision. It is an art in itself to be able to create time and space wherein this reflection about the effects of that paradox can be aired.

CHAPTER EIGHT

Rituals of revenge

Martine Groen

I n partner relationships where conflicts are being resolved in a violent manner, there is often a vast amount of resentment about the humiliation endured by the one who has been beaten, once the violence has ceased and the fear of violence has lessened. There is a substantial need for vengeance. Taking revenge precedes forgiveness and reconciliation. To take revenge in a ritualized manner where the therapist bears witness and gives acknowledgement, can stem the destructive flow without the couple returning to the downward spiral of violence.

Family history

Which factors increase the chances of violence within partner relationships? Studies show (as seen in Chapter Five) that violent behaviour seen and experienced in the family home increases the chances that such behaviour might happen in a first partner relationship: 60–80% of men who hit originate from families where violence was used as a way to solve conflicts. Thirty-five per cent of those men have seen their mother being beaten at home (Straus,

1980). Furthermore, a lot of men who hit seem to have been abused in their childhood.

There is also a connection between beating and the use of alcohol and drugs (Gelles, 1983). There have also been studies into whether boys and girls from violent backgrounds react in different ways in the long-term. Boys tend to focus the aggression outward, while girls channel their anger into self-destructive behaviour (Wolfe, Jaffe, Wilson, & Zak, 1985). Both boys and girls copy the manner in which conflicts were solved within their families and they repeat the traumatic experiences of the family home.

Self-image

A poor self-image appears to be a motive to use violence within an argumentative situation. Rows will deteriorate more often into a physical fight if one of the partners is not capable of translating the ungovernable anger that is felt into words. The different ways in which partners tend to solve a conflict might be the immediate cause of a fight starting. In general, women have learned to express their feelings better. There tend to be more beatings in cases where women have a higher social status than their male partner (Dutton & Strachen, 1987).

A characteristic interaction pattern is that men start hitting when they are no longer able to vocally express their anger and women threaten to gain the upper hand through argumentation. This interaction often occurs with couples who humiliate each other, both physically and psychologically. With men, there seems to be a connection between a lack of assertiveness in the marriage and the beating (*ibid.*). A lack of the capability to be assertive contributes to angry and frustrated outbursts. Men who hit on a regular basis often interpret their partner's behaviour as more hostile and negative than men who do not beat: their own rationalizing causes them to regard the hitting in a less negative light. This category of men is less used to reasoning or rationalizing. Their diminished capability for nuancing emotional agitation causes them to transmute hurts, jealousy, and fear into anger.

Psychologist Baumeister (1999) holds a different view on the relationship between self-awareness and violence. According to him, it is in particular those people with high self-awareness who tend to use violence most, because they are more likely to feel threatened by the words or behaviour of others. People with an already low self-esteem would not dare to use violence. Aggression, in his view, is a means to maintain the high esteem one has of oneself within a group in order not to have to face the threat to the self-image. Less self-control equals more violence. Baumeister and other researchers agree on the part diminished self-control plays in the use of violence.

Apart from the intra-psychological factors, stress is a major risk-inducing factor for violent behaviour within the family. Anger can be a reaction to stressful situations. Unemployment, arguments in the workplace, the loss of a loved one, and poverty can escalate tensions in a household.

Another factor is shame. Studies have shown that couples whose primary reaction is shame are more at risk of escalating conflicts. Men are more ashamed about social standing, while women are more ashamed when it comes to attachments. Men are more likely to show flight or offensive behaviour when they feel humiliated and women are more likely to try to ease the situation and to see to it that the bond stays in tact. Shame acts as a defender of a diminished cohesive self-image. Kohut (1971) connects deeply felt shame expressed in violent ways with narcissistic anger, which happens to people, mainly men, who feel threatened within the primary living space (the family unit). The maintenance of self-esteem and self-awareness depends either upon an unconditional appreciation which is continually reconfirmed, or on someone who is ever-present and idealized. Shame that is not felt, in particular, ignites aggression (Lewis, 1987). This is underpinned by Dutton (1995).

Relationship therapy

Which factors play a part in a successful therapy? Treatment has a higher success rate if:

- both partners are motivated to resolve arguments in a different manner, often because they do not want to lose each other;

- the partners are both convinced that they have their share in the escalating rows;
- the one who hits is prepared to be bound by contract in order to avoid the beating;
- the violence has not escalated in such a way yet that there is no going back;
- there is no talk of any psychiatric disorders, like an antisocial personality disorder;
- no weapons are being used and the violence does not have a ritualized character, as, for instance, in a violent sect (Jennings & Jennings, 1991).

Acknowledgement

Every humiliation undermines the sense of self-worth. Acknowledgement of the humiliation by the one who has inflicted it is the first step towards restoration. In reality, acknowledgement by the abuser does not appear to be sufficient. Feelings of resentment linger on, which can ignite the violence when conflicts occur. The longer a couple has been trapped within the downward spiral of violence, the more persistent the feelings of fear and resentment, even if there are no more beatings.

In therapy with these couples, agreements are made in the first phase to put an end to the violence. In most cases this is successful, but a difficult phase is reached in the therapy once the fear of violence has lessened. Often the partner who has been abused—the woman in most cases—harbours a lot of resentment and temptation looms large to take revenge in a more or less subtle way for the suffered humiliation. She wants atonement. In the next phase, the therapist tries to find ways to redress this with the couple. The search for ritualized moments of vengeance is an important part of the therapy in order to stem the anger and pain and to keep it in check.

The story of John and Jolande

The police had knocked on John and Jolande's door several times before. Up until recently, they declined any offers of help. Because

Jolande was heavily pregnant with their second child at the time another incident occurred, the officers decided that they finally had to intervene. The threat made by the police to detain John had the required effect, and this time they were prepared to ask for help.

They landed in my practice and I listened to their account. John came home drunk that night and started a row that escalated and resulted sooner rather than later in a beating. The fight led to a confession. While hitting her, he cried out that he despises himself. He felt deep remorse when he saw his pregnant wife lying on the floor, crying. Once she got up, she gathered her things and wanted to leave. She wanted to stay away for a couple of nights. Tearfully, John begged her to stay. He offered his apologies. Jolande stayed and wants to know exactly what is going on. Unusual for her, she keeps asking specific questions. Little by little, John tells her that he was sexually abused by his aunt. It started when he was twelve and lasted until he was fourteen. The abuse ceased, but he still cannot come to grips with the fact of how it could have happened in the first place. He recalls this period in his life with disgust and shame.

John is thirty-five and things have gone from bad to worse ever since the abuse. He comes from an alcoholic background; both his mother and father drank a lot. John remembers a lot of shouting and beating. He has only finished primary school, in educational terms. He got to know Jolande at a later stage in life. He did not really want a serious relationship with her, but, when she got pregnant, he married her anyway. Actually, he feels he has been tricked into it. He thinks he is a failure, both at work and in love, and he focuses his anger and frustration about this on his direct environment. Time and again he tries, by seducing women and by applying for other jobs, to prove that he is not "a loser". If he drinks, he loses control and his outbursts are more intense and violent.

Jolande's history fits John's shortcomings like a glove. Jolande is thirty; she lost her mother when she was thirteen. From then on she took care of her father and her younger sister. She completed a vocational education at secondary level and works as a secretary for the managing director of a large institution. She has one best friend, and spends a lot of time with her sister. She has been married to John for four years now and the beating started shortly after the birth of their first child, two and a half years ago. She describes her father as an egocentric man, nice to the outside world, but grumpy at home and constantly seeking attention. Her wishes, even her grief about the death of her mother, did not count for much. Jolande feels badly let down and is dissatisfied with her life. Just like her mother, Jolande's rule is "As long as he is happy". It is true that she is taken aback by her husband's outbursts of anger, but, on the other hand, she feels for him.

The first phase of the therapy: breaching the downward spiral of violence

The first phase of the therapy is outlined in Chapter Three. The cornerstone of that phase is to make a contract to put an end to the violent behaviour and to describe a time-out arrangement. It is vital to add, in this chapter, that men and women react differently towards one another. In general, women have different strategies when it comes to having a row than men.

When it comes to the initial blows, most partners are able to kiss and make up after a row. However, once the beating becomes a pattern to ease tension, the interaction between the couple changes. In such situations, women tend to retreat emotionally. Reacting to this, because of their fear that they will be abandoned, men try to exert more control on the relationship. The conflict intensifies and the fear in both partners increases. Women become afraid of getting beaten and try to create reaction patterns in order to cope with the beatings. That is, until they gather their children and walk out.

Some couples are relieved when they see the model of the downward spiral. They examine the different stages and place themselves somewhere within the spiral. "We've almost reached the last stage. It's now or never."

The second phase of the therapy: control

Experience has shown that people in general keep their side of the agreement. The next phase is meant to bring about a change at the behavioural level in order to ease the interaction between the partners. Once the contract of the first phase holds, the violence has ceased and the couple is eager to change the situation, the hard graft begins. Even though the violence has stopped, the threat lingers.

Jolande is scared to touch on any sensitive subject. She fears John's outbursts when he is feeling hurt. If she tries to talk about anything at home, for example, his drunkenness, he only has to raise his voice and she is silenced.

In this second phase of the therapy, fear dominates, and to give shape to feelings of resentment is a step too far as yet. Psycho-education about the "fight/flight behaviour" in frightening situa-tions increases understanding and therefore control over it. One of the therapeutic interventions is predicting that this phase will be the most difficult one, in order for the couple to prepare themselves.

Feelings of fear are very real indeed when one fights for survival. Fear triggers either flight or fight. Usually, women survive through flight behaviour. Sometimes they actually flee, but flight can also be seen as a metaphor for a number of other survival strategies such as disassociation, splitting off feelings, or a variant of this: to freeze inside. In this way, pain can no longer be felt. When regular and unexpected beatings have taken place, restricted awareness, loss of concentration, amnesia, and other disorders may occur. Some women flee by making up psychological excuses for their partner: "John had such an awful childhood, he hits because his aunt abused him."

Men will be more likely to react to fear and shame with fight behaviour; more often than women, they will think that they are in the right and their pride will be hurt more easily. Men are trained to voice their aggression more. Pride and loss of face are concep-tions that suit the male. Boys fight and frolic and effortlessly these conceptions gain meaning within a father–son relationship or in contacts with their peers. Failing and powerlessness equals loss of honour. Society underpins these feelings and behaviour.

Only when the violence has ceased can there be talk about the issues that are on the couple's minds. Naming the feelings of shame and providing an insight into them as a defence against the pain of humiliation is one of the subjects that will be dealt with then. Other themes in this phase are conflict control, and taking respon-sibility for the escalating behaviour. Men will have to learn to keep their hands to themselves at the right moment and to control them-selves if the tensions in the house escalate. Women will have to learn not to run after him with reproaches and to stop treading on his toes.

Once the fear of violence has subsided, a period will commence in the therapy process in which resentment and the need for atonement take centre-stage.

Revenge

In Dante's hell, those who have violated their loved ones will be submerged in a stream of swirling blood as a punishment. When the perpetrators show their heads, centaurs will shoot at them with bows and arrows. Vengeance is as old as time: revenge is an important theme in world literature.

Resentment is a feeling, a lust for revenge, and can lead to vengeance, an act. Resentment can also linger on, undetected. One can spend a lifetime feeling vindictive. One of the reasons to hold a grudge and to take revenge may be that one has been humiliated; one's sense of self-worth has been violated. By taking revenge, one will try to restore one's sense of self-worth.

The way to retaliate and the manner in which revenge is taken differs in time. Within small communities, retaliation used to be settled according to "an eye for an eye" principle. This kept further acts of vengeance in check. With time, retaliation has been taken over by the state and the judicial system in order to prevent acts of vengeance between citizens, generally known as "taking the law into one's own hands". Retribution has to provide atonement, but the sentence does not always comply with the individual or society's need for atonement. The individual is left unsatisfied when he feels that his individual interest does not coincide with the collective interest considered by the state.

Restoring the sense of self-worth is a way to ease the feelings of wanting vengeance and to create an atmosphere where forgiveness is possible. Acknowledgement by the perpetrator is most helpful and most obvious in this. If that is unachievable, for example, because the perpetrator does not value continuing the relationship any longer, there is a third party that needs recognition. In most cases, the judicial system operates as the third party, but a psychotherapist, too, can occupy this role as an exponent of society.

Revenge is retaliation for the suffered humiliations. In order to restore self-worth, atonement is vital. For a long time, abuse was considered not to be a crime, but a private matter. Although abuse within the marriage is seen as culpable now, but, just as with abuse in general, it is not a priority as a criminal offence. Therefore, the perpetrator and the victim are locked together in a resentment. In therapy with couples who solve their conflicts in a violent way, it is vital not only to look for alternative ways to handle conflicts but also to search for some kind of retaliation together with the partners. Ritualizing revenge is one of the avenues to take.

Do women have a different take on revenge than men?

Two women encountered in the Greek tragedies, Hecuba and Medea, are the icons who take centre-stage as the "revengeful ones" who could not keep their passions under control. Does this mean that women are more uncontrollable in their vengeance, more obsessed? Statements like "vengeance is mine, saith the Lord", or "the sword of vengeance", seem to indicate differently. The realms where men and women exert their vengeance are different. Men are expected to restore the family's honour, or that of the country, by taking revenge. They execute vendettas, women do not. Women take revenge within the confines of the private home. Medea is driven by jealousy: her husband wants to divorce her for political reasons and he has asked the king's daughter for her hand in marriage. Medea takes revenge by killing their children and by burning her husband and the king's daughter. Hecuba, the queen of Troy, takes revenge on her friend Polymester because he has violated her trust. His eyes are put out. Women in Euripides' plays do not take revenge to save the family's honour, but their own.

    In our time, too, one can distinguish many kinds of revenge within the realms of privacy. It is no longer permitted to take the law into one's own hand, yet there are realms where people do take the law into their own hands because they do not feel the state has played a satisfying role as the keeper of justice. In divorce cases, women often take revenge either through money or the children's visiting arrangements. Women do indeed take revenge in a different way. They tell on their husband to Social Services when he has a job on the side, or they accuse him of incest. In families where

conflicts are solved in a violent way, revenge is often the spark that
ignites and escalates the violent behaviour, time and again.

The third phase of the therapy: taking vengeance

Once a woman is convinced that her husband will no longer hit her,
all the suppressed anger will come pouring out. Women have
developed different strategies than men to get even and they often
do it in a subversive way. This subtle venom can be very obstruc-
tive and deeply destructive. Most of the time, it is difficult for the
therapist to gain a precise insight into how mutual vengeance is
taken. This is often underestimated. Jolande harbours a lot of
resentment. The couple therapy is on the brink of failure. In the
counselling room she is often angry, but not unreasonably so, as if
forgiveness is just around the corner. The depth of her anger only
surfaces when John has hit her again. Again, a time-out was
needed. The reason for this escalated conflict seems to be Jolande's
reign of terror at home. She follows John around, criticizes everything he does, he is no longer allowed to go his own way, after
work. She has turned her lust for vengeance into a boundless perse-
cution mania and suspicion. Jolande keeps blaming him continuously for having hit her. She also predicts that he will lose his job;
he will be fired.

At some point John is no longer able to keep his frustrations in
check. John acknowledges that he should not hit her, it is wrong, he
feels ashamed, but it is not enough to satisfy her. The acknowledgement of her anger too, is insufficient. I urge Jolande to voice
her anger more openly instead of following him around, nagging at
him or humiliating him. But more has to be done; her lust for
vengeance seems boundless. He has to show that he is sorry in
some way or another, she has to have atonement. One of the ways
to do this is by means of a ritual.

Ritualizing revenge

A transition ritual changes current discordant interaction patterns
by replacing them with new and qualitatively different ones (Van

der Hart, 1978). Without the aid of a ritual act, emotions may get out of hand. Hate keeps one captive and it devours energy. Resentment is a powerful feeling and, at the same time, a destructive emotion when this is turned into acts of vengeance. Letting go of such powerful emotions is harder than one may think, but ritualizing may help to channel them. Within the ritual, emotions stay in check, which makes the interaction less threatening. Besides, rituals of revenge stem the tide of anger and put it into perspective. They can serve as a transition towards possible forgiveness and a new start, or a possible divorce. The ritual that can achieve atonement takes the shape of a "community service". It is not always easy to find a suitable penalty. In order to be effective, the punishment has to be equally important as the "offence". It is almost impossible to undo the damage the offence has inflicted, but atonement can be demanded. This is a priority within modern community service. The consequences of violence cannot be erased, but handing down a community service as a punishment opens up the opportunity to make it up to the community.

The latter has to be the point of reference when handing down a "community service" sentence within a violated family unit. Such a punishment can be regarded as a ritual punishment. That is why the handing down of the punishment has to have a ritual course, too. Within this process, the penalty and a strategy are designed first. Next, we make an inventory of the behaviour of the partners in order to decide when and how the ritual punishment will be executed. Finally, we decide when the closing ritual will take place.

Devising a penalty for abuse happens through negotiation. The therapist is the third party in this, the mediator, the witness. The role of the therapist is that of a family court judge without legal jurisdiction. This seems to be awkward for a lot of therapists. Therapists tend to play down the violent behaviour, just as the couple does. One is inclined to go along with the issues the couple chooses to offer.

Furthermore, it appears that most therapists tend to be on the woman's side, which tends to negate the woman's acts of vengeance. It is important to ponder this in order to devise the right penalty, taking everyone's view into consideration. The therapist reorders and restructures within the frame of atonement and the transition ritual, trying to find a daily recurring moment when the penalty becomes a heartfelt experience and not a casual, isolated experience.

What are Jolande's demands, what is her claim, and what will be sufficient to satisfy it? In the end, three community services are decided on for John and one for Jolande. The first part of the punishment only concerns John. John and Jolande decide that he will come home earlier from his activities and, when he is home, he will play with his son, he will do the dishes, and put his son to bed. She will not interfere in the way he spends these hours. If she cannot restrain herself from tormenting him, he can send her away. Furthermore, he will have a couple of community service tasks, a punishment John is not looking forward to. He has to give his father-in-law a hand with the renovation of his house.

The second point Jolande wants to discuss is her wish to become more independent of John. That is one wish that bothers John a lot. She wants to have a monthly allowance that she does not have to account for. This would mean that he would have to take night-shifts in order to keep up the monthly income, but that is not really what she wants; she wants to have him at home more often. As an alternative, she offers to go out with her girlfriends more often.

John is jealous: he suspects that Jolande will run off with the first available man. He has been appreciative of the fact that she has been dressing down more since they met. Her clothes are less provocative than when he first met her. His low self-esteem is the source of his need to control and his angry outbursts. This makes it a rather sticky point in the course of negotiations. To differ from one another at this stage seems to increase anxiety levels and appears to be risky. Nevertheless, it is part of taking responsibility. John will undergo separate therapeutic counselling to deal with his history of abuse, to learn to differentiate feelings, and to regain his self-confidence.

John's retribution is discussed too. Jolande's persecutory behaviour will be curtailed. Strict agreements are made. If Jolande does not keep her end of the agreement, John may say "stop" and walk out. Jolande is not allowed to follow him. She will restrict some of her behaviour.

What kind of night out will incur the least level of anxiety for Jolande and what can John do to control his outburst of jealousy? To bear the jealousy is part of the punishment. In this matter,

Jolande will no longer have any consideration for him. To make it more bearable for him, this ordeal will carry the label "on the way to becoming independent partners". Jolande will organize a night out with her friends on a monthly basis. She will also take a computer course in the local community centre. Besides, Jolande plans to go and look for a job once things have settled down after the birth of the baby. The goal is for her to slowly but surely give shape to her independence, without losing the bond with John. Jolande's third demand is that John stops drinking. How achievable is this demand? He turns out to be a habitual drinker. Six beers after work is the norm. Sometimes, things get out of hand. He does not know exactly after which beer this happens. He declines any help in this matter, but we agree that if he passes the limit, he will not be allowed to enter the family home. We discuss where he might sleep off his hangover.

The closing ritual

It is vital to formulate when the punishment will end and to decide which ritual can underpin this closure. John and Jolande decide that the end will be in sight when the renovation on her father's house has finished, when he has sought help, and at the same time has spent more time with their little boy. She promises not to hold a grudge about the past when all this is done and dusted.

With John and Jolande, the community service took six months. Meanwhile, their second child was born and, as a closing ritual, they have spent a long weekend away together, without the children.

CHAPTER NINE

The reproduction of violence

Martine Groen

Children as witnesses

"Mummy has been irritated all day long and is muttering about everything we do. At the end of the day Daddy comes home. He is in a bad mood too and starts talking about his work to Mummy. They get into an argument and he threatens to hit her. She runs away and almost trips over Rob. He starts to yell, she hoists him up and throws him away. Rob just lies there on the floor. At first we think he is dead, but luckily he snaps out of it when Mummy shakes him to and fro."

Introduction

This chapter treats the subject of the abuse of children, characterized by extreme, escalating physical aggression between parents or by one of the parents, and of children who are witnessing the parental violence. Children between zero and seven years old are most at risk when confronted with the violent emotions of parents. The level of the divorce rate is very high in this phase of parenting.

Perhaps one of the factors contributing to the interactional escalation is a poor expectation of educating children, or a romantic expectation of bringing up children that is disappointed, or the pressures of managing children and work. Other reasons for the escalation of negative interactions between parents are poverty, debts, and transgenerational repetitive behaviour. Recently acquired knowledge about the influence of violent behaviour of parents or care-givers on the development of children shows how destructive this is and what the consequences could be.

Shame is one of the main emotions that causes violent behaviour of parents towards children, because it threatens the bond. Threatened or damaged bonds create an environment for conflict. Shame is an underestimated feeling, and the inability to acknowledge shame and the absence of a bond go together and escalate the spiral of conflict in families. Shame may be the most social of all emotions, since it functions as a signal of threat to the social bond (Sheff & Retzinger, 2001).

Humiliation, isolation, alienation, and resentment represent a shame–anger sequence in interactions in which anger is directed at another. These interactions weaken the bond and alienation threatens the integrity of the relationship.

There are perpetrators and victims. The position in the shame–anger sequence changes. The Conflict Tactics Scale (CTS) is an instrument that allows us to test what kind of escalating behaviour and violence we are dealing with.

- One parent abuses his partner and children.
- One parent abuses the other and the other parent abuses the children.
- Parents are violent towards each other and together abuse the children.
- One parent abuses the other and together they maltreat the children.
- Everyone in the family is shaming, humiliating, and violent towards each other, including the children towards their parents (Hamel, 2007).

Men are mostly the perpetrators because they are stronger and the beatings they can mete out are more severe. But recent research shows that women are as aggressive in violent interaction as men. They humiliate and intimidate in a similar way to men, and also abuse their control over men in the household.

This chapter describes the current knowledge regarding the influence that violence and threats between parents/guardians has on the development of children, the dynamics of violent emotions and behaviour in interaction, and the different survival strategies that children employ therein. Two case studies illustrate the counselling possibilities.

The consequences for children who have witnessed violence between parents

Children are forced into the role of witness. Literature shows (Benedek, 1985; McNally, 1993) that the feelings of disgust, shame, and powerlessness run deeper with witnesses than with perpetrators or victims, simply because children are not capable of preventing someone they love from being abused.

Four representative studies from the USA show that 11–20% of adults have memories of violent incidents within the family home (Henning, 1996). A representative study in the US from 1985 shows that 13% of adults have a memory of violent behaviour between their parents (Straus, 1992; Straus & Gelles, 1990). It is estimated that in 40–80% of the cases where violence takes place between parents or guardians, children are present (Jaffe, Wolfe, & Wilson, 1990). Despite all these figures it is difficult to know exactly how many children are witness to violence at home (Wolak & Finkelhor, 1996). The most recent research shows higher numbers. A major new study involving 453 couples with young children (Slep & O'Leary, 2005) found that bidirectional partner aggression occurred in 65% of the families, and 51% of couples engaged in both partner and child abuse.

Severe violence by father and mother and severe abuse of the child by either parent accounted for only 2% of families (Hamel, 2007).

In Holland, recent numbers of child abuse are impressive also in the light of the next generation: thirty children in 1000 are abused (Vrije Universiteit Amsterdam, 2007).

Symptoms

Almost all children who live with their mothers in a shelter for abused women can speak in detail about the violence they have witnessed (Jaffe, Wolfe, & Wilson, 1990, p. 20). Being witness to violence is often as traumatic as undergoing violence itself. In Israel, research has been done with several groups of children, those who have been beaten and those who have witnessed beatings (Sternberg, 1993). Both groups show the same score regarding complaints about depression. Yet another study shows that a child who has been a witness of violence will have more behavioural problems. Herein, two categories of symptoms can be detected: complaints that are turned inward and behavioral disorders that are turned outward.

Examples of inward-turned complaints are avoidance behaviour or falling silent, avoiding people and places where the violence has been experienced, loss of abilities they have only just mastered (such as potty-training), recurrence of just conquered fears (being afraid of the dark, for instance), sadness, depression, retreating behaviour, and extreme shyness (McNally, 1993). These children are at risk of numerous psychotic symptoms (Pynoos & Eth, 1984, 1985). Dissociated complaints occur as well: loss of memory at certain moments, unwillingness to think about it any more, derealization, depersonalization, a fragmented memory.

Outward-turned complaints are categorized under re-enactment: repetitive talking about what has happened, repeating what was witnessed, nightmares, flashbacks (Drell, Siegel, & Gaensbauer, 1993). Living within a violent family for a prolonged period of time will bring about chronic complaints of stress. Chronic stress changes the body and the function of the brain and, as a consequence, the ability to mentalize. This mental processing of emotional and cognitive functioning is blocked and disturbed and sometimes destroyed. These characteristics are typical of post traumatic stress syndrome: re-enactment of experiences of violence, extreme despair, anguish, fear, sadness, powerless anger, mood-swings, hyperactivity, hyperalertness and repetitive behaviour. To conclude, there are also complaints which are hallmarked by an autonomous state of anxiety, such as insomnia, loss of concentration, impulsivity, and seemingly uncontrollable fits of anger

(McLeer, Deblinger, Atkins, Foa, & Ralphe, 1988). Others mention worryingly nervous behaviour and physical complaints such as nausea, headaches, double vision, stomach-aches, and loss of appetite (Davidson & Baum, 1990).

This elucidation of the multitude of complaints shows the complexity of this issue and how diverse children might react to similar experiences.

Survival mechanisms

Born out of the need to survive, children are very flexible and are capable of adapting to the most bizarre circumstances. They develop ingenious survival mechanisms that offer them a chance to come out of all this relatively well. Some children have developed an enormous capacity for dissociation. Others develop all kinds of phobic or avoidance behaviour. Several theories have been developed as to why one child shows signs of behavioural disorders while another does not. A point of view within modern trauma theory (McCann & Pearlman, 1990, among others) is that the extent to which an event is experienced as being traumatic depends on the personal capacity of an individual to give experiences of violence a place in his or her life. Research literature shows that if traumatic experiences defy one's ability to find solutions from within, the chances of becoming unhinged increase tenfold. The endured pain sets biological and psychological defence mechanisms in motion. Children who have had little chance to attach themselves to the main carer have little self-awareness at their disposal. They have not learnt where their "self" is limited by others. They have had little practice in regulating feelings. These children run the highest risk of behavioural disorders.

One has studied thoroughly through theoretical models (Deblinger, McLeer, & Henry, 1990; Keane, Zimmerling, & Caddell, 1985) what it is that children learn when they are unexpectedly and randomly confronted with awful and violent situations and how they avoid the painful emotions that go with it. Children who have witnessed violence at a young age have not yet learnt how to regulate their feelings. Intensely painful feelings are conjured up without being set in order (unconditional aversive stimulus) (Kilpatrick,

Veronen, & Best, 1985). Once children have learned to set emotions in order, the feelings that are tied to the traumatic event will function as acquired behaviour. Often, children cannot remember where these intense reactions stem from when they are engulfed by fear. In everyday life, children and young adults find themselves in many situations that can function as a trigger. A trigger is a symbol that reminds one of an awful experience. It could be a minor detail: a sound, a smell, a colour, often undetectable to others.

According to these theoretical models, violent events lead to helplessness and powerless behaviour. Children will develop an impaired motivation to deal with new stressful situations; they are at risk of depression, resulting in a destroyed self-image. They feel unable to curb, as they see it, transgressive and unchangeable tensions and events (Boggiano, Barrett, Silvern, & Gallo, 1991). Several authors put the emphasis elsewhere when they write about the survival mechanisms of children who have witnessed violence. Some (Foa & Kozak, 1986; Foa, Steketee & Rothbaum, 1989) say that children no longer believe that their world is a safe place. This felt insecurity becomes the driving force behind their actions.

Children who are witness to abuse against their mother and/or siblings often play a part in the downward spiral of violence. They contribute to easing the tensions that are already present, or they take on the role of lightning rod in order to divert and stem the tensions within the family.

> Bloeme knows that her mother cannot stand her and her sister fighting. "Mummy starts yelling really loud. Daddy often intervenes. It all depends on his mood if he can stand it or not. If he feels too angered about it all he will first throw stuff around and if he has not calmed down enough, Mummy will get hit. We either look or hide in our room. Mummy starts to cry awfully hard."

The transference of aggression within families where abuse takes place is linked to the gender of the child (Jourilles & LeCompte, 1991; see Chapter Six, also). Girls tend to aim felt fear and anger inward. Boys have the tendency to behave more aggressively in reaction to their mother being abused. This image is underpinned by an American study that shows the link between aggressive and criminal behaviour of boys and a father behaving aggressively. Boys who have fled with their families and who have witnessed acts of war and butchering also have a tendency to repeat the explosive aggressive behaviour. The war situations witnessed on the streets are often re-enacted within a group.

Development phase

Children who have been confronted with life-threatening situations show, in general, the same survival strategies as adults: denial, repression, dissociation, and identification with the aggressor. Feelings of fear, despair, and helplessness form the basis for the development of symptoms. The ability to find solutions for stressful situations depends on the age, gender, development phase of the child, the child's place within the family, and the context within which a child is growing up. Research literature shows that mothers are twice more likely to abuse their children if they themselves are being abused. The abuse of children ceases or decreases once they have ended the relationship themselves (Saunders, 1993). It does not come as a surprise that mothers who are unable to stand up against violent behaviour will take it out on their children. Mood-swings and sudden outbursts of anger are part of post traumatic stress symptoms.

The development phase of children plays a role in the way they themselves handle and shape whatever they have experienced into acceptable or manageable experiences by their own standards. Very young children (28–36 months) who cannot yet speak of what has happened show agitated and unco-ordinated behaviour (Terr, 1991, p. 15).

Children between the ages of three and five who show avoidance behaviour (especially girls) tend to cling more to their parents, which makes them less able to detach themselves from their parents later on. Children avoid getting into interactions that could enhance that attachment. They avoid standing up for themselves and comforting themselves. They dissociate the painful feelings (Briere, 1992) and tend to take care of their mother or the other children. Their social skills with other children are disrupted too; the ability to make friends diminishes. This lack could become a large obstacle to coping in later life.

Primary school children re-enact with their classmates what they have seen at home. Boys, especially, can copy their parent's aggressive behaviour through bullying and fighting. They are more at risk of being shunned. Sometimes, they seem to avoid this by forming their own violent gang.

Between the age of seven and nine, children develop the ability for self-reflection. They are able to take in several dimensions of reality simultaneously. They are capable of recognizing different feelings alongside each other and of forming a judgement about the parental behaviour. This ability is, of course, limited as yet. However, children begin to understand how parents regard them and that often results in feelings being hurt and sadness. It is hard to bear for children to see rows festering within the home. They feel powerless because there is nothing that they can do about it.

Children between the age of nine and thirteen can no longer avoid the fact that something is definitely amiss at home. In most cases, they have developed a preference for one of the parents with whom they have some secret bond. They will tread cautiously in order not to hurt the other parent needlessly, and they tend to distance themselves from the battle between the parents. If the beatings by the father are on a regular basis, the temptation looms large to choose the mother's side. Choosing for one parent becomes more apparent and gender-specific in the next development phase. The hyperactive, regressive behaviour and concentration disorders, which are the consequences of the situation at home, are often hard to handle within the classroom. As said before, boys react more actively and aggressively than girls. Of course, such behaviour is noticed in the classroom and, as a result, children are often referred. They get special attention but no connection is made between their behaviour and the violence at home. Often "remedial teaching" is offered as a solution, but without much success. This comes down to the lack of expertise within the school. School doctors, who could take on the role of experts, have sadly disappeared into the background (de Savornin Lohman, 1997). If school doctors saw children more often, intervention could take place sooner.

Studies such as that by Johnston (1993) show that boys between the age of thirteen and fifteen are more likely to display behavioural disorders than girls. In most literature (Girshick, 1993; Sudermann & Jaffe, 1993) a connection is made between growing up in a violent environment and the occurrence of violent behaviour in later life, where one acts either as the perpetrator or the victim. Not everyone who stems from a violent environment will repeat the violence from their youth. On the other hand, studies show that 30% of boys who display sexual and physical aggression towards women come from a violent background. This figure coincides with the numbers that apply to adult relationships. Youths in this category show similar behaviour to that of adults who interact in a violent manner (Girshick, 1993; Walker, 1989): tension-building, outbursts of anger, and attempts at reconciliation. The violent behaviour in this age group shows a broad spectrum, from hitting and pushing to threatening, intimidation, and grave violence (Bethke & DeJoy, 1993).

The re-enactment of parental behaviour is underpinned by three theories: the theory of social learning, attachment theory, and the feminist theory about the reproduction of the imbalance of power. The first theory does not focus solely on the message of the parents that violent behaviour is an acceptable way to solve conflicts; this theory also describes the influence of the media and that of the current norms and values which surround us (Emery, 1989; Jaffe, Wolfe, & Wilson, 1990). Attachment theory is focused inward and shows just how vital parental care and protection is with regard to the development of children (Alexander, 1992; Bowlby, 1988; Cicchetti & Barnett, 1992). The main focus within attachment theory is the formation of an inner model, "the hard disc" of the computer, a mental construction within the attachment to a carer, which forms the basis of the personality. If this does not take place, the attachment process will be blocked. It is hard for children to build up self-confidence within an unsafe environment and to form a positive image of the world. The manner in which children learn to attach is repeated in adulthood; in general, one looks for whatever feels familiar. A constant effort is needed from the adult in order to overcome the consequences of experiences of violence from childhood (Dijkstra, 2002).

From the feministic perspective, the imbalance of power between the sexes and the condescending treatment of girls and women is regarded as the underlying cause of violence against women (Dobash & Dobash, 1992; Jaffe & Hastings, 1995; Miedzian, 1995). However, the paradox is that a diminishing in the imbalance of power increases the violent behaviour of boys rather than decreasing it. The balance of authority between men and women has changed. Obedience is required within a balance of authority. Wherever violence is used, authority has failed. Authority is incompatible with persuasion. Persuasion presupposes equality and is rooted in arguments. Argumentation excludes authority (Arendt, 1994). Women's emancipation has breached the obvious authority that men have over women. It has become increasingly difficult for men and boys to maintain a certain attitude when it comes to wooing girls; one can detect a cause of violent behaviour within this as well (Van Stolk & Wouters, 1983; Woltring, 1988).

Two case studies

In the following cases, the different ways in which children choose a survival strategy which is key to the surroundings in which they live are demonstrated.

Clara would like to go into counselling. She would like to be supported in raising her son. Ever since the divorce, he has displayed phobic behaviour of a compulsive character. Her son Jan is twelve years old and he is unable to leave the house before having walked up and down the stairs twenty times. He has to have three showers and to walk around his room ten times before he can do anything else. He is undergoing counselling with a psychologist who gives him behavioural therapy and who tries to discuss the ramifications of the divorce with him.

Clara is a lecturer at a university but is unable to work because of her son's behaviour and the distress caused by the divorce. She has taken sick leave. Her ex-husband is a surgeon who is very well known in the town. She still sees him regularly. According to Clara, they have a close but complicated bond, and they disagree about how to deal with their son.

In the following meeting, her ex-husband Piet attends. He is nervous and immediately grabs the bull by the horns on entering. It is not his fault that the boy, their son, shows such behaviour. He blames his wife's boundaryless behaviour. If she would toughen up her act, lay down more boundaries, then everything would soon blow over.

During the weekends that Jan spends with him and his new wife, he does not suffer from his compulsive behaviour. Clara yells that Jan, once back home from his visit, displays ritual behaviour that is tenfold worse. At my request, they recount how painful and complicated the divorce has been for both of them. He does not want to lose his son, but senses being shut out by Clara at every level. She is jealous of his new wife, and blames him for her being abandoned.

In the third session, their son Jan and his psychologist are both present as well. It is customary within our practice to invite all involved consultants. It could result in more information being available and improve co-operation. In this session, I interview both parents in order to hear how they deal with Jan's serious complaint. It transpires that the parents quarrel about how to improve the care. The father thinks a strict approach is the way to go about it, while the mother engages more with Jan's ritual acts. Jan says there is nothing to be done about it, because there is a demon within him which he can only control in this manner. To try to trace the demon, I ask where it is coming from and when he got into Jan. Jan says, "I'm not sure if I can say it here. He appears in my nightmares and orders me to do certain things every day." Jan can hardly manage to go to school. He has to rise earlier each day in order to execute the ritual acts.

Therapist: "Who will it harm if you tell us what the demon orders you to do?"

Jan: "My parents." He retreats and doesn't say another word.

Therapist: "What would happen if you let the demon tell it?"

Jan: "I don't know if the demon wants to."

Therapist: "Could you ask permission? It might be a good idea not to say it but to show it on paper or with the dolls."

Jan starts to draw, and a beating couple appears on the piece of paper. His father is hitting his mother, who is down on the floor.

Therapist: "When your parents are having a row, do they hit each other?" Jan confirms this and looks down. His psychologist encourages him. Jan says that when he was eight years old his parents had fierce blazing rows. He stood frozen at the top of the stairs and looked on and saw his mother crying and falling. His father would beat her hard, yell at her, and humiliate her. This happened on a regular basis. The image of this one row where her mother defended herself with a knife keeps coming back.

Jan tells how awful he felt about not being able to help anyone. The beatings went from bad to worse. Jan could no longer concentrate at school; he retreated and found no pleasure in school activities. His fears got the upper hand. Now he can only exist if he does whatever the demon tells him to do, then he is at peace.

Jan tries to banish the images, as it were, with his ritual acts. He does not fight, but flees, retreats, and can no longer recall that his behaviour is linked to the violent rows of his parents. His inner conflict has been suppressed and his fear emerges in another shape. His nightmares and fears are related to the images of his parents' rows. He is so scared of his father that he retreats and has to perform the ritual acts in his mother's house in order to suppress the images.

Both of Jan's parents listen with rising bewilderment to the observations of their son and they are both ashamed. The father tries to marginalize the violence. The mother becomes enraged and recounts how bad it has been.

Therapist: "Jan, in what manner do your parents argue now when they disagree about you?" Together with the parents we make an inventory of the ways in which they argue.

Jan: "He doesn't hit her so much nowadays, sometimes now and again, when they both drink too much."

Later on during the session the violent behaviour of the father, Piet, is discussed; how and when he loses self-control and what he can do to avoid it. He will walk out if he feels the tension rising in his body. An agreement is made that Clara will curb her provocative behaviour. She will limit her derogatory language and reproaches. She will write him letters in which she will try to voice her anger and pain about the divorce. Jan is asked to point out when the tension between his parents increases again. Although the responsibility lies with the parents, of course, it is important in my experience to involve children in the agreed changes in behaviour. The sense of being able to make a contribution could contribute towards recuperation from the endured powerlessness. Jan can stop the exorcizing behaviour and his psychologist can support him in coping with his pain.

In this example, one was able to ask Jan to describe the images that are going round in his mind. However, prudence is called for. It is vital not to put children in a position of betraying anything. This can conjure up a lot of guilt and worsen the complaints. On the other hand, it is good to keep asking specific questions. The safety of children has to be guaranteed, too. It is a dilemma.

Sometimes, behavioural disorders are so severe that it becomes difficult to detect what caused the development of such behaviour. A biological component might also play a part. Fear can affect all areas of life. One often forgets where they are coming from. Jan and his parents had become so preoccupied by his rituals that all attention was diverted to this behaviour. The care for Jan bonded the couple once more. On another level, it was, for Jan, a way to keep the tension in his body in check, which was, as it were, a repetition of what had taken place. The rituals that Jan developed, with an internal logic of their own, fitted this frame. He felt as if he had failed because he could not protect his mother and he was convinced that he was a coward. He had to pay for that. He had developed his rituals in such a way that they could only be performed with the greatest of effort.

Children independently develop rituals in order to cope with the fears in life. They do this especially in the transition from primary to secondary school or from kindergarten to primary school (Guggenbühl, 1996). Rituals are also developed in order to survive violent situations. Because children are incapable of controlling these situations, they try to ward off their fears by inflicting on themselves a pain that they are able to bear, for example, by hitting themselves until they can barely take it any more. Every child experiences fear when he goes from one development phase to another. Most of the time magical incantations are developed, like walking past a tree at a certain time, talking to it, or walking on the pavement in a certain manner.

If they grow up in a violent atmosphere where tension and stress are part of everyday life, they must find a way out for the despair, anger, pain, and sadness which form an extra burden on top of the fears which are inherent to growing up. It seems logical that suitable rituals will be invented.

In Western society, transition rituals have all but vanished. As described by Van Gennep (1981) and Campbell (1983), special transition rituals are carried out in many cultures in the transition from childhood into adolescence and from adolescence into adulthood. The child has to undergo a test in order to reach the next phase of life. In such ceremonies or initiation rites the boys will have to endure pain before they can be embraced into the world of adult men. They say farewell to the women's world. In the aboriginals in Arnhemland, this involves their having to lie in the sun for hours until they are almost dried out. Only then will they be initiated into the secrets of the tribe (Guggenbühl, 1996).

It is remarkable that fear plays a dominant role within all these initiation rites. Children learn, backed by a community, to conquer their fear and to bear pain. That gives self-confidence. The importance of these rites is that fear is channelled and given its place in life. It seems a pity that there are no more rituals left in modern society that make regulating fear possible. In this void, children, like Jan, are tempted to develop personal rites that will enable them to control the fears in their lives. However, these private rites are not sufficient to compensate for the lack of collective rites.

In the next case, the son tries to find another solution. In a sense, the violent behaviour is ritualized, only not focused inward, but also outward.

This case is about Norma (44), her husband Hans (40), and their son Floor (16). At the initial session I only saw Norma; Hans did not want to come yet.

Norma is tiny and slim, almost skinny. Hans is 6ft 7in, heavily built, and a former judoka champion. Their son, Floor, is heavily built as well.

The beatings had started within the first three weeks of their dating. He admits to having "itchy hands". They went through all the phases of the downward spiral of violence as described in Chapter Three. She found him to be a rock, after countless bad relationships, but she really minds the beatings; she should not have accepted it. But he always makes up for it, and after the "honeymoon" period the beatings start afresh. He works as a bouncer in the catering industry and she works at a department store. Their daily life is badly tuned to each other. He works primarily at night and she works during the day. That causes a lot of tension. Twice monthly the conflicts reach their peak. After seventeen years, Norma is fed up. She hardly eats, and she sleeps with a knife under her pillow. Their son threatens to run away, he cannot take it any more. The violence in the relationship has increased ever since she found out, a year ago, that her husband had fallen in love with someone else. She does not trust him at all now, and increasingly argues about the other woman.

After two sessions with her alone, her husband comes along, too. His physique is so impressive that one wonders why he would need to beat at all. To begin with, he says that he has beaten up eight boys who had threatened him at work. He intended to threaten the therapist, too, because he is afraid that the sessions will break up the relationship with Norma. He says that he has come along to help her. Because he took the first step into talking about beating, it is only a small step to deepen the subject. He knows that he is overstepping boundaries. He is prepared to take responsibility for this. If he feels taunted by her, especially when she treads on his toes, he will snap.

Norma: "You start hitting when I threaten to walk out, you can't stand that."

Hans: "I'm not afraid of that, but I can't stand you yelling at me all the time. I just want to shut you up."

At the end of the session the following agreement is made: they both want their relationship to improve, especially for their son, Floor. The boy is not doing well at school. He has got involved with a school gang and terrorizes the schoolyard and the school itself. The school staff have given signals that they are no longer prepared to put up with the aggressive behaviour. The police have been informed about the gang's activities, but have not intervened as yet. The boy's education is important to both parents.

She really does want to end the relationship if the rows keep escalating. She has reached her limit, especially after this affair.

During the session, it transpires that there are plenty of areas left which they share pleasurably, although this has declined significantly over the last two years.

Hans: "I can understand her, she is very angry with me because of this love-affair. It does bother me, but it has to fade away slowly, it'll take time."

We agree that they both want to improve the situation. They want to learn how to control the rows at an earlier stage. They would rather smash up a cupboard than kick or beat each other.

Floor, their son, comes along at the fourth session. His involvement in the rows is discussed.

Floor: "I often intervene and I run off once I see that look on his face. That's when I think: Let them deal with it themselves. It used to scare me, now I'm just fed up."

Floor and the father are similar in a lot of ways. Once they start talking they cannot stop; words are fired off through the room like machine-gun fire. The father does not hit Floor, but they do throw dinner-plates at one another. Floor describes in detail what happens when there is a row. Nowadays, it happens when his mother mentions the other woman's name; she becomes fierce and starts to yell. His father gets up and walks out. She goes after him and starts calling him names. He goes into the garden, into his hobby-shed, and tries to escape her voice. She pursues him and starts kicking him. He gets angry and hits her. She yells even louder and tries to hurt him.

Floor: "When I was a child, I tried to stand up for my mother, but now I realize that she is addicted to these rows, too. I don't want to have anything to do with it any more. I've wanted them to split up for so long. I find them both awful."

If there are no tensions in the home they will do anything for each other. Floor thinks his father has to control himself. He also thinks that his mother goes too far. The tendency to protect is still playing tricks on him. What can he do when things are escalating at home? Floor wants to co-operate, but he has not got a clue how to go about this. The father says he will walk out if she starts about the other woman again. She promises not to go after him any more.

Floor's behaviour at school is discussed. Floor says that he is not solely responsible for it, but that he is influenced by his friends. He, too, finds it hard to take responsibility for his violent behaviour at school. The father demands that he will draw up a programme in order to control his aggressive outbursts, just as he is doing himself.

In this case there is a clear link between the aggressive behaviour of Hans and the re-enactment of it by Floor. The parents in both cases are so preoccupied with their relational rows that they pay no attention to the importance of their son's behaviour. Jan did his utmost to ward off his fears by developing compulsive rituals and Floor wards off his fears by repetitive behaviour at school.

Conclusion

Children risk emotional and behavioural disturbances when they witness or experience violent behaviour. Survival strategies of children are stress-orientated and so the flight, fight, or freeze tendencies are seen. Emotions such as fear, despair, and helplessness often play a role in symptom forming.

The repetition of violent behaviour in adulthood is estimated at 30–80%, and this number is still being researched. What is clear is that in intimate relationships, the repetition is more often reported. Boys and girls react differently; boys primarily react more outwardly and girls more inwardly.

The reproduction of violence at school, on the streets, and at home is a concern for all of us.

To restrict the violence in the way we describe in the therapeutic setting can be of help. The contract with the partners in violence can break the spiral of violence; also, psycho-education about the consequences for their children can motivate parents to develop an other style of conflict management. If a contract is not sufficient, then the law is on our side and sanctions can follow. In the Netherlands, at present, the most extreme sanction, besides prison, is that the police can, on the decision of the mayor of a village or town, force the perpetrator out of the house for at least a month. The desire to limit shameful behaviour through education is very popular on television, and consequent in punishment and positive attention.

Rituals can be very helpful in structuring phases in education and in the lifespan, and possibly the lack of rites of passage is also due to the escalation of interactions in relationships. Rituals could be reinvented in society if there is a need for them.

The two cases featured illustrated that, for children, it is very helpful to include them in the treatment if violence is in the home.

In the USA, group therapy is developed for parents to manage stress and conflict and also for children to overcome the stress-related symptoms and to control their behaviour.

CHAPTER TEN

Of young rulers and the terror at home

Justine van Lawick

Introduction

This chapter deals with another form of violence within families: that perpetrated by children against their parents. Increasingly, there is mention of children, teenagers, and adolescents who treat their parents with violence. This goes so much against all expectations regarding normal family life that many may find it hard to believe that it occurs on a regular basis. Society's acceptance of children hitting their parents is even less than that of parents who hit. Because the abuse of parents goes against the prevailing norms, parents are often deeply ashamed when it does happen and try to hide it in every possible way. Therefore, it is a group that hardly ever has been studied. A study in the USA (Harbin & Madden, 1979) into fifteen families wherein an adolescent between fourteen and twenty years old abused the parents, shows that these parents suffer from fear, depression, and a strong sense of guilt. They try to trivialize and to gloss over their children's behaviour, and desperately try to keep up the image of a harmonious family. This denial leads to the adolescents not being sanctioned for the abuse they have committed and to the parents not seeking help. In a study by Cornell and Gelles (1982), during a representative random test of American families with a teenager between ten and seventeen years old, 9% of the parents reported at least one violent act perpetrated by the teenager against them.

Children are also capable of killing their parents. Again, statistics from the USA show that between 1977 and 1986 it appeared that one in every eleven family killings featured children who kill their parents (Heide, 1995). The children in these cases state the murder to be the result of years of abuse, sexual abuse, and humiliation by the parents. In 85% of the cases, the perpetrator is a son. Only in a small number of cases does the child appear to suffer from a mental disorder, or have an antisocial disorder (*ibid.*).

If we combine the study results with our own clinical findings, it appears to be about different groups. The first group consists of youngsters who, as children, have endured much abuse and sexual abuse at the hands of their parents and who have witnessed a lot of violence between the parents. With these youngsters, the use of violence in conflicts has become part of the behavioural repertoire. Furthermore, if the child had been seriously abused, anger and feelings of vengeance against the parents play a role.

Another group comprises children and youngsters who do not seem to accept authority and who will use violence rather easily if they are being frustrated. They cause problems at school, at home, and on the streets. With both these groups, the problem of addiction is an enhancing factor. These youngsters will terrorize their parents on a regular basis in order to fund their addiction; moreover, the use of stimulants itself will lead to aggressive outbursts (Bentinck, Duintjer, van der Post, & van Weeren, 1986).

Omer (2003) studied this group and worked with them and their families. He developed a therapy model called "non-violent resistance".

The group of youngsters who resist authority and society while they themselves have been spared the rod in their upbringing accounts for the increase in violence perpetrated by youngsters. The group who had suffered abuse themselves and who re-enact violent behaviour, appears not to have increased as such (Van den Brink, 2001).

Is there an increase in violence in the Netherlands?

If we study the statistics of registered violent criminal offences, there is a notable decrease of violent criminal offences after the Second World War up until 1975. It is safe to presume that people were scared stiff and that violence was taboo after the atrocities of the Second World War. A lot of attention went into rebuilding the country and politically it was a period of bloom for the pacifist and peace movements. Within families, too, authority, punishment, and hitting were no longer accepted and one can detect a transition from "households of orders" to "households of negotiations" (De Swaan, 1982). One worked towards a society where negotiation would lead to solutions and where violence would decrease exponentially. After 1975, this image underwent radical changes. Between 1975 and 1995, the number of registered violent criminal offences had tripled; this goes for life-threatening offences (murder and attempted murder) as much as for abuse. It is remarkable that the number of registered sexual offences has not increased and in itself does not represent a high percentage of the registered criminal offences. In 1975, the annual statistics for sexual offences was 51 per 100,000 residents, in 1995 it was 48; the annual statistics for registered abuse cases per 100,000 residents was 72 in 1975 and 181 in 1995. If we look at the statistics regarding youngsters, the discrepancy is even larger: the number of sexual offences remains at 50 reports per 100,000 residents annually, whereas the registered cases of abuse soared from 59 in 1975 to 256 in 1995 (Van den Brink, 2001; Wittebrood, 1998). For a long time, within the Mental Health Service, the emphasis had been more on sexual violence than on any other forms of violence. The statistics underpin our proposition that more attention to the problems surrounding physical violence is of the utmost importance and, frankly, unavoidable. Part of the increase in registered violent criminal offences can be explained by an improved system of registration. Specialists in this field all agree that this does not explain the strong increase as a whole. There is more to it. Previously mentioned statistics also show that violence among youngsters is on the increase more than that among adults. We feel safe in presuming that the registered violent criminal offences are just the tip of the iceberg. Most violent criminal offences are not registered. A self-report among youngsters in 1996

(Van der Laan, Essers, Huijbregts, & Spaans, 1998) shows that 34% had reported involvement in a fight or riots, 33% had taken part in vandalism, and 33% had regularly carried a weapon. Self-report also shows a strong growth in being involved in a riot or fight; the figures went up between 1990 and 1996 by 119%. This is almost exclusively a boy thing. Although violent behaviour is on the increase among girls, too, this trend is not as strong and they account for 10% at most of the total of criminal offences. This goes for both registered offences and for self-reporting.

Several explanations can be given for this. Ethologists often point out the similarity with the behaviour of chimpanzees (De Waal, 1982). Young male chimps busy themselves with obtaining the highest possible position within the hierarchy of the group. They do this through imposing behaviour, fighting, and by forming coalitions. Young female chimps busy themselves with personal contacts, involvements, and sympathy. We can detect the same with people: with boys the group seems to be of the utmost importance. A group consists of a leader and a varying number of hangers-on. Boys like to be a part of the group and "score high" within the group. Boys behave boisterously, aggressively, and "big" within the group of teenagers; they try to impress and form coalitions with the popular and powerful leaders. Girls are more interested in empathy and antipathy and prefer to have a best friend with whom to discuss things. The biological factor of the male and female hormones is often cited as an explanation for this. The male testosterone would boost aggressive behaviour. In the introduction, we have already mentioned the importance of gender differences in masculine and feminine behaviour within human relationships, but these factors do not explain the strong increase in violent behaviour among youngsters. There are several explanations possible for this increase.

In this book, we focus mainly on violence in families. I would like to limit myself here especially to the changes which have taken place within the Dutch family structure.

Changes within family life

From the 1960s onwards, much has changed in Dutch family life. Thanks to contraception, one has a larger say in the number of children one has, which makes every child a wanted child, almost without exception. Secularization has contributed as well. The authority of the vicar or the priest, who would like to have seen many "gifts from God" born into the family, weakened, and parents took their decisions autonomously in this respect. Under the influence of women's liberation, women were able to be educated and started to work *en masse*. Families became smaller, and the age at which women would conceive their first child increased steadily. Around the turn of the century, the average age for a Dutch woman to give birth to her first child was almost thirty. There is a more egalitarian division of roles between man and wife, and the raising and guiding of children is increasingly regarded as a vital and joint task of both parents. Van den Brink (2001) proposes that this, in turn, has increased self-esteem in children. There is more parental attention per child and the attention and time parents spend with their children have increased rather than decreased. Children get the message that they are important and precious to their parents. In the 1950s, most fathers had to work hard to keep the economical situation of the large family sound, and mothers busied themselves almost full-time with the time-consuming household chores. Raising the children was a marginal thing, considering all these activities. After 1960, the efforts that parents made for their children increased, and with that their expectations. The use of emotional rewards is increasing, especially with regard to good achievements. Parents appear to demand much of their children with regard to social achievements. It is no longer about helping out with the household chores or doing your bit for the family income. Parents invest longer in their children and children find themselves increasingly at the receiving end. What children can give to their parents in return is to "end up well". The relations within the family have become more egalitarian. Children have their own autonomous voice, which is heard "loud and clear". They have become more assertive and have more power. Van den Brink assumes that the increased position of power, together with increased assertiveness, will make them vulnerable and easily offended. The link to violent behaviour has been described by the American psychologist Baumeister (1997), on whose work, among others, Van den Brink has based his own. It is often presumed that violence is linked to a low self-esteem, Baumeister switches this around. Violent youngsters have a strongly developed, but, at the same time, vulnerable sense of self-esteem. If they feel threatened therein, they will proceed to violent behaviour. There is—according to Van den Brink—a field of tension between the increased self-awareness and the increase in demands that are put on children. He calls this the field of tension between the stimulated assertiveness of the child and the sociability which is simultaneously expected by its environment.

Omer (2003) has a different point of view; he found that children who are raised in a permissive educational atmosphere do not develop a steady sense of self-worth. Because the parents continuously give them the feedback that everything they do is good, they do not develop tolerance of frustration and they do not learn to overcome difficulties. When everything is good, there is no meaning to it.

All authors agree that a permissive educational climate creates vulnerable children that are not able to tolerate frustration; they act aggressively and intimidatingly when they are frustrated.

In addition, in society as a whole, tolerance towards aggressive behaviour of teenage boys seems to have diminished. In an egalitarian society, extra emphasis is laid on socially acceptable behaviour and respect for one's fellow man. Recruitment advertisements, too, show that basic social skills have increasingly become part of the normal *curriculum vitae*. Because assertiveness and aggressive behaviour of youngsters have increased at the same time, a strong growth in unwanted behaviour can be detected.

Personally, I think that there is another factor at play here. Because of women's liberation, an increasing number of girls have followed an education. They form the greater part of the higher levels of secondary education and they appear to be better at it than boys. Universities, too, show a strongly growing number of female students, and in the more traditional male studies such as medicine and law, more than half of the student population is female now. Education has become more female-friendly. On average, girls are better at languages than boys, and language has become increasingly important within education. Examination subjects, too, have many verbal assignments and talks, as do school papers; they are all part of the regular educational programme. In addition, women have a positive goal to reach for: to increase the number of women at higher positions within science, politics, and business. Through-out all layers of the population, both with the autochthonic and the migrant population, the self-awareness of women seems to be on the increase. Boys, however, appear to be less sure of their position as men: on average, they seem to be less successful in education, with regard to women they are not sure what is expected of them, and they lack a specific target to aim at. They find themselves in an existential crisis, whereas girls appear to be more self-aware. Boys compensate for this tension with aggressive, intimidating, and violent behaviour in order to restore their bruised egos.

Violent youngsters and attachment

Weerman (1998) conducted a study into criminal delinquents and concluded that the attachments of criminal delinquents with regard to their parents/carers, school, society, and work are not as tight as those of non-criminal youths. Violent delinquent boys comment more negatively about their parents; they also appear to be less bothered about them and withdraw from the supervision of parents or other carers. They are the children whom parents feel disap-pointed in and they see their parents often as distant and dismis-sive and therefore they feel neglected and rejected. They do not feel at ease at school and value an education less than non-violent youths. They also have less strong ties to the community than non-violent youths. They are not interested in politics and regard soci-ety as hostile. They find work and a career not important. The only thing that they invest in more than non-violent youths is friendship. They spend more time on friends who are part of the same crimi-nal circuit and value this more.

Weerman based his study on the theory of Travis Hirschi, who proposed in 1969 that criminality could be connected to a lack of attachment. Therefore, the attention has shifted from social circum-stances to personal factors. The hypothesis of social neglect has not been confirmed time and again. There seems to be no proven link between social circumstances and criminality. There are two notable exceptions. One is the traditional underbelly of society; these people have lived for generations in the impoverished neighbour-hoods of the towns, the parents are low-skilled, learning difficulties are common, and there is much alcoholism and unemployment. Parents often feel powerless with regard to raising their children and often resort to physical punishments; there is a lot of beating within the partner relationship, too. Children often play truant and leave school at an early age. Social services are often unable to get a grip on these families, so things hardly ever change for the better. Within this group, violence is handed down from one generation to the next, but there is no noticeable increase in violence. Therefore, these families do not fall within the analysis regarding the increase of violence among youngsters.

The other group wherein social neglect might play a part are certain allochtonous groups. There seems to be an overrepresentation of different ethnic minority groups within the criminal statistics. Especially, Antillean and Moroccan youths between the ages of twelve and seventeen show an overrepresentation in violent criminal offences (De Haan & De Bie, 1999). It is difficult to interpret these statistics correctly. Both cultural and social factors probably play a role therein. The contrast between a patriarchal, hierarchical way of raising a child within the family and the more permissive style within Dutch society also creates confusion and possible detachment with all involved. I cannot elaborate further on this within the scope of this chapter, but it is obvious that much research needs to be done in this area in order for preventative measures to be taken.

As stated before, the hypothesis of social neglect does not apply to the largest group of violent youngsters. The hypothesis of a link between violent behaviour and the quality of attachments appears to be acknowledged even more. The quality of the relationships between parents and children, the depth of mutual involvement, and the atmosphere in general appear to influence violent behaviour. Divorce seems to be a risk-enhancing factor, but this could be blamed on the bad atmosphere before, during, and after the divorce procedure rather than on the divorce itself. It appears that a lot of fighting, name-calling, and threatening to walk out have the same risk-enhancing effect, even if the parents do not divorce (Bol, Terlouw, Blees, & Verwers, 1998).

The defining factor would be how the youngster perceives the parents. It appears that parents of violent youths do not bestow less time, attention, and money on their children. However, there are more conflicts about school results and school behaviour, the company of friends, the behaviour at home, and plans for the future. Violent youngsters seem to be less bothered about the opinions and desires of the parents with regard to all this than nonviolent youngsters. It is understandable that both parents and youngsters find themselves trapped within a negative downward spiral. The youngster does not fulfil the expectations of the parents (any longer), who get increasingly frustrated that all their investments are running aground. Parents lose their grip on their child and are less willing to invest any longer. The child's school results start to suffer, and the child feels as if it has failed. To maintain its self-image, the child is increasingly defiant and starts to socialize with children who use aggression and violence. Parents become more and more disillusioned and behave dismissively. For the youngster, the path back to education and work becomes increasingly difficult to reach (Bol, Terlouw, Blees, & Verwers, 1998).

Individual characteristics

Individual characteristics appear to play a part in this. Loeber and Farrington (1998) studied individual factors which might predict violent behaviour in youngsters and came to the following risk-enhancing characteristics: complications during pregnancy and birth; hyperactivity during the primary school years; restless behaviour and problems with concentration; aggressive behaviour at a young age; reckless behaviour; and poor self-control.

Detecting problem factors that could be an indication for violent behaviour at an early stage in individual children could be important. A study by Doreleyers (1995) shows that, with delinquent youths, we should be mindful also of psychopathological factors. His study shows that there is a much higher rate of psychopathology among young criminals than in those youths who do not cross swords with the law. Attention deficit hyperactivity disorder (ADHD) often crops up. Doreleyers advocates early detection of this psychopathology in order to render an adequate treatment possible, to support parents, and to be able to work pre-emptively. I do not want to get involved in the "nature–nurture" debate, but I do assume that psychopathology is often a combination of predisposition and environmental influences. It is important not to lose sight of the aspect "predisposition" in order not to put the blame on the parents automatically: "It is because of their lax discipline that their child has become such an utter brat."

To discipline

Another important factor appears to be a lack of self-control and discipline. In the magazine *Jonas* (February 1996), there was an article by the criminologist, Chris Rutenfrans, titled: "Why are there so *few* criminals in The Netherlands?" The phrasing of the article does not stem from the fact of why people commit crimes, rather than why so many do not. This explanatory device is known as the checking perspective. The French sociologist Durkheim (1858–1917) occupied himself with this at the closing of the nineteenth century. Durkheim presumed that the needs of men are endless and unlimited and that in principle everybody will go to any lengths to fulfil those needs. In this way, the spark for criminal behaviour is present in us all and does not need specific explanation. The vital question then is why society does not succumb to criminal and antisocial behaviour. Durkheim proposes that in every society a consensus is needed about the collective norms and values. These days, wherein not society but the individual takes centre stage, the collective values have become more flexible and feeble. Due to growing prosperity, limitless needs are increasingly dipped into. According to Durkheim suicide, violence, and criminality will be increase in times when people have the notion that all their needs can be satisfied. On the one hand, there are boundless expectations, and on the other hand, there are everyday life limitations to these expectations. The bigger the gap, the greater the frustration and the tendency for criminal and destructive behaviour.

Within this theory, the central question is how people learn to curb their limitless needs. The contemporary American criminologists Gottfredson and Hirschi (1990) use the concepts of Durkheim in their theory about self-control. They propose that although inherent predispositions might play a role, the environmental influences of being raised as a child at home and those of society have a greater impact. People learn self-control mainly in their primary years from their carers, when they learn to postpone satisfying their needs and in doing so deal with frustration.

In her cynically written novel, *Monster Children and Dragon Parents*, Schöttelndreier (1995) proposes how a generation of "bourgeois" parents with didactical indecisiveness, weak dispositions, and indolent spoiling have spawned a generation of insufferable princes and princesses with whom only a quarrelling relationship remains. All this within a social context where there is an absurd abundance of babies' and children's material, from fairytale baby bedrooms to toddlers' mopeds to real-life computer games wherein people who cry "help, don't shoot" are mercilessly gunned down by the little gamer. Schöttelndreier lays the blame rather easily with the parents and has little patience for the big dilemmas these parents face within this social context (Van der Pas, 1996). We do recognize in our practice the exhausted parents who tell us seriously that they cannot handle their three-year-old son, or the parents of a ten-year-old girl who still take turns in watching over her night after night until she falls asleep around half past eleven at night. These people do not have a social life any more. You no longer entertain people when one of you is permanently upstairs with your daughter, and a baby-sitter is not accepted by her. How could they have let things come this far? Because they want to be good parents; they are afraid of damaging their daughter, she is always so scared to go to sleep. We know numerous examples where we hear how far parents are willing to go to meet their own image of being a good parent. If we ask the parents about it, they always have a philosophy to which they cling to, they do not just muddle along. They want to be child-friendly, they do not want to damage their child, they want to do it differently than their own parents, they find it hard to act in an authoritative manner, and they want to fulfil their child's every want and need. But what happens if they keep to this course? At some point they will come to us, at their wits' end, with more or less totally misfit children who demand a lot and give little.

We do not want to fall into line with the large group of culture pessimists who are of the opinion that the increase of violence within society is solely due to the decline of order and authority within the family, school, or state. We do not promulgate a return to patriarchal family structures. We focus more on the demise of clear structures where children can safely develop and wherein parents feel supported. These days there is a lot of confusion about what is expected, what is possible, what a proper upbringing is, what a good partner-relationship is, what is feminine, what is masculine, and what is of the child. Viewing it from this vantage point, society finds itself in an existential crisis. The fact that so little is defined offers a wealth of possibilities, too: for example, to bring about a change in the trusted male–female patterns. The multi-cultural society also brings new perspectives and confusion as well, with regard to norms and values. On the one hand, it is greatly beneficial to put one's own cultural values into some perspective. One realizes the limits of one's own point of view. However, it also creates confusion in several essential areas of life. Within our indi-vidualistic society, it is "not done" to meddle in the way someone else raises their child. In South-Africa, we have encountered a whole street community confronting a father who had not protected his daughter properly. Our society has become very complex indeed, and this puts high demands on families and parents who raise children in our time.

To conclude, we can propose that the increase in violence among youngsters, perpetrated against their parents and fellow citizens, is linked to a complexity of factors. The social structures are strongly prone to change, youngsters mostly grow up in small families where they get a lot of attention, and are rewarded all the time for unclear reasons, but where a lot is expected from them, too. Because society has become more egalitarian, more emphasis has been put on good manners, and former hierarchies which used to guide social association are no longer in play.

In practice

A lot of families with youngsters between the ages of fifteen and twenty come into the practice of Lorentz House (Lorentzhuis). These youngsters display many problems, varying from passive and depressive behaviour to intense acting out behaviour, where violent and criminal activities are a regular component. These are often families with modern parents who both work and who have done their utmost to raise their children properly, child-friendly and according to the latest views. They can be categorized within the group of parents written about in the theoretical part of this chapter. Despite all their efforts, the result is disastrous at times. Children no longer attend school, lounge about in coffee-shops (where soft drugs can be legally bought over the counter), have a dim or nihilistic view on life, and show little social respect.

Many of our theoretical reflections can be applied here: these children have had a great deal of attention, their voice is taken very seriously, they are assigned too much power and have developed a vulnerable sense of self-worth. At the same time, they have not learnt any self-discipline and they can only with difficulty bear the postponement of the satisfaction of their needs. Their self-image is under threat when the demands of their parents, school, and society are being raised while they grow older. They resist the changes, after which parents become disappointed. Slowly but surely they find themselves in a negative downward spiral which is hard to breach.

Omer (2003) shows how two different groups of reactions can be recognized. One point of view is that these young people need a strong and authoritarian approach. They need to learn to accept authority and rules. The other opinion is that these youngsters need understanding, they are not feeling happy, they do not feel at home in the world, they need help. Parents and other care-givers often switch between these different perspectives. At one time they are furious because of the oppositional, aggressive, and irresponsible behaviour, they fight with their child and want to win and retain control. At another time, they feel that their child is unhappy and not in a good state; they want to support and help the child. Sometimes, these positions are divided between the parents, father is fighting the son while mother supports him. Then the parents get into fights and blame the each other for the misbehaviour of their child. Omer states that both positions end in powerlessness of the parents. Youngsters love power, when parents try to control them with authoritarian behaviour and punishment, the adolescent will strongly and continuously oppose these measures. This will result in an atmosphere of ongoing war at home and everybody will suffer. Parents who try to understand and support the child without limits also stimulate extreme and aggressive behaviour. Omer suggests an approach that connects the two different perspectives.

He focuses on the well-being of the parents. When he started this work, he was confronted with the fact that most of these parents did not feel at home any more in their own house. The adolescent took over the living space, everywhere, so that the parents did not feel that there was any space for themselves. He coaches the parents to take a new position and be present in the lives of the youngsters and care better for themselves as parents. He names this position "parental presence". He invites the parents to be there in the lives of their children because you cannot fire a parent. He stimulates parents to find out where the child is, with whom, and what he does. Without screaming, without violence. Parents have to resist; it is a fight, but a non-violent fight. He invites parents to contact other parents of friends of their child, to collect mobile numbers of these parents and of friends in order to be able to find out where their child is hanging around. He stimulates parents to support each other, to go together to pubs or discothèques to find out where the youngsters are, and so on. When opposition is there and the parent him or herself gets furious, he coaches parents to postpone their reactions: "do not strike while the iron is hot". First calm down before you act.

This is congruent with our time-out model. Parents can be parents again. When children develop well parents can give freedom to the child; when a child is developing in an alarming way, parental presence is crucial. Parents can explain to the child, who will be very irritated when they are so busy knowing where he is and what he does, that more freedom will be there when their concerns are less.

We recognize much of this approach in our work.

In the next example, we show how we, together with the whole family and the social systems that surround them, can break through the negative downward spiral and put a positive development in motion.

A case

Through a case that is representative for the group with which we often work, we want to show how we link the previously mentioned views within our clinical practice.

Two desperate parents come to our practice with two sons and a daughter, aged seventeen, sixteen, and twelve. The older two sons are what they consider to be "a failure". Their development went pear-shaped at secondary school, and because their daughter is of that age now, they want help to prevent the same thing happening to this child. At first, they thought it would not happen because she is a girl. However, the mother had read in a newspaper that there are also gangs of girls and just the other day a friend of the youngest had been held at a police station after stealing a Walkman.

During the assessment, by telephone, I put the emphasis on inviting the whole family. With great apprehension, the two eldest sons came into the practice just once, and that was it as far as they were concerned. The father is not bothered about that at all; he has long given up on them. All his hopes are pinned on this youngest child. The mother thinks differently. With tears in her eyes she says that she still cares about the two eldest, that she does not want to give up on them.

The father is a physiotherapist who has his own practice, the mother is a nurse. Both parents stem from more or less large families. The father comes from a family where the business always came first. He perceived his mother as caring and long-suffering; she was often ill. As far as he was concerned, he did not have a father. He was never there. When he wanted to have an education and did not want to take over the family business, it was seen as over the top. His brothers and sisters did join the family business and adjusted better then he ever did. They all married and had children. The father did everything single-handed. He never felt any support or encouragement. He felt very lonely in his family of origin. We can, therefore, suppose that the father did not build a safe attachment to his parents. He was determined to handle it differently, to do it better with his own children. He firmly resolved to be there for them, to give them attention and love, and to encourage them in their lives and studies. The mother also stems from a large and, according to her perception, a warm family. She thought her father was dominant. She also thought her mother to be something of a doormat. Her parents had a lot of worries about a brother who did not develop properly; she herself was a well-adjusted child who rocked the boat hardly at all. She does think that she did not receive enough attention. She herself wanted a smaller family, three children at the most, who would get a lot of attention, love, and support.

These two parents were in agreement. Their children were the centre of their lives and they wanted to raise them purposefully. The mother stayed at home while the children were small. Once the youngest entered primary school, she took on her former job as a trained nurse. The father often used to come home early so that he could frolic with his boys or kick a ball about. During the summer months, he used to take them on bicycle trips. Whenever problems occurred, they tried to have it out in the open and talk about it. Once the children had mastered that, it opened the floodgates— everything was discussed. What clothes to wear, about bed-time, in fact, about every possible rule and regulation you could think of. The parents kept looking for compromises because they felt that the children's voice had to be taken into account. Numerous accounts bear witness to the children's growing ability to discuss. They were able to wangle an agreement with the one parent when the other had just refused permission, and they would get their own way time and again. If any problems arose at school, the parents would intervene and would do their utmost to resolve it for the boys. In a material sense, they lacked little. They never had to wait long to have their desires fulfilled. Slowly but surely it went from bad to worse. While they were at primary school, things could be reasonably controlled. Once they entered secondary school, it all went pear-shaped. The eldest was tested at Higher General Secondary Education level/pre-university education level. The father reckoned his son could do pre-university level, and tried to keep him at level pegging through a lot of help and meddling. Out of the blue, there were these different set of demands: homework, tests, and proper achievements. All of a sudden, things got serious. This son could not handle the change well and started to fail. Circumspect at first, playing truant one time, getting bad grades, resistance to doing homework, but much more serious later on. He slid from pre-university education level to Higher General Secondary Education level and subsequently to Lower General Education level, but he made a complete mess of it there as well. Once the negative downward spiral was set in motion, it was difficult to turn the tide. Help was sought at the Regional Institute for Mental Welfare—Youth Care (RIAGG—Jeugdzorg) and with the Advice Bureau for Youngsters and Parents (AJO). In both institutions, the counselling did not take off properly, partly due to sick-leave and resignation on the side of the counsellors and also because of a lack of motivation by Johan, the son. It went increasingly downhill. He joined a group of friends, most of whom did not attend school; some worked, or lived on social benefits. He started smoking pot and did not abide by any house or school rules. Thus, he was expelled from three different schools. Because his pocket-money no longer sufficed to maintain his habits, he started to put pressure on his parents. However, the father wanted to keep him on a short leash because of his misbehaviour. He could wangle some money from his mother, through pleading, whining, or threatening. His mother became scared of him. He also began stealing. First from his parents; he stole from his mother's purse and took his father's CDs. Later he would nick stuff from his aunts and grandmother and subsequently from shops and other people. At last, he started breaking and entering with a gang, which appeared to be a substantial source of income.

Meanwhile, his younger brother (two years younger) was following in his footsteps. They ended up in the same gang. This second son, a gentle-faced boy, had found himself on the slippery slope at school, too, and was truanting so frequently that he was automatically expelled in the end. He became criminally very active. The brothers started experimenting with drugs. The parents became increasingly desperate and felt powerless to do anything. The mother tried to reason with the boys. The father became ever more frustrated; he lost contact with both boys and retreated. The boys increasingly crossed swords with the law. One day, they organized a burglary at their grandmother's house and they stole equipment and money. Although the grandmother and the parents suspected Johan and Erik, they naturally denied it vehemently. However, this time the grandmother did file a report, and, through fingerprints, the parents' worst fears were confirmed. The Child Welfare Council (Raad voor Kinderbescherming) was called in and the Organization for Youth and Family (Stichting Jeugd en Gezin) started to get involved with the family. Erik was given a six months' suspended sentence to do community service and was put on Juvenile Probation because of the multiple cases of breaking and entering. Counselling was established as well with the organization "The Slippery Slope" ("Het Hellend Pad"), where criminal youths from Haarlem were counselled at the time. Nowadays, this task has been taken over by bureau STOP (HALT) of the police. Only much later on was there a referral to our practice through another source, not so much to counsel the two eldest, but to save the youngest daughter, as said before.

The therapy

On entering, one could observe that the parents were polite; they introduced themselves and only settled themselves down when I invited them to do so. The boys walked in surly, completely ignoring me, and flopped into a chair. The eldest put his feet on the table and the middle one stared out of the window, bored. The daughter brought her chair close to those of her parents. When I explained to the parents that they could talk to their children as they would do at home, it appeared that they did not react to the churlish behaviour of the boys. The father made it clear from the start that he only came because of the youngest child, that the two eldest only came on my insistence, but he especially wanted help in order to prevent his daughter from following in her brothers' footsteps. The eldest interrupted by telling his father: "Yes, Jan, only this once, because we had to, but no more, you promised." I made an inventory of the counselling contacts prior to mine, which showed the devastating history of the two eldest. In spite of this, I did not put their problems centre stage, because I would have passed over the request for help from the parents; besides, the odds were greatly against me that it would rub the two eldest up the wrong way immediately.

I decided to do what I often do: a "sculpting" with the family. It is a kind of family sociogram where all the family members take turns in placing each other in a space. This sculpting explained a lot. Erik started, grumbling but co-operative anyway. He put his mother, sister, and eldest brother more or less on the same line, and his father as far removed as possible. When I asked him what he wished for, he showed me that he wanted his father closer by.

Johan put the whole family on the same line, and himself far apart. He said not to want it any other way. "I am not much of a bonding type." He told me that he only had acquaintances, no close friends. He said he did not need any. His lonely position was poignantly clear after a while. To my question as to who would be most bothered about him being so distant, he answered decidedly: "My mother." I asked him to place the situation in the space when he was ten years old. He subsequently made a tight circle of all five family members. I asked what had happened for him to run off so far. His immediate answer was that his parents had turned away from him, too.

The daughter placed herself between her parents, really close to one another. She placed her brothers far away. It was her wish to keep it that way. I asked, "Wouldn't you want them closer?" "No," she said, "because they will start kicking and hitting, they will hurt me then."

The father put his wife and daughter immediately next to him and his sons at a great distance. He really pushed them away from him.

It is not hard to guess how the mother placed herself: husband and daughter on the one side, the two sons on the other, she herself in between. Tearfully, she spoke about how she was crushed. She could understand her husband's and youngest child's feelings of repulsion but she just could not give up on the other two. She kept hoping things would get better, maybe against better judgement. "I know they're not bad boys on the inside", she said, and this was confirmed simultaneously by Erik handing over a tissue to her. The father again kept his distance, saying he no longer wanted to invest in his two eldest, they had completely lost his trust, and he had given up hope for them ever to turn out right.

On questioning further, it appeared that both Erik and Johan found this to be painful: "It's your Dad after all!"

At the end of the first session I could persuade all family members to make another appointment. I was able to persuade the two eldest by asking them to come in order to assist their mother, as she could not handle the situation any longer.

During the second session, I paid extended attention to the backgrounds of the father and the mother. I have already relayed something about these backgrounds. To the sons and daughter it became clear for the first time ever that their parents themselves felt as if they had been short-changed in their families of origin and that they had tried to do better with these children. At the end of the session, all three children apologized profusely to their parents. If there were any problems at all, it was not the parents' fault; they had done it all well.

During this session I examined a bit further the position of the daughter, who seemed to have the need to do everything perfectly and to prove the parents had done well after all. For instance, while she had her school test, the advice was Higher General Secondary Education level/pre-university education level, but she said to her father, "Maybe I could do the gymnasium."

I rounded it off with a story about the link between different factors, predisposition, family, extended family, school, friends, etc. On further questioning, the father thought that the problems were 80% to do with predisposition and 20% with surrounding influences, the mother thought the precise opposite.

In the third session I was ready to gather explicit information about the behaviour of the two eldest. I wanted to know how much pot they smoked, how many other drugs they used, which criminal activities they had on their slate, how much they had stolen, and what kind of sanctions their parents had put on this. Through circular questioning, I involved everyone in the interview. But this appeared hardly possible. The eldest became downright rude when I kept asking further. He said that it was none of my bloody business, I should shut my stupid mouth, or else he would walk out. The parents proved to be powerless. When I kept on questioning, the eldest did indeed walk out ostentatiously; the second son followed suit. The mother cried and the father was grim-faced. I continued with the parents and the youngest. I heard just how far they went. The father said, "Selling on the CDs they stole from me is one thing, but to burgle the house of their own granny . . .!" Thus, it became clear how the parents had shifted their limits bit by bit. I had mostly shown my surprise, but I could understand their side of the story as well. Accounts by clients are never really incomprehensible once you have a clear insight into the motives and ideas behind their actions; seemingly absurd behaviour becomes explicable, all of a sudden. I elaborated on the rules which still apply at home and how they dealt with them. I became clear in what manner the father had given up. He had retreated in disappointment and left his wife to cope with it all. However, she showed herself to be powerless and thus a power vacuum was created into which the boys readily stepped. We have encountered this pattern

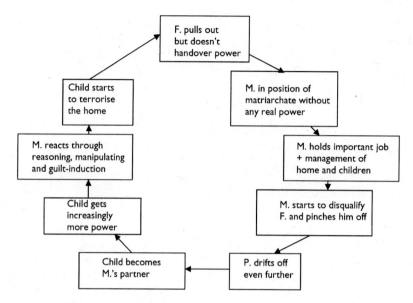

Figure 3.   The circle of the power vacuum.

often enough. We call it the circle of the power vacuum (Figure 3). I would like to point out again that the description of such an interaction circle can be regarded as a useful metaphor to make a process comprehensible. Of course, such a circle does not really exist. It is a framework wherein the individual and unique history of people can be told and understood and thus render possible new ideas and forms of treatment.

Commentary on the circle of power vacuum

As with every interaction circle, one can start at any given behavioural segment; we start at the top with the father, who pulls out, but who does not hand over power to his wife. We have already discussed this process.

It is in regard to fathers who started off raising their children in an enthusiastic and child-friendly manner, completely different from their own fathers'. They will keep this up as long as the interaction with their children generates the desired results, that is, nice, intelligent, and happy children of whom they can be proud. Once the children develop into nagging bitches, drop-outs, children of whom they feel ashamed, a lot of fathers pull out and retreat into traditional areas like work, sports, and the pub. This clearly shows how gender formation keeps trickling on and that new behaviour does not directly lead to a change of gender identity.

Mothers often persevere and find themselves more and more in the position of matriarch: after all, there is lack of a partner who at times can, and wants to, intervene. However, power has not really been handed over properly. In general, the status quo is that men are allocated more power than women (Komter, 1985). Women find themselves in the unfortunate position of the matriarch without power. They often combine a rather important job with running a household and caring for the children. These superwomen become exhausted and dissatisfied. They become more or less openly angry with their male partner, whom they feel has left them in the lurch. They start to disqualify him and shut him out. Men in general do not take kindly to being treated in such a manner, and react by staying away from home for longer periods of time. Women have no choice but to direct themselves to their children for emotional support. Thus, children can become their mothers' partners. The child's power will increase with this position. It will try more and more to have its own way at home. The mother may react with acquired "feminine" behaviour; she will try to regain control through discussion, convincing, and guilt-induction. The child is not won over that easily, and puts its own mechanics of power in motion. Violence may be used as well. Slowly but surely the terror of the child will gain strength; the mother cannot take it any more and the father pulls out even more. This completes the circle.

For that matter, we can also often see this process with migrant families where the fathers find themselves to be powerless against the rebellious and negative behaviour of their sons. They are disappointed in them and are ashamed of them. They see the root of their sons' misbehaviours outside themselves, within the Dutch society, or in the weak attitude of their wife. They increasingly flee the home, thus leaving the mothers behind with the sons they cannot handle. Here, too, power is not handed over, and thus many allochtonous mothers find themselves in a comparable situation: the matriarch without power.

Therapy

With the starting point being the powervacuum as a possible analysis, we saw a number of points to consider for the therapy.

First, it seemed vital to us not to blame any of those involved for the current situation. With the aid of the circular interview, we could test the convictions of the parents with regard to proper child-rearing. Future-bound questions in particular could help them to reflect on the consequences of their actions.

Through strategic interventions, we could introduce a different reality wherein parents could gain success experiences with collective handling of power.

Via the circular interview, we could also study the expectations the parents have of their sons and the expectations the sons have of the parents and of each other; and so illusions about ideal children and ideal parents could be discussed. One would expect that letting go of illusions would involve feelings of mourning on the one hand, and on the other hand create more space for differentiation for all involved. The bond and love for each other would get more breathing space once the disappointment and failures are on the back burner. So, too, would the numerous things which did go well in their mutual history. Talking about the sense of loss about the good old days often is a good starting point.

A good opportunity arose to put these plans into action through interventions when I got a phone call after the third session from a colleague in my practice. He had received new clients that afternoon, one of whom, a woman, had reported her wallet had been stolen from her coat pocket. I immediately understood the perpetrators to be Johan and Erik. Nobody else had been on the premises that afternoon, and I did hear them loitering about after they had left the room. I called the parents and told them what had happened. If the people involved filed a report, it would indeed look grim for Erik, because he was on probation. I proposed to the parents to have their sons give account of this at once. The mother found this hard. "You are not completely sure about it." I said that I was convinced, and suggested to them to play safe this time. This proved to be hard; they were so used to asking, which would always lead to denial and endless discussions. Despite all this they decided to go ahead. The parents both stayed up and when the boys came home at 2 a.m. they were confronted by two hopping mad parents who ordered them to see to it that the wallet was returned immediately. Of course, Johan and Erik tried to persuade their parents that they knew nothing about it, but this time they did not stand a chance. All of a sudden, the parents were capable of putting their foot down, and once they noticed that it worked, they became more convinced that what they did was right. In the end Johan and Erik went back to the park were they had got rid of their booty and they had to crawl around on their hands and knees in the dark, looking under the bushes until they found the wallet. The money was all spent, of course, but they had to compensate it out of their own pockets.

I think this was an important breakthrough in the therapy, although there were still hard times ahead; the sons no longer wanted to go to that bloody woman and her stupid family therapy.

Around the same time, it came to light that Erik had committed an even worse offence. This had taken place before we had established contact, but it had only just emerged. He had, together with a friend, broken into a pensioner's house at night. The burglary was deliberately planned and prepared. When the pensioner awoke, they threatened him at knife-point. They also stole the gold watch that he was wearing. It was clear that this crime would have serious judicial consequences as well.

Erik was sentenced to a four-month unsuspended sentence, two months probation, and a fine. He would be placed in an institution for juvenile offenders as soon as there was an available place. Until then we would continue our therapy in the Lorentz House.

We proceeded on to a professional consultation. Once several different professionals are involved in the one case, it is often advisable to arrange consultation in order for it to be clear to everyone where each person's responsibility lies.

In the helping professionals consultation the following were represented: the GP, the family guardian, the probation social worker, and the systemic therapist of the Lorentz House. It seemed vital to us all that the individual counselling of the boys as well as the family therapy would find an outlet. In order to persuade the boys to continue with the family sessions, a request would be made to the judge to include family therapy as a special condition in the sentencing. The social worker, who had a good rapport with the boys, wanted to make it mandatory.

This gave me some space. I no longer needed to tread carefully and it would be a positive push for the parents, too. A psychological examination scheduled for Erik. The conclusion of this examination was that his intelligence level was above average, but he had an inadequate impulse control and a lacunally developed conscience. Chances of reoffending were deemed highly probable. Despite the results of the individual psychological examination of Erik, we decided not to proceed to individual psychotherapy. The current package was enough of a burden for Erik. We, as professionals, agreed to meet on a regular basis.

After this period, the parents did manage to exercise authority better. They had readjusted their convictions about proper child-rearing. Acting and taking effective measures were part of the package now. Intense clashes occurred, especially with the eldest son, who could not accept the new regime. In the end, it led to a violent confrontation with the father, who kicked him out of the house. Although the mother found it hard, she did agree with it. The relationship between the parents improved and they started doing things together again.

Johan lives on his own now, but has his dinner regularly at his parents' house. This way, they keep in touch, but with a lot more positive moments. Johan appears to arrive on the dot every time for dinner. He holds down his job, and although he kept smoking pot, there have been no more criminal activities. There have been no more run-ins with the law.

Erik has served his time in jail and is back home now. He works in a supermarket and is thinking about going back to college. He sticks to the home rules.

The final session was with the father and the two youngest; the mother was ill and the eldest could not get time off work. The relaxed atmosphere was tangible. The contact with the father had visibly improved. Erik tried to relax the rules of curfew and smoking pot. Father kept his foot down firmly but lovingly, on which I complimented him profusely.

The daughter became defiant and no longer wanted to come along. I was relieved to find that obviously some space had been created for her to start acting up—within reason, of course.

Afterword on this case

This case is almost in its entirety a transcript from the first print of this book, because we thought it still illustrates our work method very precisely. Around the time of the first publication (1998), the therapy had only just come to an end. The other day (five years after the therapy had ended), I bumped into the eldest, quite by accident, in a supermarket. He recognized me before I recognized him. "Hey there, Ms Van Lawick!" he called out enthusiastically. It was a pleasure talking to him again. He told me that he had had a job for years now, and that he was living with a woman. The contact with his parents is good. His younger brother worked, was attending college too, and doing well. His sister was about to sit her Higher General Secondary Education exams; she was also a handful, "but nothing compared to me!" This reflection and the evident self-perception were the clearest indications that the positive change had been followed through.

Conclusion

In the theoretical part, we argued that the changes within the family unit and society can be linked to the growing violent behaviour among youths. We have tried to illustrate this with an example from the clinical practice. Due to the negative downward spiral of mutual resistance and disappointment, family members have turned away from each other. Parents and children felt that they have failed and were ashamed about their failings. Breaching the negative downward spiral was possible because the parents started to co-operate again and because they were able to regard disciplining and taking actions as proper parenthood and loving behaviour. Within this growing partnership and structure, it became possible to focus on the positive qualities again, and thus for the sons to reconnect once more. This reinstated the contact between parents and children and proved to be much more influential than the actions of the police. The point of change has to be a proper bond with the therapist, wherein all family members feel respected and supported.

Afterword

After the first publication of this book, much has changed in the work with problematic adolescents and their parents. New approaches have been developed. Most acknowledged is the approach from Omer (2007), who I mentioned earlier. He invites parents to be more present in the lives of their children with a position of parental presence. Also, in the case described above, the parental presence of mother who felt powerless, and father who had withdrawn as a parent turned out to be crucial. Omer has elaborated on this theme. He made a manual for parents and supports parents. He forms a counterbalance to the media, which blame parents for the misbehaviours of their children because they do not control their children. This culture of blame only adds to feelings of shame and the powerlessness of parents. Omer goes against the populist call for more authority. He thinks that we have to reflect on new forms of authority which fit the present time and context, with internet, cyberspace, and information technology.

In a workshop in the Netherlands, in May 2008, he demonstrated the scheme set out in Table 1.

These new forms of authority are necessary to help parents and children to find their way in the present complex world.

Table 1. The contrast between traditional authority and new authority.

Traditional authority	New authority
Based on distance and fear	Present, close, and involved
The other one is responsible	Everybody is responsible for their own part
Need to control	Obligation to set limits
Secrecy, no space for criticism	Transparency and social support
Direct reactions	Postpone reactions
Top down	Rooted in a social network
Revenge	Reconciliation after conflict
Looking after and controlling	Being touched and asking questions

Source: Omer, 2008.

CHAPTER ELEVEN

The therapist as a person

Martine Groen

Processes of transference and countertransference

Countertransference in team groups: the toll of empathic ability

A t the beginning of the 1980s I worked in an all woman team. We all worked with clients who had suffered the serious consequences of violence. At the time, we did not truly grasp the impact this had on our team, but, in hindsight, certain patterns emerged. Each and every one of us got stuck in repetitions of unaccepted events in our own lives.

We argued, could not say "no", became overstressed in turn, repeated patterns of torment, chased each other in anger or, on the contrary, with powerlessness or victimized behaviour which belonged somewhere else but which was now projected on to colleagues. The dynamics which come with working in a team came under great pressure. The powerless anger enhanced the border-crossing behaviour of team members, which, in turn, was fed by the high demands of the subsidiary. The concept of co-traumatization has been the subject of discussion before, but only briefly. More often than not, the extreme stress was dealt with on an individual basis; it was not regarded as a structural theme which was recurring. Furthermore, we did not recognize that contamination had taken place within the team and that it was possible to drag each other into a powerless downward spiral.

Only in the last couple of years, stimulated by counsellors on all levels of social areas, was it acknowledged that counsellors who had to deal with the consequences of violence and disasters (e.g., policemen, fire-fighters, rescue workers, social workers, employees in centres for asylum-seekers, psychiatrists, and psychotherapists) run high risks. This chapter deals with those risks. After a general description, we specifically target the countertransference symptoms in working with couples in which the man abuses the woman in escalating conflicts. We discuss the several different reactions of counsellors with the aid of a schedule. Finally, we deal with the prevention of burn-out and secondary traumatization.

The distinction between burn-out and secondary traumatization

Everyone within the Mental Health Care system who has come into contact with the consequences of violence will, at some given moment, be confronted by stress complaints. Listening to gruesome accounts seeps through into the unconscious and conscious life of the listener.

More often than not the social worker will suffer, at some stage, from complaints that can be categorized as symptoms of burn-out. These complaints could be both psychological and physical and have an impact on behaviour. Often the social worker will take sick leave, or is sent home to take some rest, and that will be the end of it. A social worker often feels isolated with her or his complaints and she or he tends to take the blame on her/himself and will put the complaints down to psychological incapacity or unsuitability to do the job. The change in behaviour could have an impact on the social worker's surroundings. If the social worker is part of a team, isolation could be one of the illness-inducing factors of the negative downward spiral of stress, but it has its reverberations in private life as well: for example, the social worker becomes irritable.

It is crucial to make a distinction between symptoms of burn-out and trauma-specific stress symptoms, because different interventions are needed to help the person in question. An example from another context follows.

> Officer Andreé arrives at the station, growls, and behaves unreasonably towards her colleagues. This is uncommon; she is usually friendly and quick-witted. Her colleagues ask her what is the matter, but she does not respond. Her behaviour continues without anyone understanding what is going on. She retreats, and others avoid her. Conflicts arise with her close colleagues and this reaches some kind of climax. In the end, she takes sick leave. She is not promoted in the next round of reorganization. At first, she takes it rather well. Comments from her closest colleague reveal that she had been involved in a case of child abuse which had gone off the rails and led to the death of the child. She has a small child herself.

This could be someone who is burned out or someone who suffers from secondary traumatization.

The distinction is not always easily made. The complaints are strongly similar, but a number of characteristics belong specifically to complaints which point to secondary trauma.

General complaints of stress are: increase of emotionality, decrease of mental elasticity, feelings of helplessness and powerlessness, complaining behaviour, growling, headaches, stomach upsets, heart problems, neck problems, eating and drinking more, trouble with sleeping, sexual problems, and lack of concentration.

Trauma-specific stress symptoms are: nightmares, feeling unsafe, recurring flashbacks, oversensitivity to violence, detachment from loved ones, change in identity awareness, change in sensorial awareness, lack of concentration, and reacting in an over-alert manner.

Social workers who suffer from trauma-specific stress symptoms need the same approach as their clients. The flashbacks and nightmares will disappear if one addresses it in a specific manner. Talking about it helps. Offloading one's feelings could help to clarify why certain images linger on. Often it has something to do with some event from the therapist's personal life, but it may also be connected to the content of the traumatic account, with the organization in which the therapist works, or the education which the therapist has followed.

Therapists find it hard to talk about abuse within a partner relationship. The same used to be the case, in the past, for accounts about incest or rape. After the Second World War, no one wanted to know exactly what went on in the concentration camps. It is a human trait to avoid accounts about violent behaviour, connected to fear about dying or death itself. Similarly to their clients, therapists do not like accounts which render them powerless. Of course, they have been trained to deal with it. They do not avoid it on purpose, but they seem to be mal-equipped to deal with it. Often, they do not want to believe that there could be more than what the client tells them, even though the signals are loud and clear.

In cases of both abuse and incest, secrecy plays a significant role. The shame that a disclosure can bring about prevents a much needed openness between therapist and client. Unintentionally, a conspiracy may develop, in which the therapist takes over the shame, as it were, and she/he avoids asking specific questions. That which one does not want to hear or see will not be spotted. Avoiding, ignoring, denying, and disbelief are phenomenona which are part of countertransference symptoms and which characterize confrontations with traumatized people.

Countertransference and secondary traumatization

"Some images are burned onto my mind's eye. Months later they are still there."

"My mental space is filled with filth, if I walk outside every man I encounter is a dirt-bag, capable of anything, a suspect being."

Sympathy and antipathy are the intuitive undercurrents that come into being either at the first moment of contact or later in the process. Some people evoke sympathy from the moment they arrive, while others stir antipathy from the start. It is fascinating to investigate on what these preferences are based. During training sessions, social workers say that they find helpless and powerless women the hardest to deal with. The passive victim evokes much aggression. The perpetrator conjures up vengeful fantasies within the fantasy of the overly identified social worker.

Cultural differences and class background also play a part. If one expects there to be more beatings in working-class families, one will be more tolerant towards clients from such backgrounds than one would be towards clients from different social backgrounds. It appears to be very hard to believe that well-educated people holding good positions also cannot keep their hands to themselves and terrorize their wives. Temptation looms large to deny that beatings and abuse occur with these couples.

The concepts of transference and countertransference indicate feelings evoked between clients and therapists within a therapeutic process. These could be negative feelings, such as fear or annoyance, and positive ones, such as admiration and warmth. The phenomenon of transference deals with the feelings clients have about a therapist. Those feelings refer to wishes, fears, and longings. They are projected by the client on to the therapist. Within a psychotherapeutic process, these feelings are "reworked" in order for them to be given a place within the existence of the client.

Countertransference is the reversed process. It deals with the feelings of the therapist as a reaction to the client. Therapists are faced with complicated dilemmas within countertransference.

Counsellors who listen to the horrifyingly frightening and painful accounts of their clients are often just as shocked as their clients. Fierce emotions, such as anger, fear, powerlessness, and feeling unsafe, are conjured up. In studies, a distinction is made between reactions of counsellors which could be related to their own history and reactions of a more general nature, somewhere between subjective and objective reactions (Gorkin, 1987).

Many counsellors who work with traumatized clients will be motivated to do so in one way or other. A study in the USA shows that half of all counsellors have had a traumatic experience themselves, for example, a childhood riddled with alcohol abuse and violence (Hartman & Jackson, 1994; Howe, Herzberger, & Tennen, 1988; Jackson & Nuttall, 1993; Nuttall & Jackson, 1992). In order to be able to work with difficult cases, it could be an advantage if one had also experienced pain. One has a better understanding of how intensely clients experience existential incidents. However, a therapist's traumatic experiences can be a disadvantage as well. If these have not been dealt with, they could block the therapeutic process. They become visible both in the desire to deny the tough accounts of clients and in the tendency to identify with them.

A female counsellor with a telephone emergency service heard the following account.

> Mrs X was afraid to leave the house. The day before, a man had forced her at knife-point to go into the bushes with him. While he kept the knife at her throat with one hand, he undressed her with the other and raped her. Hurt and in a state of shock she had stumbled home.

> The social worker who heard this account was alone at the office in a large and dark building. As her shift ended, she wanted to go home. She found that she actually did not dare to go through the building. She kept seeing intruders everywhere intent on causing her harm. Once outside she remained afraid. She called her husband, who came and picked her up.

Even though she had been an employee with the telephone helpline for many years, it was this story that made an impact on her at that precise moment.

It could be the voice of the victim, or a specific detail in the account that evoked the stress that lingered inside her. During supervision talks, it emerged that the woman was, in fact, actualizing an early childhood memory. As a child she was grabbed by a group of boys. The powerlessness and the fear that she had experienced then came flooding back because of this re-enactment.

The setting and context wherein one works partly contributes to the manner in which counsellors react. For example, working in a shelter for traumatized women and children is of another order than working in a Regional Institute for Mental Welfare (RIAGG) with victims of incest. The latter differs again from working with traumatized refugees of war, or working with violence between couples in a private practice. It also depends on the organization itself, which stories are told and which are not, which stories are believed and which are not.

Clients look for a safe place to unload their confusion and feelings. The function of the therapist is, among others, to listen empathically within a boundaried surrounding, in order to give clients the opportunity to do justice to their emotions. In this process, the personality of the therapist is at level pegging with the personality of the client. The force of the feelings that are being unloaded can be so intense at times that they *have* to have an effect on the feelings of the counsellor. If one works in groups, this force could multiply and intensify even more. In our experience, if the counsellor is not supported in some way or other to deal with such feelings, the therapeutic contact will be lost and ruptures will appear between what the client wants and what the therapist has to offer. The emotional stress of the therapist acts as a hindrance.

Wilson and Lindsey (1994) have developed a theoretic model in order to assess the countertransference symptoms, specifically in dealing with trauma. In our training sessions for counsellors we use this model, which we call the counsellors' cross (Figure 4).

Wilson and Lindsey distinguish two main types within the range of possible reactions to trauma accounts. The two main groups are over-identifying with clients as an active reaction and identifying with the powerlessness as a passive reaction. An example of an active form of over-identifying follows.

> A counsellor says that during the course of an intervision she was unable to control the anger she felt towards the husband. "You are wrongly beating your wife, sir." She openly chose for the wife. The trust of the couple was obviously so shaken that they did not show up for the next appointment.

Saving	Professional façade
wanting to do it all	talking a lot about the client
wanting to save the client	this is not part of our job
wanting to reach the unreachable	aiming for diagnosis
acting in the client's name	referring client
'love'	

becoming		*keeping a*
overly involved		*distance*

Powerlessness	'Blaming the victim'
becoming gloomy and despondent	not taking problems seriously
feeling a victim oneself	trivializing
not being able to help	the client whines
to give up on counselling	they can do it themselves
	aggressive, sadistic, masochistic

Figure 4.   The counsellors' cross.

An example of a more passive form of over-identifying is:

During a supervision meeting, Maaike speaks about how angry she feels towards her client, who has gone back to her husband. On the other hand, she is also very concerned. Beaten black and blue, the woman had ended up in a shelter. Now that she has recovered, she has returned home with her children. The counsellor feels disheartened and powerless and doubts the meaning of her work.

On the other side of the line, avoidance takes centre stage in every shape imaginable, keeping one's distance. In the active sense, the referral of clients who are deemed to be too difficult and categorizing clients. In a passive way, to distance oneself, the client is blamed. The social worker runs the risk of becoming cynical. Examples of actively keeping a distance are:

Therapist: "Madam, if you would only adjust and learn to listen to your husband, you would not be punished that much."

A psychiatrist describes, deeply ashamed, how it is not uncommon to diagnose women who have experienced violence as borderline patients and to refer them to a structured kind of therapy.

An example of passively keeping your distance is:

"Women exaggerate and whine. They've probably had it coming. Nothing can be done about couples like that."

Most counsellors react to shocking accounts with over-identifying, and they start to react overly concerned. In asking specific questions, it often appears that the institution where one works allows this. If the culture in the institution is more distant, as in hospitals, police stations, or fire departments, one would be more likely to react in a more detached manner, would rather become cynical and blame people themselves for what has happened to them.

Over-identifying: prejudices and myths
surrounding the traumatic account

For a long time, identifying with the victim—from the women's liberation side as well—has been the tool to use in order to find solutions which are directed towards a divorce. Victimhood is often associated with weakness and passiveness. Reality has taught us that driving a wedge between couples is not always the right solution. Once they have caught their breath, women often return to their husbands and leave the counsellors behind, confused.

Victimhood has become controversial. There is some grain of truth in all prejudices. It is deeply embedded within Western culture that women and images of femininity primarily represent victimhood. Men and masculinity exclude victimhood. Laying victimhood at women's doorstep goes hand in hand with aggression. Images and testimonies of this can be found both in literature and paintings. Violence perpetrated against women is enacted and depicted. Such a deeply rooted cultural inheritance is not that easily erased from our network of prejudices and points of view (Römkens & Dijkstra, 1996).

Violence within relationships often takes place in a very complex situation. It is difficult to determine each partner's individual part. Prejudices play a role, for example, "In general men hit and women nag." Counsellors often tend to agree with this division of roles and thus react with their own prejudices. The most common and often heard reactions are: "She could just walk out", or "She is just asking for it."

> Yvonne and Mohammed have relationship therapy. Twelve sessions on end his problems with integrating in the Netherlands are discussed. He hails from Morocco. She holds a successful job as a nurse. They have two children who are suffering from stress, mainly, as the therapist reveals, because of his shouting. His jealousy is one of the problems. He had hit Yvonne because she talked to another man at a party. The therapist can imagine his jealousy because he himself finds Yvonne very attractive. The man's reaction is smoothed over and defended.

In this case, the counsellor identifies himself with the traditional opinions of the husband with regard to the role of women. He confirms the myth that the man is allowed to own his wife and is responsible for her sexual satisfaction. What was not discussed in the therapy, was how Yvonne is systematically beaten and raped by her husband. The therapist has obviously become blinded by his own prejudices.

This case is a perfect example of the manner in which men can be caught up in stereotypes about women. In Mohammed's reaction his wife (or women in general) appears to be an alien creature, barely controllable and having an all consuming sexuality which threatens him in his fantasy. The image of feminine sexuality is not limited to this specific case only, but is expressed in numerous myths, legends, stereotypes, and behavioural rules (Nicolai, 1992, p. 63).

A second way to excuse the beating of women is to offer a difficult childhood as an excuse: "He must have had a hard time as a child. He has been seriously damaged in childhood and she pushes him too much. He cannot control his strength, he doesn't know his own strength, he suffers from a childhood trauma."

It is rather striking that in all these examples the wife or the mother is blamed. Everybody recognizes these prejudices, both men and women. They obstruct one's view of what is really going on. Thus, both parties can avoid a real confrontation.

Prejudices in relation to men that point towards an over-identifying with abused women can muddle a discussion just as much. Prejudices such as "Men are incapable of taking about sensitive subjects, they just lash out. It is all about power with men. Sessions with couples in these cases are impossible because the woman will live to regret it afterwards. He may say that he will keep his hands to himself, but he will not succeed anyhow. She has to divorce this man immediately." In these situations, male counsellors will tend to take on the "saviour's role". They identify themselves easily with the male client with regard to earning a living, sexuality, dominance, and work, but they do get snared by taking sides with the miserable spouse. The opposite happens as well: the male therapist feels so connected to the male partner that the contact with the woman disappears from the equation.

Psychologizing the offender is another factor. Looking for the causes in someone's childhood is excusing incomprehensible violent behaviour. Empathy, the most important tool for counsellors, is tested to the limit by violent clients. A third reaction from counsellors to the abuse of women is a deep hostility towards the man who cannot control himself. Colleagues often become incensed if fellow counsellors keep retelling the details of abuse cases. Another often observed reaction is fear, which can manifest itself in avoidance behaviour during the session. Female counsellors often show a very special reaction. They bask in their role as "saviour", meaning that the untamed aspects of the men need to be conquered.

Voyeurism

Sometimes, clients' accounts might just evoke forbidden feelings and fantasies in the social workers (see Chapter Five for more detail). Often this titillating of the senses will be covered in shame and guilt. This could mean the development of additional complaints. In the following example, the therapist is on sick leave. She calls it being confused and overstressed. After some time, she asks for counselling.

> During a supervision session she says that she hardly sleeps; she lies in bed tossing and turning. She is worried about the wife of a couple she is treating. The beatings have worsened. Furthermore, the woman is raped during these violent outbursts. The therapist has done all she could to somehow ensure the woman's safety. Despite this, the images keep coming. Especially the image of the rape: he fucks her anally and the woman says that she is in a lot of pain. He keeps doing it while he grabs her breasts hard. At home, the therapist becomes incensed with this man; she would like to hurt him as much as possible. On the other hand, the image excites her too. The therapist feels ashamed and loses herself in worry.

For many people, violence, fear, and excitement go hand in hand. Sometimes, perverse images of dominance awaken primitive motives. A high state of excitement is part of the experience of violence. This same excitement manifests itself with deaths and births and conjures up feelings that change the perceptions of time and space.

The therapist tends to over-identify with her client. She projects her feelings on to her and acts accordingly. Her coping mechanism expresses itself in being overly responsible and she loses sight of her own boundaries within the counselling. Her empathy spills over and blocks her view of the survival strategies of her female client. She considers herself, in this case, the saviour of her client and "the trauma specialist" *par excellence*.

Rape does occur within violent relationships. The threshold for asking specific questions about it is high. In general, one is already satisfied if the fact that beatings occur is discussed. The symptoms which could point out to the therapist that there is more under the surface are ignored, such as, for example, hyper-sexuality, an enormously erotically charged counsel, over-alertness, self-destructive tendencies, the incapacity to protect oneself, restricted awareness, tendencies to dissociate, and the loss of self-awareness and time (Burgess & Holstrom, 1974; Foa & Kozak, 1986; Herman, Perry, & Van der Kolk, 1989). It is known that some therapists do not have an eye for these symptoms. This is remarkable, since they are known to be feature in post traumatic stress syndrome. Furthermore, this negation has a harmful effect on the clients, as they have the tendency to re-enact traumatic events permanently.

Keeping a distance and avoidance

A social worker relates that he no longer dares to ask questions in a session with a couple. They tell him that he beats her regularly when a conflict arises and she, in turn, says that she does not spare the rod with her children on a regular basis. He backs away from this information and avoids questioning any further.

> In a supervision session, it emerges that the social worker himself has been witness to the abuse of his mother. He has often intervened, but to no avail. He discovers why he freezes during the therapeutic sessions with this couple, why he does not dare to ask specific questions. He is afraid that he might attack the husband. All the old feelings of guilt and powerless anger resurface, so palatable that he is lost. He has never confronted his father with his rage. This unsolved conflict renders it difficult, if not impossible, for him to work with abuse within a couple relationship. He has the tendency to refer clients.

This social worker was overwhelmed by fear, and he felt insecure and guilty. He defends himself by retreating during the session. He minimizes the trauma. His coping strategy is a passive rejection and a denial of responsibility. He is unable to unravel the trauma account of the abuse.

He entered, together with her, for an initial session. He was tall and enormously muscular, a P.E. teacher with a black belt in karate. She, tiny and slim, worked in the catering industry. On entering, he said that he was not afraid of anyone and suggested that, if need be, he would take on the therapist as well. The female therapist reacted with admiration to his extremely well-toned body, and simultaneously with fear because he had warned her not to over-step his boundaries. She noticed that the woman was very tense and that she reacted nervously. She could barely sit still and hurriedly told what took place at home when they were having an argument. The woman's signals were loud and clear. However, both the admiration for and the fear of the man prevented the social worker from asking specific questions about the suspicion that he had sex with her against her will. The therapist was intimidated by his strength and feared his anger. She was afraid to lose contact, but this obviously did happen.

It is common knowledge that, in general, women find it more difficult to set boundaries in their work, to react assertively, and to deal with their anger in a constructive manner. Scientific research regarding women's socialization shows that they find it hard to openly express annoyance, criticism, and anger. The most quoted explanation for women restraining themselves is the fear of losing contact with the other. Women are socialized with the message to look after the other, to voice the emotional aspect within the family system. Within this frame, the bond with the mother is given as one of the obstacles to learning how to set boundaries, daring to say no, to compete, and to promote oneself. Thus, these images have been ratified within society. For a long time the division of labour has been organized along these lines: there is work for men and there is women's work, and the latter commands a lot less respect and power. To women's work belongs the emotional maintenance of a network, whether it is the family or work.

Women have learnt better how to attach and to voice a "we". Some women do speak of "we" when they talk about themselves. Therapists do this as well, and are caught up in the "we" with the woman who is being abused. They begin to feel and express the anger that should have been felt and expressed by their female client.

Maria had become deeply involved with the couple. Some improvement could be detected. He controlled himself and she was a little bit more relaxed. Then the beatings started again. The illusion is shattered. The woman, sitting depressed in her chair, can barely utter a word; the tension builds. He apologizes for the umpteenth time. The woman feels defeated and represses anger. Maria becomes annoyed during the therapy session.

Within countertransference, it is vital to be ready for the possibility of confrontation. This is needed to establish boundaries, to point out what is and what is not permissible, to express feelings of power and powerlessness, and to show feelings of horror.

The qualities of previously mentioned therapists are rather different. Some of them are highly qualified psychotherapists with the capability to follow the therapy process to the letter and to reflect upon it in a systemic manner. Others lack this particular capacity, but are highly experienced in working with violent couples. Their cognitive system differs from that of a trained therapist. Identifying and using countertransference symptoms is less familiar to them. Therefore, they are more vulnerable in the confrontation with violence and they run more risks of becoming co-traumatized.

Anger and revenge

It differs somewhat if women are able to defend themselves properly. If they can explain their own behaviour, if they are capable of protecting their children, and still harbour some hope for the relationship to improve, it is a radically different situation from the one where they just sit there and let their male partner do all the talking.

Such differences play a major part within countertransference. The reaction of the children is important, too, as is the manner in which decisions are being made and the way in which the relationship is defined. Time and again, the therapist is reminded of the problems other couples have who are being treated by him or her, couples who may not beat each other but who do show the same dynamics of power. Finally, the arguments in the personal life of the therapist play a part too.

There is an argument about who does what in the house and there is a small child involved. He earns the lion's share of the family income, she holds a part-time job for three days a week. She would like to further her career, but, given the work and the expected doubled responsibility, not much will come of it. She does everything and he hardly lifts a finger in the house. He controls the spending. She is chronically unsatisfied. They both talked about "the baby" in a detached manner. There are frequent arguments, twice a week. She starts throwing things and he humiliates her. "You are stupid, you are the spitting image of your stupid mother." In the end he hits her, hard. He cannot stand to be seen as useless. The fighting starts when she wants to leave.

The therapist is having a hard time with this couple. They are more or less in the same situation as he is. The awful battle about the daily chores, the rubbish bags, the ironing. During the session, he identifies with the man. He finds her a bore, someone who is always nagging. He instantly becomes allergic to the woman and the counselling session goes off the rails. Only in hindsight does he realize what has gone wrong. During the supervision session, he first unloads his anger about the powerless battles he has at home and then he comes to realize that he sees his own wife and his client as "castrating". Meanwhile, he has learnt little about the frequency and the level of seriousness of the beating and possible sexual abuse. Furthermore, no agreements have been made to reverse the violence.

The absent or split-off anger can be tangible within a therapy room, but will usually stay hidden beneath shame and guilt. As I said before, this is a pitfall of the first degree. Powerlessness and helplessness are hard to bear. They tempt the therapists into quickly finding solutions in order to ward off these feelings, or to unload them in the shape of powerless anger. An experienced therapist, too, may come adrift and voice his feelings of anger, for example, by expressing his annoyance about not keeping appointments, whereas he should have discussed a totally different matter.

Therapists are constantly invited to take on the powerlessness of clients. If the client is incapable of establishing boundaries while angered, the therapist is asked indirectly to do this for her or him. Fear and anger are ever present in a therapeutic session. It all depends on the alertness and baggage of the therapist as to how it is dealt with.

Another tricky situation arises for the therapist once the violence has ceased and the couple really wants to improve their relationship. A situation will develop wherein especially the woman will look back in anger and sadness. Women can become so angry in the therapy room that it will become very hard for men, as for the therapist. Wanting to take revenge and getting atonement precede the process of forgiveness.

> She comes in swearing. "All men are bastards. My mother told me so, they are not to be trusted and you least of all." She keeps on ranting and recounts all the violent incidents of which she has been the victim. She wishes him the very worst. He starts to defend himself. The therapist feels the need to defend him against so many grievances. After all, he is doing his best to improve the relationship.

Tempering anger and thoughts of vengeance are part of the therapist's defence mechanism. She is not able to deal with so much overdue anger.

The organization of counselling

The organization of counselling with regard to the issue of violence within relationships also plays a part in secondary traumatization with counsellors. The manner in which supervision and intervision are organized, the attention paid to, and the experience with, the issue of violence and the way it is dealt with are contributory to the well-being of counsellors. We now discuss a number of situations, knowing full well that a great many of counselling variants are not taken into account.

The Regional Institute for Mental Welfare (RIAGG) and social work

The counsellor, the psychotherapist, the psychiatrist, and the social worker are all at risk if they work within a setting where they are on their own. The statistics of burn-out are higher in this sector than anywhere else (de Volkskrant, 1997). In this situation, staff, and with them the clients, are being sacrificed to the detrimental workings of the market. Production standards have to be met and thus quality standards are slipping.

Research regarding work processes which lead to burn-out shows that an excess of stress in the workplace and a lack of energy resources will inevitably lead to burn-out. More specifically, burn-out is the end result of two separate processes. In the first process, many demanding tasks at work lead to an ongoing sense of over-burdening and, in the long term, this could lead to chronic fatigue or exhaustion. In the second process, the lack of energy resources, such as coaching by superiors and a lack of autonomy, hinders the reaching of targets. In the short term, this leads to frustration, and in the long term towards a cynical, detached work attitude (demotivation). If both processes occur simultaneously, burn-out is possible. Research has shown that burn-out has a negative impact on the functioning of employees in terms of health, sick leave, commitment, and achievements (Bakker, 2002).

The search for, and organization of, energy resources within an organization acts as a buffer to prevent a fall-out. Energy resources can be found the level of:

- the organization (career improvement possibilities, salary, job-security);
- interpersonal relationships (support from superiors, colleagues, and team spirit);
- the work organization (for instance, clarity regarding one's role, participation in the decision making);
- the level of the task (for instance, feedback about how one functions, alternating the use of capabilities and autonomy).

These energy resources are preconditions within an organization to prevent primary and secondary stress, as well as counteracting burn-out.

Detecting energy leaks

Isolated talking to a couple in a room by oneself has its pros and cons. The check on the actual work is limited; only clients may blab. Colleagues only hear the watered down versions at an intervision. One often plays up to another in a language that is acceptable and fits within the beliefs of the work setting. Counsellors who are often confronted with the consequences of violence and who work with couples where the wife is being abused will not easily fall back on colleagues. It is difficult to discuss and to share the intensity of feelings that are part of cases of violence. The price of empathy can be high.

Of course, counsellors will tell each other the horrifying accounts, in the hallway or in the office, probably to the secretary. But one story will sound more serious than the other.

> "I keep my mouth shut if I hear her talking about the awful tortures in South America, I don't have such stories. I almost feel ashamed for being troubled about something."

One assumes that one has been trained to deal with trauma-specific symptoms of transference, that it is part of the job. Care for the employees is organized in intervisions, but does not suffice when it comes to the debriefing of traumatic accounts.

During supervision and team support sessions, we encounter traumatized teams who react with avoidance and cynically towards the behaviour of the traumatized. Traumatized teams react in the same manner as their clients: alert, tense, over-involved in the suffering of their clients, and with anger which is aimed outward or taken out on colleagues, without it ever being discussed. In our experience, it is difficult to co-operate when insecurity is increasing. Minor issues are being intensely fought over, a sure sign of a stressed-out team or organization. In such an atmosphere, it is easy to look for a scapegoat. Something that can often happen is a division within a team: for instance, a group that is in favour of or against a certain approach with a client. Several more reactions can be mentioned which are related to the reactions of the team in trauma counselling. The counsellors' cross, shown in Table 2, could be a good indication for a team, too.

Teams could offer protection against secondary and primary trauma-related stress if they function properly. Trauma reactions within teams could be seen as signals of a high level of insecurity. The emotional danger of contamination is high within such teams. The functioning of the group is highly dependent on the level to which that group has been secondarily traumatized. The capacity of a group to solve problems is determined by the quality of the group and the quality of the management. In every phase of the group's development, a need will arise for specific strategies to face up to the problems with which the group is confronted. The team also needs support and preconditions from the organization to act as a buffer and a safe haven in order for employees to function. Furthermore, the quality of the style of management plays an important role. Every phase of the team's development needs a different approach in management. If there is a lack in this adjustment, the group can no longer act as a safety net for channelling the built-up stress.

A shelter

In the downward spiral of violence, as described in Chapter Three, women regularly flee for a short while to a shelter after phase nine. We will discuss this form of counselling too, because it is a much-used safe haven, by describing the situation in a particular institution.

The staff of the shelter has a monthly supervision to keep the processes of counter-reference in check. There are twenty-five women from different cultures in the house. They all have been abused and are traumatized, and they live there with their traumatized children. The staff, too, is multi-cultural. There are different ideas among them about abuse and sexual abuse and about women's rights.

At times it is difficult for the counsellors to try to understand why the women keep returning to their abusive husbands or family system. Nowadays, more knowledge has been gathered and there is more understanding for the love–hate relationship which hallmarks such relationships.

There are regular conflicts between the women, which may result in an actual fight. Sometimes, children are involved, or they are the very reason for the conflict.

During the supervision sessions, it becomes clear that the tension for the counsellors often boils over. In the past couple of years, many counsellors stayed home with complaints related to stress. This was an indication for the board to research whether this kind of tension is predictable and could be prevented. During the course of the supervision process, the question arose as to whether one can come up with interventions which would have a de-escalating effect on the spiral of heightened tension. First, we tried to make an inventory of the group's processes which arise within this artificial community. It is quite a task to judge each varying bond, sub-groups, the differences in language and habits, on their own merits. This also goes for the effects those sub-groups have on others. It is not easy to uncover precisely when chronically occurring tensions will lead to conflicts, which in turn will spread like wildfire.

> Miriam regularly yells at her housemates if something does not appeal to her. She came to the house at the same time as two others. They are sometimes able to calm her down quickly, but this time they did not succeed. Due to her impossible outbursts, she is in danger of becoming the black sheep. On the grounds of these threats, different sub-groups have formed against her. Miriam feels she is at risk and turns to the staff for help. A couple of counsellors feel for her and want to protect her against the threat of exclusion. Within the staff, the process seems to mirror itself: some have taken sides with the woman, but others are against her because she determines the atmosphere and creates an unsafe climate.

> Miriam shows her best side when she is with her counsellor. She shows insight into her behaviour and promises to be less aggressive. During team sessions, the counsellor declares that there is perspective in Miriam's stay in the house. The next evening, however, she starts an enormous row, which escalates into a fight with other housemates. Miriam's counsellor runs the risk of being shunned by the staff because she maintains her support for her client, even now that she has breached the rules. She does not want to expel her.

Implementing rules in order to guarantee safety is a recurring battle between staff and the admitted women and children. Within a multi-cultural climate, it is a daily given fact that the several partisan views are played out against each other. Some inhabitants demand a special position on the basis of religion or other cultural issues. Within the staff as well there are differences in approach, which are surrounded by a whole series of arguments. For example, are you allowed to touch clients or not, how many times, and where? Which habits lower the threshold of fear and are part of a culture, and which induce fear and are border-crossing? If comfort is given, through touch and massage, how will the other women in the shelter react to it? Often the discussion is about which exceptions can be made and which cannot. In times of high-rising tensions, maintaining the rules becomes a problem. All of a sudden, it appears that different counsellors interpret the rules in a different manner, just to keep the peace. The counsellors feel powerless and everybody does whatever seems to be the right thing to do. Some counsellors believe that their approach is the only right one and secretly they will give in more than is acceptable.

There are limits to the possibilities of these kinds of shelters, which get more than their fair share of the most desperate problems and the most difficult cases. The abuse of women and children evokes all kinds of different reactions of over-identification or avoidance in teams.

There are innumerable factors at play that draw the counselling in a shelter into a desperate and exhausting battle. The staff is not only contaminated with the history of the traumatized, but also with the ever present acting-out behaviour. Little wonder that counsellors within this setting become regularly secondarily traumatized and need time to catch their breath. In some houses, this is met with sympathy, in others you are met with disdain if you dare to take sick leave.

Conclusion and recommendations

Reactions such as over-identification and avoidance can also be detected in other professional groups such as the police and primary health care workers, where one is confronted first hand with the consequences of violence within relationships. It is striking that nowadays, within the police force, a lot of attention is given to the employees in order to prevent secondary trauma. There are teams of co-workers specially trained to help colleagues in need. In mental health care, too, one runs the risk of becoming co-traumatized if one does not have the opportunity, on a regular basis, to voice that which has been silently haunting one's mind. Breaching the silence is a condition in order to be able to keep on working in a healthy climate.

One can formulate a couple of personal, professional, and organizational conditions in order to do this job and (almost) get away with it in one piece.

Personal. It is vital to give priority to your private life and not to slacken the bonds with the ones who are close to you. Empathic fatigue is one of the characteristics of secondary traumatization and it could result in avoiding friends and social activities. Furthermore, no one wants to burden their loved ones with awful accounts from work.

What might help is keeping a diary of emotional reactions. It could be useful to keep a friend informed about reactions at work. Try to organize some relaxation time in everyday life: sports, massages, sauna, hobbies, going to the theatre. It often helps to go and see or hear something beautiful after hearing violent, destructive accounts. Beauty makes up for a lot. Take regular short breaks if possible.

Professional. Following a course in learning therapy, or the possibility of making an appeal to a supervisor who is familiar with the symptoms of co-traumatization. For someone who works independently within a team looking after the consequences of violence, it is vital to breach the isolation. This is not easily done because colleagues, like most people, are not eager to listen to horrifying stories. In these situations, it is necessary to have the backing of a good supervisor and to keep colleagues informed once in a while.

If reactions are fierce, it is good to discuss them with someone with whom you can unravel them. Feelings of insecurity, despair, powerlessness, and sorrow can be given a place once more. Repetitive behaviour, linked to former traumatic experiences, also can be stopped if help is available.

Furthermore, it is wise to organize a varying practice wherein the treatment of the consequences of violence is spread out more.

Organizational. Within the institution and the intervision network, support has to be offered where the emphasis is laid on the therapist as a person and not on the treatment and institutional procedures. Intervision sessions are indispensable within private practices. One can even decide on a one-to-one debriefing with a colleague and *vice versa*.

Within the team, agreements have to be made as to what the signals are for secondary traumatization and what one can expect from each other if tensions are boiling over. In the previously mentioned shelter situation, it helps the employees a great deal to predict tensions and foreseeable reactions.

The safety of counsellors needs to be actively addressed by installing an alarm system or by seeing to it that colleagues are around if any escalating violence looms.

If institutes are less than supportive, rigid, or downright dismissive of requests for support, the employees run the risk that they will be sent home with burn-out symptoms.

CHAPTER TWELVE

Apprehensive heroes

Martine Groen

T he emphasis in this book is particularly placed on border-crossing behaviour within families and the consequences for children who grow up in violent, quarrelling families. The scale and size of this behaviour demand reflection. What is going on? In this chapter, different views are discussed surrounding the authority crisis within the primary living system and its consequences on the regulation of aggression of our youth, the future generation. This process of undermining was been set in motion immediately after the Second World War, and it has consequences for the manner in which we relate to the aggression we encounter every day on the streets, in public transport, and in the therapy room.

The manner in which aggression is regulated between people differs through time and history and is linked to the then ruling values, norms, and developed systems of punishment (Berlin, 1990). Nowadays, there is a growing "zero-tolerance" towards violent behaviour. The debate on norms and values has found its way into the political agenda once again. One has become aware that boundaries are crossed at all levels, and that no one has an answer at the ready.

There is attention, too, for violent behaviour within families at the Department of Justice, where research is being funded. Insecurity on the streets is an issue, too, and a study has been commissioned to find the connection between the violence on the streets and the witnessing of violence at home.

There are so many contradictory movements visible that it is hard to believe that one can expect an unequivocal answer. In short, there is more to it than that, but what? A great many things have changed in the past decades. The relationships between men and women have become very problematic indeed. Children are growing up within shifting family circumstances. The positions have changed place. The demands on men and women differ from those of the 1950s generation.

What is going wrong with the socialization of youngsters? What causes them to feel that they have the right to use violence casually and what causes them not to be able to restrain themselves? Is it fear which causes aggression to escalate in such a way, and, if it is, how and what is it linked to? How and in what way do mothers come into it, and whatever happened to the fathers and grandfathers?

The rising aggression; the current pedagogic failure

The shift over the past couple of years is particularly notable in the rise of juvenile delinquency. In both public and private life violent offences are on the increase. (You will find statistics on this in Chapter Eight.) Every day, the papers run headlines such as, "Three youngsters wilfully murder a forty-year-old woman". The Netherlands was shocked when some youngsters—under the influence of alcohol—kicked a man to death in Leeuwarden. A boy in Venlo was beaten to death because he was defending an elderly woman. Despite public outcry, the abuses continue.

Aggressive speeds on the roads, and in public life boys between twelve and twenty-one, with their destructive forms of aggression, determine the level of fear on the streets. Girls in a similar age group nowadays also contribute to making public places unsafe, although this does not compare to the rise in criminality among boys. However, the number of abuses among girls is increasing more rapidly than that among boys. Fifty-seven per cent are boys and 39% girls, and boys are more often victims of violence than girls, but girls feel far more unsafe in public areas. What has changed, and what has gone wrong?

Because we mainly deal with young men here, Enzensberger refers in *Oog in oog met the burgeroorlog* (1994) (Face to Face with Civil War) to the eroded patriarchy.

> Secret male societies were a time honoured tradition. Their task was to channel the testosterone driven energy surge of the youngsters, their competitiveness and thirst for blood by ways of initiation rites. The up and coming macho was expected to show proof of courage and display his fighting skills. With this, stringent codes of honour had to be taken into account. These concepts are alien to the current violent perpetrators. A new masculinity has raised its head. One would think that its name would be coward, but that is an overestimate. [p. 94]

Enzensberger fulminates on and on, feeling powerless against these forms of barbaric violence.

Van den Brink (2001) assumes that people's feeling of self-worth has grown strongly over the past thirty years. Most children have been given more attention from their parents than ever before, and much attention has been bestowed on the individual, compliments of the welfare state. Van den Brink reasons that citizens are extremely assertive and that neither the state nor the police have a proper response to it. The violence, in his opinion, derives from the fact that citizens are at a loss with their assertiveness and fall back on senseless violence or other violent behaviour. Threatened assertive citizens no longer have a say in the political debate or in the civil administration. The gap is too wide, thus frustration looms large.

This reasoning in itself is interesting but there is a lot to be said about it. Van den Brink assumes that a lot of attention makes children more assertive. But does it? Other scientists (Mooij, 2002; Verhaege, 1998) propose the exact opposite. Precisely because children have been given so much attention, a generation has emerged that is not able to deal with blows, but has learnt only to consume and to demand. And if every need is not immediately satisfied, there will be anger, and the new citizen will scream out his rights as a toddler would. The focus has shifted to the satisfaction of the "Me", and empathizing with the "Other" has been put on the back burner.

The decline of authority

Theories have been developed from all sides; hypotheses have been shaped to explain these possible changing and toughening processes within our society. From an ethical point of view, one blames the decline of morality and the loss of authority on the loss of a religious structure that offers people something to hold on to. The systems of values on which life goals are based are no longer distinct. There is no set of rules about how one is supposed to live, what the tasks are supposed to be for women and men, and how they should conduct themselves. A renewed debate about norms and values has been initiated to restore authority. However, the question is whether there is any point in this; the process of erosion was set in motion a long time ago, is rather complex, and covers almost all fronts.

Family life has become more unstable, the divorce rate has increased, the division of roles is under discussion, and the expectations men and women have of each other have become increasingly unclear. Women have gained greater independency and they have a stronger foothold in the labour market. The number of women working outside the family home has risen dramatically, compared to twenty years ago. The position of fathers within families has shifted and weakened. Only 38% of children still live in the original family unit. The changing relationships between partners have caused boys to be raised mainly by women. The concept "absent father" became relevant after the war. Literally disillusioned, hurt, and traumatized men returned home from the war. The rebuilding and the subsequent hard graft played a part, too. Figuratively, the process was set in motion long before that.

Hannah Arendt regards the collapse of all traditional authorities as an authority crisis which had been set in motion at the beginning of the twentieth century. The gravity of the crisis had spread its tentacles towards the domain of child-rearing and education. The relationships between adults and children, teachers and pupils, have become unclear. This means that all old, honourable meta-phors and models of authority have lost their credence (Arendt, 1994).

These days, boys are confronted with the loss of a structure wherein they could learn how to become a man in a civil manner, how to control aggressive behaviour, how to conquer their fears, how to behave towards women, how to find their way in a chang-ing society where physical strength is no longer needed, but where other qualities are valued. They can no longer fall back on this image of fatherhood. On the other hand, there is a small-scale movement that concerns itself with caring fatherhood, and boys are presented with a different model. The confusion is great. Tears have appeared in this fabric of the rite of passage for boys.

Images and myths

Young adolescents speak animatedly of how exhilarating they find beating someone who is weaker (Enzensberger, 1994). The sense of power is based on the conviction that you have the upper hand through sheer physical power. This sense of power is not solely endowed by their peers; teachers, fathers, and mothers all contribute. Perhaps this violence at this particular point in time is less extreme than it used to be. Nowadays, the violent behaviour appears to be without rhyme or reason, without any links to a community or meaning. The most remarkable examples are those of youngsters between the age of twelve and eighteen forcing elderly people out of the tram without any bystanders intervening.

It will probably become more understandable if one closely examines the circumstances in which the violence increases and which role parents or surroundings have in it.

Brute physical force and a big mouth are no longer a matter of course, and yet boys learn from an early age that this separates them from girls. Remarkably, it is especially the mothers who emphasize this difference (Chodorow, 1980). Psychoanalytical theo-ries and anthropological research offer interesting material on this issue. An example of the latter is the work of the anthropologist Gilmore (1994). In De man als mythe (The Man as a Myth), he describes how in different parts of the world the initiation rites form an important part of becoming a man. With most peoples known to anthropologists, true masculinity is a treasured and wavering status that reaches way beyond being a man. It is a stimulating image to which boys and men want to conform because their culture demands it. In his book, Gilmore combines cultural legacy, social role, and a psychoanalytical view on the social construct of masculinity. He distinguishes how the different contexts determine the images of masculinity. Life at work, the office, and the demands that are put on men have their impact on the private domain. Even though men personally do not feel powerful, they are allowed to move in a space that is reserved solely for them. Their own domain is often the result of a prolonged training which differs between cultures and locations.

In the UK there were boarding schools that would turn boys into men. Cruel tests, physical violence and terror, were the instruments of older male students. Parents believed that this would lead the way to the social status of masculinity. Military service had a similar role in the Netherlands. There were other customs in Germany. George Steiner writes in *Anno Domini*:

> In the summer months we learned how to become a man. We were made to stand on a chunk of wood, side by side, and beat, in turns, the crap out of each other. The one who ducked first was a coward. [1974]

Learning to be tough, controlling aggression, withstanding fears, and taking on pain without shedding a tear, these are the ingredients to make a man out of a boy and to distance yourself as a boy from your mother. Soldiers do not need mothers; that will only be a burden to them. The gentleness that is associated with the longing for mothers is a handicap in tough public life. Boys have to be turned into warriors, ready for battle. These are the violent myths that are a role model for boys.

Another point of view is underpinned by Whitmer in her book *The Violence Mythos* (1997), in which she proposes the thesis that our heroic images are traumatized men, who suffer from post traumatic stress syndrome. Banishing pain, splitting feeling and logic, lack of empathy, and repeating traumatic experiences are all elements which explain to her that our cultural images are drenched with sick heroes. This account coincides with the findings of Dutton (1998), who also describes traumatized men who can no longer take the tensions and start hitting (see Chapter Nine for more detail).

The psychoanalysis

In most societies, the awareness of the boy leads to some form of independence which clarifies that there is a difference between him and his mother. At a certain point, he will find that he differs from his mother and that other behaviour is expected of him. In order to break free from his mother, the boy has to be put to a test which severs the bond with her. He will have to relinquish his bond and find his own way. According to this theory, danger for the boy lurks in his mother, in not getting away from her, and not his punishing father. Not getting away from the mother, the ineradicable wish, the longing for the motherly symbiosis, obstructs the way to adulthood for boys.

Male constructed images can be interpreted from this psycho-analytical perspective as a defence mechanism against regression. All children have the tendency to long for the safety of their mother's lap in times of danger. This childish tendency is never really absent in adults.

The theory of the psychoanalyst Kohut (1971) sheds an interesting light on the ambivalence that surrounds the socialization of boys. According to him, masculinity develops along two poles. The one pole represents the mother, the bond, and the longing for intimacy. The other pole carries the male ideal, and it targets the development into accepting responsibility, as society demands. Kohut says that boys have to give up the first pole, breaching the bond with the mother, and hardening themselves in accepting tasks. This is an almost inevitable choice that boys have to make. The culture offers them nice myths and stories to get through the ordeal in order to reach the masculine ideal. Percival used to be the role model; nowadays it is the Rambos and the Schwarzeneggers who are the role models.

Men have to prove their manhood; in most cultures, they have to be able to maintain the family, they have to be sexually active and potent, be serviceable, and perform. The man proves himself through public deeds. In the image of masculinity the same opinions return over and over again: controlling his wife's sexuality, the protector of the family honour, the family as an important beacon for the "male honour".

In the modern heroic stories, these coding elements play their part, too. Their meaning may ring somewhat hollow; on the other hand, the lack of a father, for example, is precisely the reason for youngsters and adolescents to fall back on old archaic images. The media and computer games gladly exploit this gap in the market. We see the return of strong, violent heroes in games and on the television screen.

The lack of a father, according to the Belgian psychoanalyst Verhaege (1998), causes the sons to lose their central identity and thus they are doomed to remain in the position of a son. We can detect youngsters of thirty and adolescents of forty. The amount of fear in these sons can be found in the resulting aggression.

With youngsters who are born in the Netherlands but whose parents hail from Turkey, Morocco, the Antilles, Surinam, or a country from which they have fled, the expectation gap plays a major part. The expectation is that, on the one hand, the youngsters have to fulfil the tasks of the parental home and, on the other hand, they want to maintain themselves among their peers. The codes of honour in such families are less hollow, loss of face is a serious matter, shame is extremely painful, and is often followed by anger. In cultures where shame is the foremost guide for behaviour, boys are legitimized in revenging themselves in the group to which they belong.

Rituals

The place of women, men, and children within a traditional society is embedded in rules and regulations, in rituals, and in the manner in which religion proscribes how to behave. Rituals underpin this division in the social order and give it sense and meaning. Part of these rituals have been lost and have probably been replaced by other practices, but we do not really know. Rituals, as common acts, used to limit the violence within the family. All that has changed now.

Different meanings are given to the relationships between the sexes. The distance of power between women and men has diminished and there are no new codes to steer these shifts in the right direction.

We suspect that ritualized practices have been developed, but their effect is not clear. It is therefore important to know the meaning these customs now have, which role they play in the transference, and in the image surrounding masculinity. Are they a useful instrument to refute violent behaviour?

Different definitions are given of rituals in anthropological studies. A ritual is an acknowledgement of the unity of a community against the frictions, the tensions, and the rivalry of social life; in the words of Turner (1968), it is a creative anti-structure which distinguishes itself from the strict enforcement of the social order and hierarchy and of other traditional forms of control.

In general, rituals are meant as an expression of the faith in symbolic "ways"; they have to be reaffirmed constantly in order to have the desired effect. This happens, for example, while internalizing the images of masculinity and femininity. Constantly recurring daily rituals unconsciously confirm the images, thus imprinting them.

The "formal" character of the rituals is important. One does not have to believe them in order to participate. This does not apply to myths: you cannot retell myths over and over again without believing in them. Rituals, therefore, cannot be traced back to linked opinions of faith which are shared by the participants. The "workings", the effect they have, is induced through the activities of a ritual *per se*. This insight can also be applied to the relationship between rituals and power. Rituals do not hide or cover up power. They are an expression of power; they make people do things and set them in motion.

In this opinion, ritualizing is first and foremost a strategy to construct certain types of power relationships. A remarkable exponent of this opinion is the French philosopher Foucault (1995), who supposes that the subject derives from a network of strategic power relationships. Ritualizing is a strategy to call power relationships into being. It enhances the power of those who control and check the process of ritualizing. That power is not without its limits. Ritualized practices always need the consent of the participants, but, at the same time, they pave the way for a reasonable degree of resistance. This resistance is limited because there is not much to gain in a ritualized power relationship. Ritualizing supposes set patterns wherein the margins for participants to the ritual are extremely limited.

Another opinion about ritualizing puts the emphasis on the symbolic modelling of the social order. Turner and Douglas (Turner, 1968) are the exponents of this opinion and they presume that the imagery (or iconic) quality of the ritual forms the basis of its effectiveness.

Ritualizing masculinity

Against the backdrop of these different opinions about rituals and ritualizing, it is worth the effort to see how boys turn into men and what has shifted in the last decades within this process.

In the Western world, there are hardly any ritual acknowledgements to be found (see Chapter Seven for more details). Youngsters will have to find their own way to becoming a man. The anthropologist Dijk found that use of alcohol and fighting in bars in Canada and on the island of Tuck were a ritualized way to gain masculinity. Fighting spirit here is a substitute for proof of power through war and plunder. The use of alcohol, fighting, smoking pot, and showing off are pre-eminent proofs of masculinity within the working-class cultures in the industrial Western world. After they reach the age of twenty-five, the lives of most men will become more tranquil.

Most road accidents happen to people between the age of eighteen and twenty-five. One tests one's limits, the dangers, and death itself. These are personal tests nowadays; youngsters look for acknowledgement herein and they seek admiration. Enzensberger presumes that gaps have occurred in the transition from adolescence into adulthood. Youngsters are no longer able to find a new grip and they do not learn to deal with their feelings in another way. They fall back on age-old images and their reflections: who is the strongest, who can take the most drink, who can beat or shoot the most boys. They continue to reproduce this type of violence.

Other examples include the fact that the referee in amateur football is increasingly called names and threatened. He no longer receives the acknowledgement of distinction on the pitch. Authority has failed wherever violence is used. Rules are no longer respected or taken into account. Sport was pre-eminently meant to create a healthy mind in a healthy body. This, too, no longer rings true.

There seems to be a link between playing sports intensively and violent and criminal behaviour. Rules which used to be highly important in combat sports are no longer so. Self-control, in combat sports like judo and karate, is no longer held in high regard outside the gym. Boys measure their strength without any ritual meaning in the broader community.

At home, too, the violence of children perpetrated against their parents can get out of hand, especially in families where reason and control are the magic words. It is striking that especially in so-called civilized families, children can terrorize their parents in the extreme, even through violent behaviour. Not drawing lines and keeping up unclear relations are contributing factors.

The empty marriage and the short-term relationship

What does the rite of passage of men entail for marriage; what is the meaning of romance? How have men learned to solve and to settle disputes with women? Which images play a part in this? How do men behave if they are threatened with abandonment?

They lose their grip; familiar patterns are lost. The traditional codes that define personal existence and social life are being eroded. There are no new codes, as yet, to which they can conform. For men (and women, too) this means, more than ever, having to fall back on their individual resources and this is beyond their reach. Verhaege (1998) blames this failure on the disruption of the monotheistic patriarchy which holds men in the grip of fear for their existence. According to Verhaege, this fear does not only strike men, but women, too, but for men it takes a specific, sexualized form. He describes this fear as the fear of getting lost in the female body and, simultaneously, a longing to lose oneself.

Verhaege's analysis owes a lot to the philosophy of Jaques Lacan, according to whom men's existence is marked by a fundamental and insoluble shortcoming. The human subject is never entirely autonomous, it never falls into place with itself; in its longing it is always dependent on others. This longing cannot be fulfilled. In this lies the human shortcoming. This shortcoming is epitomized by what Lacan calls the symbolic order. This concept refers to the existence of an abstract order of symbols such as the concepts of man and woman. The concrete identity of men and women must be defined in relation to these concepts. Once these concepts begin to shift, set free from their place in the symbolic order, it becomes difficult to develop a clear picture of one's own identity as a man or a woman. Under these circumstances, according to Lacan, the human subject has the tendency to belie his shortcoming and to escape into imaginary images, deceptive images wherein men and women try to find a grip in order to make their existence bearable. However, these images do not help.

In relationships between people, this relapse forces them to a continuous adjusting of the images each has from the other. These are stiff demands. The force of that symbolic order has diminished. Imaginary balances of power remain highly volatile and can tip over at any point. By not accepting the shortcoming, there is an insatiable longing that keeps finding its way via the other, who will never be able to fulfil this longing; the right to happiness via the other, or the compelling demand put on the other to satisfy a need. Men give a different import to this longing via the other than women do.

In denying the differences, some other order has developed within the marriage. This means the increase of more and more tormented relations, relationships in which people manipulate and threaten each other in order to be recognized and satisfied in their longings.

How often do we hear in our practice that couples do not understand each other any more, that they speak a different language? Especially when relationships are based on performance and competition, there is a constant battle for balance: who admires whom the most, and who disappoints whom the least? The fear of not being up to scratch is a driving force behind this dynamic within couple relationships.

Men feel vulnerable, scared, and they think this entitles them to use violence. Men who deny their dependency on women, who are ashamed, also find cause to react in a violent manner. Within imaginary relationships, the images that men and women have of each other have their impact on all levels of the relationship. The longing can be projected without limits on to the other with the aid of imagery which hails from the age-old symbolic relationships, but which have been completely eroded.

Other meanings have taken over control. A study conducted by Van der Avort (1987) clearly shows that marriages which have clear boundaries and marked out tasks and fields have a more harmonic course than the modern romantic marriage in which the dual merger is valued highly. The battle, or competition about who has what to say about whatever, is often fought to the limit. In our estimate, beatings in these kinds of relationships are often more cruel and boundless.

One in three marriages end in divorce. Love is no longer a lifelong adventure; a marriage is easily broken up. A quick end has come to high expectations. Many cultural scientists are worried about this trend. They talk of a culture of consumption: you eat away at your relationship, you finish the chapter, and you move on to the next. They warn about the demise of meanings of solidarity and loyalty in communities (Idenburg, 1983; Lasch, 1977; Zijderveld, 1983). Lasch, especially, is gloomy and says that the primary relationship no longer has any meaning in the public domain. This does have its consequences for raising the next generation.

Mooij (2002) underpins this train of thought in his book *Psychoanalytisch gedachtegoed* (Psychoanalytical Line of Reasoning). He pictures the retreat of the symbolic, the creation of a culture of images in which he sees an accumulation of examples that encourage people towards rivalry and competitiveness. This leads, according to Mooij, to a self-image that is closely linked to the idolized imagery of a narcissistic nature about one's own supremacy, not aimed at the future, but which has to be realized here and now.

Envy and aggression form the core features that are of narcissistic origin. In Mooij's perspective, such an imaginary culture of images leads to a strong desire to control and a focus on performance. The realization of inevitable failure is either pushed aside or denied. The capacity to take a blow has been lost, and with it the ability to suffer and mourn losses. One feels one is entitled to happiness and, if one does not have it, it has to be demanded. In public life, there are no new heroes to be detected who could act as a role model for vulnerability. The model is the strong individual who guarantees his own development. Loss equals failure, failure is shameful. Whenever shame becomes unbearable and is denied, it could lead to angry outbursts (Tangney & Dearing, 2002).

A power vacuum has been created. Its causes are probably manifold: women's liberation, the anti-authoritarian upbringing strategies which were important in the 1970s, the democratization of family life where the child's voice takes centre-stage, the erosion of the father's authority. Men especially suffer because of this power vacuum. Their authority is no longer accepted as a matter of course; they flee outward and cling on to their jobs. Life is work; passion is transferred into work.

Vulnerability and impotence

As said before, talking about one's feelings is a woman's domain and is less developed in men. Expressing emotions is not a skill that would have had priority in the upbringing of men, except for the expression of aggressive feelings: herein, men are especially encouraged and trained, and women are not. The silence of fathers, the lack of contact in the relationship between father and son, the incapacity of fathers to maintain an intimate relationship with their sons, is currently described in several different therapeutic books as "the vacuum". Nowadays, something different is expected of men in heterosexual relationships. It is often the demand for more intimate contact, learning to express feelings.

Highly educated men who lose their self-control during a row and beat their wives, come up with the excuse that they can no longer reason about what is going on. Women accuse their husbands of talking with their heads only and not with their hearts. The differences in expressing oneself seem unbridgeable. She starts throwing his beloved things around, hits him, and he hits back harder. Sometimes, couples declare this to be their most intimate form of contact. The man shows remorse and is ashamed, especially once the storm has blown over and the wounds have been licked. Sons who are confronted by such escalating forms of rowing regard the inability of their father to maintain contact in another way as a model.

The message boys receive while growing up is: keep silent, do not interfere, work hard and do not whine. Respect depends on performance, loyalty is shown to the company, honour is derived from work.

Ever since women have become no longer economically dependent on them, men have become extra vulnerable. Even their sperm is no longer really needed. Once physical strength is no longer a thing which society values, the organization of the world remains the vital pillar of male dominance. Within relationship therapy, it transpires that men who feel insecure about their position either hit harder or become the most depressed. As concluded before, if the roles are unclear, the most obvious reaction is a desire to return to the old and trusted.

Recent statistics about domestic violence have made their impact. Especially remarkable are the intentions and attempts by the government, police force, and the Department of Justice to intervene in the customs and habits in the domestic circle. Can private relationships be pacified by control and the authority of the government? Can "authority" ever put in place again "the border" which was lost and aid people in dealing with their conflicts in a peaceful manner? Or are the limits of reasoning already reached?

The "individualization" within our society is a silent revolution with vast consequences for the community. Who is allowed to say something about whom? Voices are being heard asking for authority to be devolved to local communities in the larger cities. The community has the right to interfere if there is violent behaviour on the streets or in the home. Experience, however, has shown that interference on the streets often leads to renewed violence and to new victims.

There are no answers

Many explanations have been given for increased aggression over the past decade: political, sociological, ethical, psychoanalytical. They are partly contradictory and partly supplement each other. Whether more or less violence was used, say, about a century ago, is unclear. We do not know exactly how violence and aggression manifested itself then. It is clear, however, that these were phenomenona which were part of society and were regarded as ways of dealing with conflicts. The violence was presumably less personal, and it was part of the family, the clan, the village, the nation. It was more or less taken for granted that the larger communities were allowed to rule over the lives of their members whenever vital issues were concerned which threatened the social or national structure.

People were not acknowledged as autonomous individuals. This applied to all, but to women and children in particular, who were not regarded as equal members of the several social systems. Power was solely a male thing. One may assume that there were clear guidelines as to situations where violence was permitted. This would probably be in situations that we would qualify as having got out of hand, such as public drunkenness and pub and fairground brawls. There, too, the violence was coded and ritualized in a way. It was the prerogative of certain groups, adolescents especially, and it was limited to certain situations. Outside this it was not tolerated, and presumably severely punished.

The ritualization and coding of violence and aggression did not mean that there was no large-scale violence. Compared to our society as it is now, post two world wars and the Holocaust, there was massive and manifest violence.

Nowadays, after sixty years of peace in Western Europe, the violence seems to be directed more inward and harder to trace. It is more specified, unruly, built-in, like road-rage, or the boasting behaviour of drunken youngsters, or aggression at school.

What plays tricks on us is the fact that public space has become more diffused, empty, indefinable. There are fewer and fewer rules, and, at the same time, there is an abundance of rules, but these do not seem to be internalized. It is no longer clear to whom the public space belongs, the parks, the streets, the squares, and who can freely move around there under what conditions. Street violence is not only caused by a lack of norms (of decency) but also by the fact that public space is no longer acknowledged as public property. People behave less as public persons; they do not regard the space as part of the community to which they belong. Public space is increasingly flooded by private interests, office buildings, shops, and terraces; thus public space loses its identity.

People have become consumers, holiday-makers who mainly eat and drink and are not in the least bothered about the mess they leave behind. The codes of behaviour for the use of public space have become empty and diffuse. People no longer know which rules to abide by. Manners in public spaces are still bound by formal rules (e.g., traffic rules), but they are no longer embedded in sociological or psychological norms. Groups going through rites of passage no longer know how to behave and constantly tend to test what is permitted and what is not.

Inside and outside

It seems to be conceivable that external aggression will partly turn inward and invade the private space. Some research has been done into the interaction from the outside to the inside, but up until now not on a systematic level. However, one may conclude that there is a link between the violence that is experienced at home and the violent behaviour of youngsters outside the family home.

Nevertheless, it has become clear that the small family unit, or comparable forms of co-habitation, no longer acts as the safe haven that it should be against the violence and toughness of the outside world. The frustrations and insecurities which people experience outside the family home put extra pressure on the family relationship. The pressure is not, or only partly, channelled. It is too vast, and the family is not equipped to deal with it. Family relations have grown in a less complex and much more orderly world; its range and elasticity do not reach far enough to withstand the pressure of "another" social surrounding, let alone deal with it.

The family no longer suffices as a safety net for the inner world, too. The existing codes and rituals are, partly and in some areas, so worn out that they offer insufficient grip. There is little experience of how to respond to new conflicts in a fitting manner. Insufficiently adequate control mechanisms have been developed within smaller systems as well. One has to rely on "talking", on the agogic, understanding conversation. However, many people are unable to do so, and, besides, a discussion is often too thin and poor to cover up the sense of fear and aggression that can constantly overwhelm people who lead an insecure existence.

Men and women become increasingly harried by the work pace; there has to be an increase in productivity, there is less time, no peace and quiet. Employability has its grip on all. This heightened pressure is almost unbearable. What we actually need is a cartography of the pressures. This cartography should show where line-crossings occur and in which schedules pressures develop. When and in which situations are people no longer able to know what to do? The question is how to find a way out of this situation.

A way out?

A way back is no longer an option and would only lead to repetition. The untangling of the images which represent "the male" could be a first step. It enables young men to mirror themselves in other forms of masculinity than those associated with power and violence. They offer a possible alternative to compensate for the loss of the former symbolic meanings. The fact that there is a great need for different images is obvious in the interest youngsters have in the media. There they find their icons, whom they worship as heroes, but in general they only confirm traditional masculinity and the old-fashioned macho ideals.

A second way out could be to discuss the role women have in the socialization of boys. Women still do play a major part in keeping up the image of masculinity. Women's liberation has questioned the image of the woman, but little attention is given to the other aspect. It is vital to make the next move and to change the part that women have in socialization. First, it is about the retreat of women. Due to the erosion of current relationships, their role has become harder and vaster. There is just cause to lessen that role and to engage men more in the tasks of care and the raising of children. In some way or other men should even more clearly be made responsible in the judicial, socio-economical sense, should they try to pass the buck.

A third way out could be to let go of the notion of the autonomous child, the pedagogic ideal of the "emancipated" child. Temptation looms large during a crisis for all concerned to choose for themselves: men do, women do it, too (but less so), and children do it as well. For complex questions, which includes the transition of children towards adulthood, this autonomy is not the answer. Hannah Arendt made a plea in the 1960s to reinstate the raising of children with the status of authority and respect and to shape youngsters in such a manner that they are capable of renewing a communal world. Arendt thinks it imperative to separate the domain of raising children from other domains, in particular those of public and political life. She pleads for the reinstatement of authority. Children and adults are not on an equal footing. Authority does not equal discussion. To argue renders authority useless.

Arendt's plea is important because, nowadays, there are no images left regarding the manner in which one can prepare children for public life. The "age of the child" has created a shift, not only in pedagogics, but also in the balance of authority between parents and children, teachers and pupils. The concept of raising has been eroded, the inner world of the child has taken centre-stage and is leading a life of its own. Children are almost treated as authorities, autonomous and emancipated. However, they are not. They are stunted in their socialization process if one treats them as such. Arendt's plea for reinstating authority in child-raising is not a call to return to the old ways, but to give meaning again to the elementary codes and values which are instrumental for socialization.

Learning to deal with conflicts in a different way is part of this. It is about developing new relations, new structures, and new codes, through which youngsters can secure a bond with the intimate world during the rites of passage and pacify their fears and aggression. One of the ways to modulate the violence within partner relationships has been discussed extensively. More research is needed, and we should experiment with other forms of solving conflicts.

We are glad to say that research has been set in motion in the Netherlands as well. On the website www.huiselijkgeweld.nl, one may find all recent studies, all activities, and publications. However, a new form of conflict-solving remains a challenge to us.

These three ways out will not lead to an abolishment of violence in our society. Violence is part of humanity, but civilization demands that we find some way to deal with it.

Conclusion

I n *Intimate Warfare*, we describe how tensions can build up
within families and in the end lead to violence. We point out in
different ways how to curb the violence and how people can be
taught different ways of dealing with conflicts. We have tried to
analyse violent behaviour within families from different points of
view. We discussed the changing shifts in the positions between
men and women and the confusion and tension that go with it. Men
no longer have a clear role model, many marriages are stranded,
and a lot of children grow up in single-parent units with their
mother. Some scientists, like Verhaege, expect more violence within
partner relationships and families in the future.

We live in a period of transition, a time where confusion could
change into fear, insecurity, and aggression. Serious conflicts often
arise within families in times of transition, for example, during a
shift in the balance of power. Apart from the theoretical analysis
about violence within families, we have described methods for
working therapeutically with violence issues within families. On
the one hand, it demands a brief and more formal approach in
order to end the violence, on the other hand, we concentrate on the
approach which assumes that the whole family suffers because of

the violent behaviour and we choose to involve the family members, whenever possible, with the process of de-escalation. Putting the violent behaviour into context has high priority in our working method. Contexts are never static. They are constantly moving and manifest themselves in changing configurations. Not only does the context appeal to the analytical capacity of the therapist, but also on his/her capability for shaping it. Putting into context is looking for a new balance and tiny shifts (Kuijpers, 2002). A family acts as a social system; the behaviour of people is conducted in relationships to others and is guided by mutual expectations, opinions, and codes. In systemic therapy, methods have been developed to bring about shifts precisely in the context of the social system, within the area of family relationships. Asking circular questions is one of the most effective ways to put a family on the right track and to inspire members of that family to deal with conflicts and tensions in another manner than violence.

This approach is diagonally different from the current trend to treat patients according to a method that is characterized as evidence-based. The protocol approach is based on the conviction that short-term treatments, linked to the right diagnosis, would yield quick results. One opts for speed and short-term results over treatments that require more time and that are focused on a more equal co-operation between client and therapist within the frame of determining the issues and finding new solutions for all involved. The protocol approach is client-focused and does not take into account the context in which people live their lives, and work. However, this context is vital in order to effectively combat psychological complaints. From this perspective, we plead for a contextual approach. Complaints often point towards other problematical social structures. The current labour market is such a structure, wherein psychological tensions arise. Research of the Donner Commission into the nature and scale of dropping out and incapacity to work, show that a third of all drop-outs (300,000 people) show problems of a psychological nature. These problems appear impossible to be classified according the *DSM-IVR*, the psychiatric system of classification. They receive treatment, if any, on an individual basis, while a great number of the outflow is due either to labour conflicts or to frictions in the tension-field of family life and work. A client-focused approach with this category of drop-outs is

fragmented, narrows people, and makes them responsible for influences that are way beyond their reach, like a re-organization or
changing demands at the workplace. We do not wish to individu-
alize the issue of violence within a family in this way.

We have tried to point out the relationship between the violence
which is happening within the broader context of the public
domain, the market and the institutions, as is also made visible in
the media. Many questions remain, and there is an abundance of
possibilities for further research. The link between street violence,
at school, and within the family still needs further research.
Bullying and violence at school and the workplace have their reper-
cussions on the family unit. Besides research into these connections,
research is also needed into the effects of the contextual approach,
which we favour. However, the future for our field of expertise does
not look rosy. We fear the detrimental effect "tunnel-vision" will
have if the proposal of the final report of the National Commission
for Mental Health, *Zorg van velen* (Care for Many), is adopted. In
this proposal, the first line (GP, community work, and social work)
will be mainly responsible for the reception of and primary deal-
ings with complaints, among which are violent offences and their
consequences. Further care, the second line, will take place in
hospitals. Psychiatric care for people who show proper psychopathic, deviant behaviour according to the book, will take place in
the third echelon, where psychiatrists and psychotherapists will
provide treatment.

Our plea is directly opposite to this advice. We cannot agree
with these recommendations, which are thought up by people who
are so far removed from everyday practice. We stand for adequate
help, specialized help, too, which is easily available to people. The
families that we have described in this book have found their way
to us via the police, GP, or another institution. It is remarkable that
the road which leads to the official institutions of the mental health
care, the Regional Institutes for Mental Health Care (RIAGG), is
often avoided. These institutions are pressured under the regime of
short-term treatments, and are mainly orientated to the individual
approach, with few exceptions. More is the pity, because the primal
intention of the RIAGG used to be to act as a Community Health
Centre, with a low threshold and amid a local surrounding. This,
unfortunately, never came into being, also due to the fact that the

RIAGG has modelled itself according to a medical–individual model. Furthermore, they had to bear a vast administrative burden over the past couple of years, due to the registration of short proto-colled treatments. Apart from that, they have become involved in mergers on a grand scale, which have made them slower and less flexible in their functioning. Owing to this development, the coun-sellors have turned inward, as it were. If the proposal of the National Commission is adopted, the isolation will only increase. Within the daily practice of the counsellor, there will no longer be any institution which deals solely with the co-operation between counsellors. Things will go wrong if that co-operation does not exist, because families who are in trouble usually have to deal with more than one institution.

Under these circumstances, we have to assume that the RIAGGs, due to aforementioned impediments, will no longer be able to fulfil this function of co-operation. It is imperative to develop other forms of co-operation that are alert and are flexible enough to work with people's concrete problems, right through all levels of institutes. The first steps in that direction have been made, for example, in projects surrounding domestic violence wherein police, social work, GPs, probation officers, Community Health Service, care for drug addiction, and specialized help, work together. This so-called "chain of care" stands an excellent chance nowadays. The reins are in the hands of the municipal government, which sees to it that all participants co-operate and tune their activ-ities to each other. The client stands centre-stage within the chain of care, and one tries to put the interests of waging an effective war against domestic violence above the procedures of the different institutions. This vision fits nicely within the implementation of a domestic ban for perpetrators by Minister Donner. On the basis of this measure, it is within the mayor's jurisdiction to proceed to displace perpetrators of domestic violence. The domestic ban for perpetrators was introduced in the Netherlands following the policy of Austria.

Since February 2006, when the law for a domestic ban on domestic violence was implemented, a municipal government may decide to ban the perpetrator from entering his house for a maxi-mum period of four weeks. Keeping in mind the effectiveness of such a decision, it is advisable that counselling should be wrapped tightly around the family involved for the first ten days. The perpetrator has to be treated, either forcibly or voluntarily. The same goes for the wife and children. They, too, need help in order to breach the downward spiral of violence. One has to avoid the battle flaring up again. The wife and children could also learn to control their resentment and grudges. Only then will they be able to start all over again with their husband or father. The space will not always be there. If it is a question of revenge of honour, as with certain migrant groups, the counselling will be limited in its possibilities. Revenge of honour is a sacred duty, which has to be fulfilled at any cost because otherwise the clan and the family members will be exposed to eternal damnation. One can only try to protect people against these kinds of beliefs; not only the wife and her children, but probably her family members as well. More help is not possible in these cases. For this group, shelters where they can stay anonymously remain a necessity.

There is no institution which can effectively battle domestic violence single-handedly. The police force, the public prosecutor, the probation officers, Youth Care, women's shelters, social services, and other aid organizations form a chain together and they will have to formulate a fitting approach together. Some things have been put in motion over the last couple of years. In dozens of municipalities and regions, co-operatives for "domestic violence" have been set up. Co-operation is mostly laid down in convenants. A survey of the convenants which have been agreed upon with the establishment of thirty-six points in The Netherlands where you can get advice and report violence; the *Advies- en Meldpunten Huiselijk Geweld* (advice and information centres for domestic violence) can be found on www.movisie.nl, the current centre of knowledge regarding domestic violence.

Establishing convenants is important, but it does not guarantee a proper co-operation. This takes a lot more. The differences between the several protocols that the institutions work with form the biggest obstacle. Intake procedures and diagnostic systems do not link up (as yet). This is one of the biggest hurdles in realizing effective chains of structure. Little experience has been gained as yet. Rules and protocols run deeper into the identity of an organization than one tends to think. Co-operation is too often looked for in the disposition of the professional employees of an organization.

However, a moral appeal to these employees does not suffice in most cases. It is extremely difficult to breach the daily routine and formal certainties. Real co-operation is only conceivable with the insight that the specific interest of an organization will receive justice if it is subordinate to a fitting system of care for the client. In the world of policy and aid, this insight is heralded with conviction. However, it seems to be not that easily put into practice. There is a need for "best practices", for unorthodox models and daring experiments. Ways have to be found as well to pass on knowledge and experience to professionals who are involved in the chains of care. The reinforcement of expertise is not only necessary for the professionals in the aid profession, but also for lawyers, members of the police force, judges, and public prosecutors. The emphasis has to be put on the work that is being done close to the fire, close to people in need.

REFERENCES

Ainsworth, M. D. S., Blehar, M. C., Waters, E., & Wall, S. (1978). *Patterns of Attachment. A Psychological Study of the Strange Situation.* Hillsdale, NJ: Erlbaum.

Alexander, P. C. (1992). Effects of incest on self and social functioning: developmental psychopathology perspective. *Journal of Consulting and Clinical Psychology, 60*: 185–195.

Alon, N., & Omer, H. (2006). *The Psychology of Demonization. Promoting Acceptance and Reducing Conflict.* Mahwah, NJ: Lawrence Erlbaum.

Arendt, H. (1994). *Tussen Verleden en Toekomst.* Leuven, Apeldoorn: Garant.

Baartman, H. E. M. (1993). *Opvoeden met alle geweld.* Utrecht: SWP.

Babcock, J. C., & LaTaillade, J. (2000). Evaluating interventions for men who batter. In: J. Vincent & E. Jouriles (Eds.), *Domestic Violence: Guidelines for Research-informed Practice* (pp. 37–77). Philadelphia, PA: Jessica Kingsley.

Babcock, J. C., Green, C. E., & Robie, C. (2004). Does batterers treatment work? A meta-analytic review of domestic violence treatment outcome research. *Clinical Psychology Review, 23*: 1023–1053.

Bakker, A. B. (2002). Hoe werkomstandigheden van invloed zijn op burnout: het web-model. In: C. A. L. Hoogduin, W. B. Schaufeli, C. P. D. R. Schaap & A. B. Bakker (Eds.), *Behandelingsstrategieën bij Burnout: Cure & Care.* Houten: Bohn Stafleu van Loghum.

Bancroft, L., & Silverman, J. G. (2002). *The Batterer as Parent*. Thousand Oaks, CA: Sage.

Bateson, G. (1972). *Steps to an Ecology of Mind*. New York: Ballantine Books.

Baumeister, R. (1997). *Evil. Inside Human Cruelty and Violence*. New York: Freeman.

Baumeister, R. (1999). Eigenwaarde is nutteloos. *NRC Handelsblad*.

Benedek, E. (1985). Children and psychic trauma. A brief review of contemporary thinking. In: R. Pynoos & S. Eth (Eds.), *Post-Traumatic Stress Disorder in Children* (pp. 3–16). Washington DC: American Psychiatric Press.

Bentinck, A., Duintjer, F., van der Post, L., & van Weeren, P. (1986). Gezinstherapie met verslaafden. *Tijdschrift voor Psychoterapie, 12*: 32–42.

Bentovim, A. (1988). *Child Sexual Abuse Within the Family: Assessment and Treatment*. London: Butterworth.

Berlin, I. (1990). *Het kromme hout waaruit de mens gemaakt is*. Kok Agora/Pelckmans.

Bethke, T. M., & DeJoy, D. M. (1993). An experimental study of factors influencing the acceptability of dating violence. *Journal of Interpersonal Violence, 8*: 36–51.

Boggiano, A., Barrett, M., Silvern, L., & Gallo, S. (1991). Predicting emotional concomitants of learned helplessness. The role of motivational orientation. *Sex Roles, 25*: 577–593.

Bograd, M., & Yllo, K. (Eds.) (1988). *Feminist Perspectives on Wife Abuse*. Beverley Hills, CA: Sage.

Bol, M. W., Terlouw, G. J., Blees, L. W., & Verwers, C. (1998). *Jong en gewelddadig. Ontwikkeling en achtergronden van de geweldscriminaliteit onder jeugdigen*. Den Haag: WODC.

Bowlby, J. (1988). *A Secure Base. Parent–Child Attachment and Healthy Human Development*. New York: Basic Books.

Braithwaite, J. (1989). *Crime, Shame and Reintegration*. Cambridge: Cambridge University Press.

Briere, J. (1992). *Child Abuse Trauma. Theory and Treatment of the Lasting Effects*. Newbury Park, CA: Sage.

Burgess, A., & Holmstrom, L. (1974). *Rape. Victims of Crisis*. Bowie, MD: Robert J. Brady.

Campbell, J. (1983). *The Way of the Animal Powers*. London: Harper & Row.

Chodorow, N. (1978). *The Reproduction of Mothering: Psychoanalysis and the Sociology of Gender*. Berkeley: The University of California Press.

Chodorow, N. (1980). *Waarom vrouwen moederen. Psychoanalyse en de maatschappelijke verschillen tussen vrouwen en mannen.* Amsterdam: Sara.

Cicchetti, D., & Barnett, D. (1992). Attachment organization in maltreated preschools. *Development and Psychopathology, 3*: 397–411.

Cooper, J., & Vetere, A. (2005). *Domestic Violence and Family Safety: A Systemic Approach to Working with Violence in Families.* London: Whurr / Wiley.

Cornell, C. P., & Gelles, R. J. (1982). Adolescent to parent violence. *Urban Social Change Review, 15*: 8–14.

Dahl, R. (1978). *De reuzenkrokodil.* Baarn: De Fontein.

Dallos, R. (2002). Narratieve hechtingstherapie: toepassing van de narratieve aanpak en hechtingstheorie in systeemgerichte gezinstherapie bij eetstoornissen. *Gezinstherapie wereldwijd, 13*: 195–224.

Davidson, L. M., & Baum, A. (1990). Posttraumatic stress disorder in children following natural and human-made trauma. In: A. J. Sameroff, M. Lewis, & S. M. Miller (Eds.), *Handbook of Developmental Psychopathology* (pp. 215–251). New York: Plenum.

De Haan, W. J. M., & De Bie, E. F. A. E. (1999). *Jeugd & geweld. Een interdisciplinair perspectief.* Den Haag: Ministerie van VWS.

De Savornin Lohman, J. (1997). *de Volkskrant,* 20 October 1997.

De Swaan, A. (1982). Uitgaansbeperking en uitgaansangst. Over de verschuiving van bevelshuishouding naar onderhandelingshuishouding. In: A. de Swaan (Ed.), *De mens is de mens een zorg. Opstellen 1971–1981.* Amsterdam: Meulenhoff.

de Volkskrant (1997). Daily Journal.

De Waal, F. (1982). *Chimpansee politiek. Macht en seks bij mensapen.* Amsterdam: Becht.

Deblinger, E., McLeer, M. D., & Henry, D. (1990). Cognitive behavioral treatment for sexually abused children suffering post-traumatic stress. Preliminary finding. *Journal of the American Academy of Child and Adolescent Psychiatry, 29*: 747–752.

Delfos, M. (2001). *De schoonheid van het verschil: waarom mannen en vrouwen verschillend en hetzelfde zijn.* Lisse: Swets & Zeitlinger.

Delpeut, H. (2002). Inner and outer voices in therapeutic conversations. Verslag van een workshop met Tomm Andersen. *Tijdschrift voor Psychotherapie, 28*: 351–354.

Dijkstra, S. (2000). *Met vallen en opstaan. Hoe vrouwen en mannen betekenis geven aan geweldservaringen uit hun kindertijd.* Delft: Eburon.

Dijkstra, S. (2002). *Stemmen van clienten met (seksuele) geweldervaringen*: Middelburg.

Dobash, R. E., & Dobash, R. P. (1992). *Women, Violence and Social Change.* New York: Routledge.

Doreleyers, T. A. H. (1995). *Diagnostiek tussen jeugdstrafrecht en hulpverlening.* Arnhem: Gouda Quint.

Draijer, N. (1988). *Seksueel misbruik van meisjes door verwanten. Een landelijk onderzoek naar de omvang, de aard, de gezinsachtergronden, de emotionele betekenis en de psychische en psychosomatische gevolgen.* Den Haag: Ministerie van SZW.

Drell, M. J., Siegel, C. H., & Graensbauer, T. J. (1993). In: C. H. Zeanah Jr (Ed.), *Handbook of Infant Mental Health* (pp. 291–304). New York: Guilford Press.

Dutton, D. G. (1995). *The Domestic Assault of Women,* Vancouver: University of British Colombia Press.

Dutton, D. G. (1998). *The Abusive Personality.* New York: Guilford Press.

Dutton, D. G. (2005). *Rethinking Domestic Violence.* Vancouver: British Columbia Press.

Dutton, D. G., & Strachen, C. E. (1987). Motivational needs of power and spouse-specific assertiveness in assaultive and non-assaultive men. *Violence and Victims, 3:* 145–146.

Dutton, D. G., Golant, S. K., & Pijnaker, H. (2000). *De partnermishandelaar. Een psychologisch profiel.* Houten: Bohn Stafleu Van Loghum.

Dutton, D. G., Van Ginkel, C., & Starzomski, A. (1995). The role of shame and guilt in the intergenerational transmission of abusiveness. *Violence and Victims, 10:* 121–131.

Elias, N. (1978). *Het civilisatieproces.* New York: Pantheon.

Elias, N. (1982). *Het civilisatieproces. Sociogenetische en psychogenetische onderzoekingen.* Trecht: Het Spectrum.

Ellian, A. (2001). *de Volkskrant,* 17 February.

Emery, R. E. (1989). Family violence. *American Psychologist, 44:* 321–328.

Enzensberger, H. M. (1994). *Oog in oog met de burgeroorlog.* Amsterdam: De Bezige Bij.

Enzensberger, H. M. (2006). *Schreckens Männer Versuch über den radikalen Verlierer.* Suhrkamp.

Fallaci, O. (1980). *Een man.* Amsterdam: Uitgeverij Bert Bakker.

Foa, E. B., & Kozak, M. (1986). Emotional processing of fear. Exposure to corrective information. *Psychological Bulletin, 99:* 20–35.

Foa, E. B., Steketee, G., & Rothbaum, B. O. (1989). Behavioral/cognitive conceptualizations of post-traumatic stress disorder. *Behavioral Therapy, 20:* 155–176.

Fonagy, P. (2001). *Attachment Theory and Psychoanalysis.* New York: Other Press.

Fonagy, P., & Target, M. (1997). Attachment and reflective function. Their role in self-organization. *Development and Psychopathology, 9*: 679–700.

Fonagy, P., Moran, G. S., & Target, M. (1993). Aggression and the psychological self. *International Journal of Psychoanalysis, 74*: 471–485.

Foucault, M. (1995). *Breekbare Vrijheid.* Amsterdam: Krisis/Parresia.

Gelles, R. J. (1983). An exchange/social control theory of intrafamily violence. In: D. Finkelhor, R. Gelles, G. Hotaling, & M. Straus (Eds.), *The Dark Side of Families* (pp. 119–130). Beverly Hills, CA: Sage.

Gelles, R. J. (1997). *Intimate Violence in Families.* Thousand Oaks, CA: Sage.

George, C., Kaplan, N., & Main, M. (1996). *The Adult Attachment Interview.* Department of Psychology, University of California, Berkeley.

Gilmore, D. E. (1990). *Manhood in the Making. Cultural Concepts of Masculinity.* New Haven, CT: Yale University Press.

Gilmore, D. E. (1994). *De man als mythe.* Amsterdam: Muntinga.

Girshick, L. B. (1993). Teen dating violence. *Violence UpDate, 3*: 1–6.

Goldner, V. (1985). Feminism and family therapy. *Family Process, 24*(1): 31–47.

Goldner, V. (1997). *De genderdialoog. Passie, macht, subjectiviteit en therapie.* Amsterdam: Van Gennep.

Goldner, V. (1998). The treatment of violence and victimization in intimate relationships. *Family Process, 37*(3): 263–286.

Goldner, V., Penn, P., Sheinberg, M., & Walker, G. (1990). Love and violence: gender paradoxes in volatile attachments. *Family Process, 29*: 343–364.

Gomperts, W. (2000). Dyscivilisatie en dysmentalisatie. De ontsporing van het civilisatieproces psychoanalytisch bezien. *Tijdschrift voor Psychoanalyse, 6*: 193–213.

Gorkin, M. (1987). *The Uses of Countertransference.* Northvale NJ: Jason Aronson.

Gottfredson, M., & Hirschi, T. (1990). *A General Theory of Crime.* Stanford, CA: Stanford University Press.

Gottman, J. M. (1999). *The Marriage Clinic.* New York: Norton.

Goudsblom, J. (1997). *Het regime van de tijd.* Amsterdam: Meulenhoff.

Graham-Kevan, N., & Archer, J. (2003). Patriarchal terrorism and common couple violence: a test of Johnson's predictions in four British samples. *Journal of Interpersonal Violence, 18*: 1247–1270.

Groen, M. A. (2000). Een geritualiseerde vorm van vergelding bij slaande ruzies in partnerrelaties. In: H. Goudswaard (Ed.), *Vergeven en vergelden*. Amsterdam: Van Gennep.

Groen, M. A. (2001). *Geweld en schaamte*. Utrecht: Advies- en meldpunt een veilig huis.

Guggenbühl, A. (1996). *Fascinerend geweld*. Rotterdam: Lemniscaat.

Hamel, J. (2007). Domestic violence: a gender-inclusive conception in family interventions in domestic violence. In: J. Hamel & T. L. Nicholls (Eds.), *Family Interventions in Domestic Violence* (pp. 247–275). New York: Springer.

Harbin, H., & Madden, D. (1979). Battered parents: a new syndrome. *American Journal of Psychiatry, 136*: 1288–1291.

Hare-Mustin, R. T. (1978). A feminist approach to family therapy. *Family Process, 17*(3): 181–194.

Hartman, C. R., & Jackson, H. (1994). Rape and the phenomena of countertransference. In: P. J. Wilson & J. D. Lindsey (Eds.), *PTSD*. New York: Guilford Press.

Heide, K. M. (1995). *Why Kids Kill Parents: Child Abuse and Adolescent Homicide*. Thousand Oaks, CA: Sage.

Henning, K. (1996). Long-term psychological and social conflict between parents. *Journal of Interpersonal Violence, 11*(1): 35–51.

Herman, J. L., Perry, A., & Van der Kolk, B. A. (1989). *Trauma and Recovery*, J. L. Herman (Ed.). New York: Basic Books.

Howe, A. C., Herzberger, S., & Tennen, H. (1988). The Influence of personal history of abuse and gender on clinicians' judgments of child abuse. *Journal of Family Violence, 3*(2): 105–119.

Idenburg, Ph. A. (1983). *De nadagen van de verzorgingsstaat. Kansen en perspectieven voor morgen*. Amsterdam: Meulenhoff Informatief.

Jackson, H., & Nuttall, R. (1993). Clinician responses to sexual abuse allegations. *Child Abuse and Neglect, 17*: 127–143.

Jacobson, N. S., & Gottman, J. M. (1998a). *When Men Batter Women: New Insights into Ending Abusive Relationships*. New York: Simon & Schuster.

Jacobson, N. S., & Gottman, J. M. (1998b). *Breaking the Cycle. New Insights into Violent Relationships*. London: Bloomsbury.

Jaffe, P. G., & Hastings, E. (1995). Preventions programs in secondary schools. In: E. Peled, P. G. Jaffe, & J. Edelson (Eds.), *Ending the Cycle of Violence. Community Responses to Children of Battered Women* (pp. 232–254). Thousand Oaks, CA: Sage.

Jaffe, P. G., Wolfe, D. A., & Wilson, S. (1990). *Children of Battered Women*. Newbury Park, CA: Sage.

Janssen, J. (2002). 'Gek en gevaarlijk'. Trends in de forensische psychiatrie. Verslag van een studiedag. *Tijdschrift voor Psychotherapie, 28*: 73–82.

Jasinski, J., & Williams, L. (1998). *Partner Violence. A Comprehensive Review of 20 Years of Research*. Thousand Oaks, CA: Sage.

Jennings, J. P., & Jennings, J. L. (1991). Multiple approaches to treatment of violent couples. *The American Journal of Family Therapy, 19*: 351–362.

Johnson, M. P. (1995). Patriarchal terrorism and common couple violence: two forms of violence against women. *Journal of Marriage and the Family, 57*: 283–294.

Johnson, M. P. (2000). The differential effects of patriarchal terrorism and common couple violence: findings from the National Violence Against Women Survey. Paper presented to the Tenth International Conference on Personal Relationships, Brisbane.

Johnson, S. M. (2004). *The Practice of Emotionally Focused Couple Therapy: Creating Connection* (2nd edn). New York: Brunner-Routledge.

Johnston, J. (1993). Children of divorce who refuse. In: *Visitation in Nonresidential Parenting*. London: Sage.

Jourilles, E. N., & LeCompte, S. H. (1991). Husbands' aggression toward wives and mothers and fathers' aggression toward children. Moderating effects of child gender. *Journal of Consulting and Clinical Psychology, 59*(1): 190–192.

Keane, T. M., Zimmerling, R. T., & Caddell, J. M. (1985). A behavioral formulation of post-traumatic stress disorder in Vietnam veterans. *Behavior Therapist, 8*: 9–12.

Kernberg, O. F. (1975). *Borderline Condition and Pathological Narcissism*. New York: Aronson.

Kik, H., & Baars, J. (2000). Systeemtherapeutisch behandelen van fysiek geweld in partnerrelaties. *Systeemtherapie, 12*(3): 162–179.

Kilpatrick, D. G., Veronen, L. J., & Best, C. L. (1985). Factors predicting psychological distress among rape victims. In: C. L. Figley (Ed.), *Trauma and Its Wake* (pp. 113–141). New York: Brunner/Mazel.

Kimura, D. (1992). Mind and brain. *Scientific American* (Special Issue), September: 118–125.

Kohut, H. (1971). *The Analysis of the Self*. New York: International Universities Press.

Komter, A. (1985). *De macht van de vanzelfsprekendheid. Relaties tussen mannen en vrouwen*. Den Haag: Vuga.

Kuijpers, P. (2002). *Rapport Zorg voor Velen*. Commissie Geestelijke Gezondheid.

Lamers-Winkelman, F. (2000). Protocol behandeling van de gevolgen van seksueel misbruik bij kinderen. In: P. Prins & N. Pameijer (Eds.), *Protocollen in de jeugdzorg. Richtlijnen voor diagnostiek, indicatiestelling en interventie* (pp. 227–242). Lisse: Zwets & Zeitlinger.

Lansky, M. (1987). Shame and domestic violence. In: D. L. Nathanson (Ed.), *The Many Faces of Shame* (pp. 335–362). New York: Guilford Press.

Lasch, C. (1977). *Haven in a Heartless World.* New York: Basic Books.

Lasch, C. (1981). *Haven in een harteloze wereld.* Amsterdam: De Arbeiderspers.

Lewis, H. B. (1971). *Shame and Guilt in Neurosis.* New York: International Universities Press.

Lewis, H. B. (1987). The role of shame in depression over life span. In: H. B. Lewis (Ed.), *The Role of Shame in Symptom Formation* (pp. 29–50). Hillsdale, NJ: Erlbaum.

Loeber, R., & Farrington, D. (Eds.) (1998). *Serious and Violent Juvenile Offenders. Risk Factors and Successful Interventions.* London: Sage.

Luepnitz, D. A. (1988). *The Family Interpreted. Feminist Theory in Clinical Practice.* New York: Basic Books.

Mastenbroek, S. (1995). *De illusie van veiligheid, voortekenen en ontwikkeling van geweld tegen vrouwen in relaties.* Utrecht: Jan van Arkel.

McCann, I. L., & Pearlman, L. A. (1990). *Psychological Trauma and the Adult Survivors. Theory, Therapy and Transformation.* New York: Brunner/Mazel.

McLeer, S. V., Deblinger, E., Atkins, M. S., Foa, E. B., & Ralphe, D. L. (1988). Post-traumatic stress disorder in sexual abused children. *Journal of the American Academy of Child and Adolescent Psychiatry, 27*: 650–654.

McNally, P. F. (1993). Stressors that produce posttraumatic stress disorder in children. In: J. R. T. Davidsen & E. B. Foa (Eds.), *Posttraumatic Stress Disorder. DSM-IV and Beyond* (pp. 567–572). Washington, DC: American Psychiatric Press.

Mernissie, F. (1985). *Beyond the Veil: Male–Female Dynamics in Modern Muslim Society.* London: Al Saqi Books.

Meulenbelt, A. (1984). *De schillen van de ui.* Amsterdam: Van Gennep.

Meulenbelt, A. (1990). *Casablanca of de onmogelijkheden van de heteroseksuele liefde.* Amsterdam: Sara/Van Gennep.

Meulenbelt, A. (1997). *Chodorow en verder. Over de psychopolitiek van sekse.* Amsterdam: Van Gennep.

Miedzian, M. (1995). Learning to be violent. In: E. Peled, P. Jaffe, & J. Edelson (Eds.), *Ending the Cycle of Violence. Community Responses* to Children of Battered Women (pp. 10–24). Thousand Oaks, CA: Sage.

Mooij, A. (2002). Psychoanalytisch gedachtegoed. Een modern perspectief. Amsterdam: Boom.

Morrison, A. P. (1989). Shame. The Underside of Narcissism. Hillsdale, NJ: Analytic Press.

Nicolai, N. (1992). Vrouwenhulpverlening en psychiatrie. Amsterdam: Sua.

Nicolai, N. (2001a). Hechting en psychopathologie: een literatuuroverzicht. Tijdschrift voor Psychiatrie, 43: 333–342.

Nicolai, N. (2001b). Hechting en psychopathologie; de reflectieve functie. Tijdschrift voor Psychiatrie, 43: 705–714.

Nuttall, R., & Jackson, H. (1992). Personal history of childhood abuse among clinicians. In: J. P. Wilson & J. Lindy (Eds.), Countertransference in the Treatment of PTSD. New York: Guilford Press.

Olivier, C. (1993). De kinderen van Jocaste. Amsterdam: Arena.

Omer, H. (2003). Non Violent Resistance A New Approach to Violent and Self-Destructive Children. Cambridge: Cambridge University Press.

Omer, H. (2007). Geweldloos verzet in gezinnen. Een nieuwe benadering van gewelddadig gedrag. Houten/Diegem: Bohn Stafleu van Loghum.

Pynoos, R. S., & Eth, S. (1984). The child as witness to homicide. Journal of Social Issues, 40(2): 87–108.

Pynoos, R. S., & Eth, S. (1985). Children traumatized by witnessing acts of personal violence. homicide, rape or suicide behavior. In: R. Pynoos & S. Eth (Eds.), Post-Traumatic Stress Disorder in Children (pp. 17–44). Washington, DC: American Psychiatric Press.

Richters, A. (2000). Geweld als Modiaal Fenomeen (Violence as a global phenomenon). lezing.

Römkens, R. G. (1989). Onder ons gezegd en gezwegen. Geweld tegen vrouwen in man-vrouw relaties. Rijswijk: Ministerie van WVC.

Römkens, R. G. (1991). Geschonden grenzen. In: E. Spruyt (Ed.), Psychologie van het gezin (pp. 279–300). Utrecht: Stichting Teleac.

Römkens, R. G. (1992). Gewoon geweld? Omvang, aard, gevolgen en achtergronden van geweld tegen vrouwen in heteroseksuele relaties. Amsterdam: Swets en Zeitlinger.

Römkens, R. G., & Dijkstra, S. (1996). Het omstreden slachtoffer. Baarn: Ambo.

Rutenfrans, C. (1996). Waarom zijn er zo weinig criminelen in Nederland? Jonas Magazine, 2 February 1996.

Saunders, D. (1993). Custody decisions in families experiencing woman abuse. Social Work, 39: 51–59.

Scalia, J. (2002). *Intimate Violence. Attacks upon Psychic Interiority*. New York: Columbia University Press.

Schokker, J., & Schokker, T. (2000). *Extimiteit, Jacques Lacans terugkeer naar Freud*. Amsterdam: Boom.

Schöttelndreier, M. (1995). *Monsters van kinderen, draken van ouders*. Amsterdam: De Balie.

Sheff, T. J. (1987). The shame–rage spiral: case study of an interminable quarrel. In: H. B. Lewis (Ed.), *The Role of Shame in Symptom Formation* (pp. 109–149). Hillsdale, NJ: Erlbaum.

Sheff, T. J., & Retzinger, S. M. (2001). *Emotions and Violence, Shame and Rage in Destructive Conflicts*. An Authors Guild Backinprint.com Edition.

Sheinberg, M., & Fraenkel, P. (2001). *The Relational Trauma of Incest: A Family-Based Approach to Treatment*. New York: The Guilford Press.

Siegel, D. J. (2001). Toward an interpersonal neurobiology of the developing mind: attachment relationships, "mindsight" and neural integration. *Infant Mental Health Journal, 22*: 67–94.

Slep, A., & O'Leary, S. (2005). Parent and partner violence in families with young children: rates, patterns, and connections. *Journal of Consulting and Clinical Psychology, 73*(3): 435–444.

Smeulers, J. (1985). Overeenkomsten en verschillen tussen de (late) gevolgen van de Tweede Wereldoorlog en die van andere vormen van geweld. In: Dane, J. (Ed.), *Problematiek van oorlogsgetroffenen* (pp. 71–78). Utrecht: ICODO.

Stark, E., & Flitcraft, A. (1996). *Women at Risk: Domestic Violence and Women's Health*. Thousand Oaks, CA: Sage.

Steiner, G. (1974). *Anno Domini*. London: Faber & Faber.

Stern, D. N. (1985). *The Interpersonal World of the Infant*. New York: Basic Books.

Sternberg, K. L. (1993). Effects of domestic violence on children's behaviour problems and depression. *Development Psychology, 29*(1): 44–52.

Stith, S., Rosen, K. H., McCollum, E., & Thomsen, C. J. (2004). Treating intimate partner violence within intact couple relationships: outcomes of multiple versus individual couple therapy. *Journal of Marital and Family Therapy, 30*(3): 305–318.

Stoller, R. J. (1968). *Sex and Gender*. New York: Science House.

Straus, M. A. (1992). Children as witnesses to marital violence. A risk factor for lifelong problems among a national representative sample of American men and women. Paper presented to the Twenty-Third Roundtable on Critical Approaches to Common Pediatric Problems.

Straus, M. A. (1999). The controversy over domestic violence by women, In: X. Arriaga & S. Oskamp (Eds.), *Violence in Intimate Relationships* (pp. 17–44). Thousand Oaks, CA: Sage.

Straus, M. A., & Gelles, R. J. (1990). *Physical Violence in American Families. Risk Factors and Adaptations to Violence in 8,145 Families.* New Brunswick, NJ: Transaction.

Sudermann, M., & Jaffe, P. G. (1993). *Violence in Teen Dating Relationships. Evaluation of a Large Scale Primary Prevention Program.* London, Ontario: Centre for Children and Families in the Justice System.

Tangney, J. P. (1991). Moral affect: the good, the bad, and the ugly. *Journal of Persdonality and Social Psychological Bulletin, 18*: 199–206.

Tangney, J. P. (1995). Recent advances in the empirical study of shame and guilt. *American Behavioral Scientist, 38*: 1132–1145.

Tangney, J. P., & Dearing, R. L. (2002). *Shame and Guilt.* New York: Guilford Press.

Tannen, D. (1990). *You Just Don't Understand. Women and Men in Conversations.* New York: William Morrow.

Terr, L. (1991). Childhood traumas. An outline and overview. *American Journal of Psychiatry, 148*: 10–19.

Tomm, K. (1987). Interventive interviewing: Part II. Reflexive questioning as a means to enable self healing. *Family Process, 26*: 167–183.

Tomm, K. (1988). Interventive interviewing: Part III. Intending to ask lineal, circular, strategic or reflexive questions? *Family Process, 27*: 1–15.

Tomm, K. (1994). Interviewing the internalized other. Workshop papers, not published.

Turner, V. W. (1968). *The Drums of Affliction.* Oxford: University Press.

Van den Brink, G. (2001). *Geweld als uitdaging. De betekenis van agressief gedrag bij jongeren.* Utrecht: NIZW.

Van der Avort, A. (1987). *De gulzige vrijblijvendheid van expliciete relaties.* Tilburg: University Press.

Van der Hart, O. (1978). *Overgang en bestendiging.* Deventer: Van Loghum Slaterus.

Van der Laan, P. H., Essers, A. A. M., Huijbrechts, G. L. A. M., & Spaans, E. C. (1998). *Ontwikkeling van de jeugdcriminaliteit: periode 1980–1996.* Den Haag: WODC.

Van der Pas, A. (1996). Recensie A. Van Schöttelndreier, monsters van kinderen, draken van ouders. *Systeemtherapie, 8*: 254–258.

van der Veer, G. (1998). *Hulpverlening aan vluchtelingen*. Baarn: Uitgeverij Intro.

van Dijk, L. (1997). Macht en machtsstrijd in partnerrelaties en therapeutische systemen. *Systeemtherapie, 9*(3): 165–178.

van Gael, M. (2002). De missing link tussen trauma en borderlineproblematiek. Een benadering vanuit de hechtingstheorie. *Tijdschrift voor Psychotherapie, 28*(5): 365–384.

van Gennep, A. (1981). *Übergangsriten*. Frankfurt: Campus.

van Ijzendoorn, M. H. (2002). Drie generaties holocaust? Over gehechtheid, trauma en veerkracht. *Tijdschrift voor Psychotherapie, 28*: 183–205.

van Lawick, J., & Groen, M. (1998). *Intieme oorlog*. Amsterdam: Van Gennep.

van Lawick, M. J., & Sanders, M. (1994). Vaders in gezinnen. *Systeemtherapie, 6*: 202–214.

van Stolk, B., & Wouters, C. (1983). *Vrouwen in tweestrijd, tussen thuis en tehuis*. Deventer: Van Loghum Slaterus.

Verhaeghe, P. (1998). *Liefde in tijden van eenzaamheid*. Leusden, Leuven: Acco.

Vetere, A., & Cooper, J. (2007). Couple violence and couple safety: a systemic and attachment oriented approach to working with complexity and uncertainty. In: J. Hamel & T. L. Nicholls (Eds.), *Family Interventions in Domestic Violence* (pp. 381–397). New York: Springer.

Vrije Universiteit Amsterdam (2007). Scholieren onderzoek over mishandeling.

Walker, L. E. (1984). *The Battered Woman Syndrome*. New York: Springer.

Walker, L. E. A. (1989). Psychology and violence against women. *American Psychologist, 2044*: 695–702.

Weerman, F. (1998). *Het belang van bindingen. De bindingstheorie als verklaring van verschillen en veranderingen in delinquent gedrag*. Groningen: Rijksuniversiteit Groningen.

Weijers, I. (2000). *Schuld en schaamte*. Houten: Bohn Stafleu Van Loghum.

White, G. M. (1992). Ethnopsychology. In: T. Schwartz, M. White, & C. Lutz (Eds.), *New Directions in Psychological Antropology*. Cambridge: Cambridge University Press.

White, M., & Epston, D. (1990). *Narrative Means to Therapeutic Ends*. London: Norton.

Whitmer, B. (1997). *The Violence Mythos*. Albany: State University of New York Press.

Wierzbicka, A. (1994). Emotion, language, and cultural scripts. In: S. Kiayama & H. R. Markus (Eds.), *Emotion and Culture* (pp. 133–196). Washington, DC: American Psychological Association.

Willy, J. (1975). *De partnerrelatie*. Rotterdam: Ad Donker.

Wilson, J., & Lindsey, J. (1994). *Countertransference in the Treatment of PTSD*. New York: Guilford Press.

Wittebrood, K. (1998). *Cijfers omtrent geweld. Biopsychologische determinanten van antisociaal en crimineel gedrag*. Den Haag: RMO.

Wolak, J., & Finkelhor, D. (1996). *Children Exposed to Partner Violence*. London: Sage.

Wolfe, D. A., Jaffe, P., Wilson, S., & Zak, L. (1985). Children of battered women. The relation of child behavior to family violence and maternal stress. *Journal of Consulting and Clinical Psychology, 53*: 657–665.

Woltring, L. (1988). *Jongens tussen branie en verlegenheid*. Culemborg: Lemma.

Zijderveld, A. C. (1983). *Steden zonder stedelijkheid*. Van Loghum Slaterus Lemma.

INDEX

abuse
  child, xi, xvi, 19, 24, 62, 84, 87,
    107, 110, 173, 183, 185, 189,
    202, 231, 249
  domestic, 132
  emotional, 107
  of parent(s), 201–202
  parental, 184, 202
  partner/spouse
    abused, xi, 20, 22, 115, 162, 172,
      185, 188, 231, 246
    abusive, xi, 19, 22, 56, 67, 104,
      108–109, 115, 126, 162, 231,
      247
  physical, xvi, 1, 107, 155
  prolonged, 66, 113, 155
  psychopathic, 24
  sexual, xvi, 66, 107, 110, 155, 173,
    202, 243, 247
  substance, 11–12, 34, 86, 94, 96,
    111, 233
  woman, 19, 24, 38, 87, 103, 108,
    125, 186, 238, 241, 246, 249
addict/addiction, xvi, 11–12, 19, 21,

34, 77, 96, 198, 202, 276 *see also*
  abuse, substance
Adult Attachment Interview, 80, 88,
  91
Advice Bureau for Youngsters and
  Parents (AJO), 216
aggression, 3, 11, 16–17, 21, 45, 58,
  64, 84–85, 108, 115, 117, 127,
  156, 158, 164, 170–171, 175, 183,
  185, 188–191, 197–198, 202, 204,
  206–207, 209, 213, 232, 237, 248,
  253–254, 257–258, 260, 265–269,
  271, 273
Ainsworth, M. D. S., 80, 279
alcohol, 11, 34, 50, 94, 96, 111, 117,
  170, 173, 208, 233, 254, 262 *see
  also*: abuse, substance
Alexander, P. C., 191, 279
Alon, N., 70, 279
Amnesty International, xii
Andersen, T., 79
anger, 29–32, 37–38, 45, 58, 60–61,
  67, 75–77, 79, 82, 85–86, 94, 108,
  114, 119–122, 125, 133–134,

143–144, 146, 152–153, 155–156,
158–163, 166–167, 170–174,
178–180, 184, 186, 188–189, 191,
194–195, 197–198, 202, 222, 229,
233, 235–236, 240–244, 246, 255,
260, 266 see also: rage
Arab Human Development Report,
101
Archer, J., 3, 283
Arendt, H., 192, 256–257, 271, 279
Atkins, M. S., 187, 286
attachment, 5, 16, 71, 88, 91–92, 160,
171, 187, 189, 191, 207–208, 241
see also: Adult Attachment
Interview
figure(s), 80–81, 91, 191
patterns, 79–80, 83, 87
relationship(s), 81, 86
safe, 11, 13–14, 46, 80–81, 83, 86,
215
theory, 46, 80, 85, 191
unsafe, 162
attention deficit hyperactivity
disorder (ADHD), 107, 209
autonomy, 11, 82, 103, 130, 160, 186,
205, 245, 264, 268, 270–271

Baars, J., 2, 114, 285
Baartman, H. E. M., 14, 279
Babcock, J. C., 5, 20, 27, 279
Bakker, A. B., 245, 279
Bancroft, L., 2, 77, 280
Barnett, D., 191, 281
Barrett, M., 188, 280
Bateson, G., 91, 280
Baum, A., 187, 281
Baumeister, R., 170–171, 205, 280
Benedek, E., 185, 280
Bentinck, A., 202, 280
Bentovim, A., 7, 280
Berlin, I., 253, 280
Best, C. L., 187–188, 285
Bethke, T. M., 191, 280
Blees, L. W., 208–209, 280
Blehar, M. C., 80, 279
Boggiano, A., 188, 280

Bograd, M., 2, 280
Bol, M. W., 208–209, 280
Bowlby, J., 191, 280
Braithwaite, J., 164, 280
Briere, J., 189, 280
British Crime Survey, xii
Burgess, A., 240, 280
burn-out, 230, 244–245, 251

Caddell, J. M., 187, 285
Campbell, J., 195, 280
case studies/vignettes
Ahmed, 115
Angela and Ricardo, 75–78, 85
Bianca and Harry, 28–33, 36–44,
47–55, 58–61, 68–69
Bloeme, 188
Clara, Piet and Jan, 192–195, 198
Ella and Peter, 25–26
Erik and Johan, 215–220, 223–226
Jacqueline and Peter, 35
Jolande and John, 172–175, 178,
180–181
Marina and Arjan, 53–56
Miriam, 248
Mrs A, 103
Mrs X (1), 109–110
Mrs X (2), 234
Norma, Hans and Floor, 196–198
Officer Andreé, 231
Patrick, 34
Pherian and Pedro, 143–144
Sanne and Pierre, 48, 53–56
Safdia and Nusret, 145–146
Yvonne and Mohammed, 237–238
Zamir and Mohammed, 120–124
Child Welfare Council (Raad voor
Kinderbescherming), 217
Chodorow, N., 51, 64, 257, 280–281
Cicchetti, D., 191, 281
circular questions, 87–88, 90, 92,
220, 274
Common Couple Violence (CCV),
3–4
Conflict Tactics Scale (CTS), xxvi, 2,
4, 184

Cooper, J., 2, 281, 290
Cornell, C. P., 202, 281
countertransference, xii, 125, 133,
    167, 229–230, 232–233, 235, 242
    see also: transference
culture(s)
    Antillean, 75, 100, 126, 129, 208,
        260
    Arab, 101–102
    Creole, 9, 104, 115–116
    Dutch, 2, 9, 13, 80, 99–101,
        103–105, 108, 115, 126–129,
        131, 139–140, 165, 204–205,
        208, 222
    Hindustani, 102, 104, 130, 134
    Islamic, 102–103, 120, 133
    Moroccan, 13, 100, 102–106, 126,
        128–132, 134, 208, 237, 260
    Surinamese, 100, 104, 115, 126,
        129, 260
    Turkish, 10, 43, 100, 103, 105–106,
        115, 120, 126, 128, 130, 132,
        134, 260

Dahl, R., 63, 281
Dallos, R., 92, 281
Davidson, L. M., 187, 281
Dearing, R. L., 159–160, 163, 266,
    289
De Bie, E. F. A. E., 208, 281
Deblinger, E., 187, 281, 286
De Haan, W. J. M., 208, 281
DeJoy, D. M., 191, 280
Delfos, M., 9, 281
Delpeut, H., 79, 281
depression, 11, 26, 56, 59, 147, 152,
    161, 186, 188, 201, 212, 242,
    267
De Savornin Lohman, J., 190, 281
De Swaan, A., 13–14, 203, 281
de Volkskrant, 99, 244, 281
De Waal, F., 204, 281
Dewar Research Government
    Statistics on Domestic
    Violence, xii
Dijkstra, S., 87, 191, 237, 281, 287

dissociation, 16, 45, 186–187, 189,
    240
divorce, 10, 20–21, 23–24, 42, 46, 89,
    103, 105–106, 109, 113, 115, 123,
    131–132, 141, 155, 177, 179, 183,
    192–194, 208, 237–238, 256, 265
Dobash, R. E., 105, 191, 282
Dobash, R. P., 105, 191, 282
Doreleyers, T. A. H., 209, 282
Draijer, N., 67, 282
Drell, M. J., 186, 282
Duintjer, F., 202, 280
Dutch Bureau of Statistics (CBS),
    100
Dutch Federation of Social Work
    (AMW), 122
Dutton, D. G., 2, 4–5, 23, 87, 115,
    160–162, 170–171, 259, 282

Elias, N., 15, 113–114, 156, 282
Ellian, A., 99, 282
Emery, R. E., 191, 282
Enzensberger, H. M., 102, 255, 257,
    262, 282
Epston, D., 72, 290
escalations, xvii, 3–4, 6, 20–21,
    26–27, 31–34, 37, 40, 59, 69–73,
    76, 79, 85, 93–98, 106, 132, 141,
    143, 159–160, 166, 171–173, 175,
    178, 183–184, 197–199, 230, 248,
    251, 254, 266, 274
    violent, xii, 3, 7, 11, 44, 93, 98, 132
Essers, A. A. M., 204, 289

Fallaci, O., 137, 282
Farrington, D., 209, 286
feminism, 4–5, 91, 191
Finkelhor, D., 185, 291
Flitcraft, A., 2, 288
Foa, E. B., 187–188, 240, 282–283,
    286
Fonagy, P., 11, 80, 84, 88, 282–283
Foucault, M., 261, 283
Fraenkel, P., 67, 288
Freud, A., 13
Freud, S., 8, 13

frustration, 4, 16, 31, 45, 58–59, 67, 70, 93–95, 97, 105, 145, 170, 173, 178, 202, 206, 209–211, 217, 245, 255, 269

Gallo, S., 188, 280
Gelles, R. J., 2, 12, 14, 170, 185, 202, 281, 283, 289
gender identity, 1, 7–9, 222
genogram, 47, 50,
George, C., 80, 88, 283
Gilmore, D. E., 10, 77–78, 257–258, 283
Girshick, L. B., 190–191, 283
Golant, S. K., 2, 23, 87, 282
Goldner, V., 2, 5, 27, 37, 44, 51, 60–61, 283
Gomperts, W., 80, 85, 283
Gorkin, M., 233, 283
Gottfredson, M., 210, 283
Gottman, J. M., 2, 78, 85, 283–284
Goudsblom, J., 114, 156, 283
Government National Plan for Domestic Violence, xii
Graensbauer, T. J., 186, 282
Graham-Kevan, N., 3, 283
Green, C. E., 5, 279
Groen, M. A., ix–x, 2, 16, 23, 27, 62, 67, 69, 87, 166, 284, 290
Guggenbühl, A., 195–196, 284
guilt, 14, 32, 37–38, 44, 51, 56, 59, 61–62, 75, 77, 85, 110, 112–113, 137–139, 141, 145, 153–154, 158–159, 162–167, 194, 201, 222, 239–240, 243

Hamel, J., 184–185, 284
Harbin, H., 201, 284
Hare-Mustin, R. T., 5, 284
Hartman, C. R., 233, 284
Hastings, E., 191, 284
hate, 40, 156, 179, 247
Heide, K. M., 202, 284
Henning, K., 185, 284
Henry, D., 187, 281
Herman, J. L., 240, 284

Herzberger, S., 233, 284
Hirschi, T., 210, 283
Holmstrom, L., 240, 280
Holocaust, 83, 268
Howe, A. C., 233, 284
Huijbrechts, G. L. A. M., 204, 289
humiliation, xv, 1, 3–4, 7, 10, 35, 71–73, 76–77, 82, 85–87, 93, 108, 112–116, 118, 121, 127, 132, 137, 145, 151–154, 158–160, 162–163, 165, 169–172, 175–176, 178, 184–185, 193, 202, 243

Idenburg, Ph. A., 265, 284
incest, 6–7, 67, 110, 177, 232, 234
Institute for Forensic Psychiatry (De Waag), 122–123
intervention, ix, 12, 42, 53, 70, 106, 118, 122, 144, 165, 188, 190, 197, 216, 222–223, 230–231, 240, 248, 257, 267
  medical, 70
  physical, 21
  police, 132, 173, 197
  psychological, 21
  sexual, 21
  therapeutic, 63, 151, 165, 175
Intimate Terrorism (IT), 3–4

Jackson, H., 233, 284, 287
Jacobson, N. S., 2, 85, 284
Jaffe, P. G., 170, 185–186, 190–191, 284, 289, 291
Janssen, J., 86, 285
Jasinski, J., 1–2, 285
jealousy, 114, 116–117, 134, 170, 177, 180, 237
Jennings, J. L., 172, 285
Jennings, J. P., 172, 285
Johnson, M. P., 3, 285
Johnson, S. M., 11, 46, 285
Johnston, J., 190, 285
Jourilles, E. N., 188, 285

Kaplan, N., 80, 88, 283
Keane, T. M., 187, 285

Kernberg, O. F., 160–161, 285
Kik, H., 2, 114, 285
Kilpatrick, D. G., 187–188, 285
Kimura, D., 8, 285
Kohut, H., 160, 171, 259, 285
Komter, A., 222, 286
Kozak, M., 188, 240, 282–283
Kuijpers, P., 274, 285

Lacan, J., 74–75, 77, 263–264
Lamers-Winkelman, F., 7, 67, 286
Lansky, M., 159–160, 286
Lasch, C., 2, 265, 286
LaTaillade, J., 20, 279
LeCompte, S. H., 188, 285
Lévi-Strauss, C., 74
Lewis, H. B., 158, 160, 167, 171, 286
life
    family, 78, 147, 201, 204, 256, 266, 274
    personal/private, 230–231, 242, 250, 254
    political, 156, 271
    social, 25, 134, 211, 261, 263
Lindsey, J., 235, 291
Loeber, R., 209, 286
Lorentz House, 27, 212, 224
Luepnitz, D. A., 5, 286

Madden, D., 201, 284
Main, M., 80, 88, 283
Mastenbroek, S., 49, 286
McCann, I. L., 187, 286
McCollum, E., 21, 288
McLeer, M. D., 187, 281
McLeer, S. V., 187, 286
McNally, P. F., 185–186, 286
mental health care, xviii, 70, 203, 230, 249
mentalization, 82, 84, 87–89
Mernissie, F., 133, 286
Meulenbelt, A., 7, 46, 51, 58, 286–287
Miedzian, M., 191, 286–287
Mooij, A., 157, 255, 265, 287
Moran, G. S., 84, 283

Morrison, A. P., 160–161, 287
mourning, 64–65, 70, 223, 265
Mutual Violent Control (MVC), 3–4

narcissism, 157–158, 160–161, 171, 265
narrative approach, 91–02
National Commission for Mental Health, 275–276
Nicolai, N., 80, 238, 287
Nuttall, R., 233, 284, 287

O'Leary, S., 185, 288
Olivier, C., 51, 287
Omer, H., 70, 202, 206, 213, 227, 287, 279
Organization for Youth and Family (Stichting Jeugd en Gezin), 217

Pavese, C., 102, 108
Pearlman, L. A., 187, 286
Penn, P., 2, 27, 37, 283
Perry, A., 240, 284
Pijnaker, H., 2, 23, 87, 282
post traumatic stress
    disorder/syndrome, 65, 124, 138, 161, 186, 189, 240, 258
projection, 37, 158–159, 163, 229, 233, 239, 265
Pynoos, R. S., & Eth, S., 186, 287

rage, 62, 76, 94, 109, 112–114, 116, 134, 141, 144, 194, 240 see also: anger
road, 268
Ralphe, D. L., 187, 286
rape, xv, 1, 62, 104, 110, 112–113, 115, 134, 137–138, 155, 232, 234, 237, 239–240
reflective
    capacity, 72, 83, 91
    function, 82, 87–88
Regional Institutes for Mental Health Care (RIAGG), 123, 216, 234, 244, 275–276

repression, 15, 113, 136, 158, 189, 242
Retzinger, S. M., 184, 288
revenge, 134, 165–166, 169, 172, 176–179, 227, 242, 244, 260, 277
see also: vengeance
Richters, A., 106, 287
ritual(izing), xviii, 57, 74, 78, 105, 169, 172, 177–179, 181, 193–196, 198–199, 260–263, 268–269
Robie, C., 5, 279
romantic
expectations, 46, 49, 52, 69–70, 184
ideal, 45–47, 53, 63–65, 69–70
illusions, 57, 70
love, 46
marriage, 265
myth, 45, 57
Römkens, R. G., 2, 27, 37, 237, 287
Rosen, K. H., 21, 288
Rothbaum, B. O., 188, 283
Rutenfrans, C., 210, 287

Sanders, M., 51, 290
Saunders, D., 189, 287
Scalia, J., 2, 288
Schokker, J., 74, 77, 288
Schokker, T., 74, 77, 288
Schöttelndreier, M., 211, 288
self, 45, 65, 79, 81, 158, 160–161
-control, 5, 15, 34, 37, 71–72, 75, 77, 114, 123, 156, 166, 171, 194, 209–210, 263, 266
-esteem, 26, 135, 171, 180, 205–206
image, 66, 81, 83–84, 92, 158–161, 170–171, 188, 209, 213, 265
reflection, 148, 190
worth, 159–161, 172, 176, 206, 213, 255
shame, xii, xvii, 12, 15–16, 23, 30, 32, 59–60, 63, 66, 73, 77, 82, 85–87, 103–104, 108–110, 112–114, 116–117, 119, 122, 125, 130, 137–138, 141–142, 144–145, 151–167, 171, 173, 175, 178,

184–185, 194, 199, 201, 222, 226–227, 232, 236, 239, 243, 246, 260, 265–266
Sheff, T. J., 113, 167, 184, 288
Sheinberg, M., 2, 27, 37, 67, 283, 288
Siegel, C. H., 186, 282
Siegel, D. J., 79–80, 288
Silverman, J. G., 2, 77, 280
Silvern, L., 188, 280
Slep, A., 185, 288
"Slippery Slope" ("Het Hellend Pad"), 217
Smeulers, J., 137, 288
Spaans, E. C., 204, 289
splitting, 15, 42, 45, 60, 65–66, 175, 243, 258
Stark, E., 2, 288
Starzomski, A., 160, 282
Steiner, G., 258, 288
Steketee, G., 188, 283
Stern, D. N., 81, 288
Sternberg, K. L., 186, 288
Stith, S., 21, 288
Stoller, R. J., 9, 289
Strachen, C. E., 170, 282
Straus, M. A., 2, 169, 185, 288–289
Sudermann, M., 190, 289
symbol(-ic), 51, 74, 84, 133, 188, 261–262, 264–265, 270
order, 46, 73–74, 77, 264

taboo, ix–x, 2, 15–16, 133–134, 203
Tangney, J. P., 159–160, 163, 167, 266, 289
Tannen, D., 9, 289
Target, M., 84, 88, 283
Tennen, H., 233, 284
Terlouw, G. J., 208–209, 280
Terr, L., 189, 289
therapy
couple, xvii, 4–5, 21–22, 24, 34, 90, 178
relationship, 24, 56, 58, 65–66, 69, 152, 171, 237, 267
systemic, xvi, xviii, 4–6, 26–27, 87, 224, 274

Thomsen, C. J., 21, 288
time-out programme, 38–43, 71–73,
    75–79, 87, 92, 96, 119–124, 144,
    146, 174, 178, 214
Tomm, K., 88, 90, 289
transference, xii, xviii, 77, 83–85, 87,
    133, 148, 188, 229, 233, 246, 261,
    266 see also:
    countertransference
Turner, V. W., 261–262, 289

Van den Brink, G., 202–203,
    205–206, 255, 289
Van der Avort, A., 265, 289
Van der Hart, O., 178–179, 289
Van der Kolk, B. A., 240, 284
Van der Laan, P. H., 204, 289
Van der Pas, A., 211, 289
van der Post, L., 202, 280
van der Veer, G.,137, 290
van Dijk, L., 2, 290
van Gael, M., 80, 84, 290
van Gennep, A., 195, 290
Van Ginkel, C., 160, 282
van Ijzendoorn, M. H., 83, 290
van Lawick, J., ix, 2, 68–69, 226, 290
van Lawick, M. J., 51, 290
van Stolk, B., 192, 290
van Weeren, P., 202, 280
vengeance, xviii, 153, 155, 165, 169,
    172, 176–179, 202, 244 see also:
    revenge
Verhaeghe, P., 255, 260, 263, 273,
    290
Veronen, L. J., 187–188, 285
Verwers, C., 208–209, 280
Vetere, A., 2, 281, 290
violence see also: abuse, escalations
    domestic/intimate, ix–xii,
        xv–xviii, 1–2, 4, 15, 24, 105,
        110, 117, 120, 124–125, 133,
        144, 267, 276–277
    intra-family, 303
    physical, 3–4, 6–7, 13, 15, 21, 23,

    27, 43–45, 60, 71–73, 84, 101,
        106, 145, 203, 258
    psychological, 2–4, 7, 71, 73, 87
    sexual, 6–7, 61–62, 65, 110,
        137–138, 203, 310
Violent Resistence (VR), 3–4
Vrije Universiteit Amsterdam, 185,
    290

Walker, G., 2, 27, 37, 283
Walker, L. E. A., 2, 191, 290
Wall, S., 80, 279
Waters, E., 80, 279
Weerman, F., 207, 290
Weijers, I., 154, 162, 164–165, 290
White, G. M., 156, 290
White, M., 72, 290
Whitmer, B., 258, 290
Wierzbicka, A., 157, 291
Williams, L., 1–2, 285
Willy, J., 46, 291
Wilson, J., 235, 291
Wilson, S., 170, 185–186, 191, 284,
    291
Wittebrood, K., 203, 291
Wolak, J., 185, 291
Wolfe, D. A., 170, 185–186, 191, 284,
    291
Woltring, L., 192, 291
Women's Aid, xii
world
    inner, 84, 87–90, 98, 160, 269, 271
    outside, 58, 63, 66, 118, 131, 152,
        160–161, 173, 269
    war
        Second, 83, 203, 232, 253, 268
Wouters, C., 192, 290

Yllo, K., 2, 280

Zak, L., 170, 291
Zijderveld, A. C., 265, 291
Zimmerling, R. T., 187, 285
Zorg van velen (Care for Many), 275